PRAISE FOR *TESTIMONIES TO THE TRUTH*

This is McGrew's best book to date! Not as technical as her previous ones, it ranges widely over all kinds of evidence within the Gospels that points to their reliability—from undesigned coincidences to unnecessary details to unexplained allusions to incidental consistency of personalities and much, much more. McGrew dips back into nineteenth-century observations long forgotten, stirs in better-known recent ones and adds a few of her own discoveries for flavor. Rather than interacting with her critics or those with whom she disagrees, McGrew has written a uniformly positive work, making it that much more valuable.

Craig L. Blomberg, Distinguished Professor of
New Testament Emeritus, Denver Seminary

Lydia McGrew has again written a very helpful and insightful book for those interested in examining the reliability and trustworthiness of the New Testament Gospels. McGrew identifies what might appear to be incidental elements that together weave a complex tapestry that reveals a clear portrait of Jesus. This book is ideally suited for individual and group use, since it includes study and discussion questions (and suggested answers in the back of the book!). Both confirmed believers and those with questions will find this book of great benefit.

Stanley E. Porter
President, Dean, Professor of New Testament,
Roy A. Hope Chair in Christian Worldview
McMaster Divinity College, Hamilton, ON, Canada

In this overall synthesis of her previous critiques of critical biblical scholarship, Lydia McGrew raises probing questions that modern scholars have failed to address. In keen philosophic analytical form, she reverses the positivistic question: from verification to falsification. How do we *know* that there is nothing historically reliable in the Gospels? We don't, overall. If the Gospels do *not* reflect historical memory, whence the grounded verisimilitude, the realia of customs and culture, the undesigned coincidences, the unnecessary details, the unexplained allusions, the unexpected harmonies, and the unified personalities of the Gospels—let alone an unmistakably distinctive Jesus of Nazareth? Another plank in the platform of the Fourth Quest for Jesus—one that includes the Gospel of John, instead of leaving it out!

Paul N. Anderson
Author of *The Fourth Gospel and the Quest for Jesus*
Co-editor of *John, Jesus, and History* (Vols. 1–3)

Lydia McGrew concisely and carefully presents a cumulative case that the Gospel writers were faithful reporters rather than inventors. With wide-ranging evidence *Testimonies to the Truth* again and again points to the reliability of the Gospel accounts, and ultimately the reliability of their portraits of Jesus. With chapter summaries, discussion and study questions (and answers), numerous real life illustrations, objections dealt with along the way, and pointers to further resources (including website links), McGrew's *Testimonies to the Truth* can be confidently given to anyone, believer and skeptic alike. This book could easily be used as an evangelistic tool on a University campus, a textbook for a survey class on the Gospels, or a guide for youth or church seminars and personal study. A convincing and edifying book!

Alan J. Thompson
Head of New Testament Department,
Sydney Missionary and Bible College, Australia
Author of *One Lord, One People: The Unity of the Church in Acts* (LNTS),
The Acts of the Risen Lord Jesus (NSBT), *Luke* (EGGNT),
and *Colossians and Philemon* (TNTC)

I've been teaching apologetics for decades and I couldn't imagine another much-needed book demonstrating the reliability of the Gospels. But then comes along Lydia McGrew who has presented compelling arguments that had never even occurred to me. In *Testimonies to the Truth* McGrew puts together her years of research in readable and persuasive evidence that regularly surprised me. Skeptics will be hard pressed to escape her robust reasoning, and Christians will be emboldened in their confidence in the testimonies about Jesus. This is a wonderful book and I highly recommend!

Clay Jones
Visiting Scholar, Talbot School of Theology
Chairman of the Board, Ratio Christi
Author of *Why Does God Allow Evil?*
Compelling Answers for Life's Toughest Questions

A superb book. Lydia McGrew not only knows the relevant scriptural and historical issues extremely well, but brings to her analysis the precision of an analytic philosopher. At the same time, she writes with an admirable lucidity and sense of humor that make the book accessible and enjoyable to non-specialists.

Edward Feser
Professor of Philosophy, Pasadena City College

Is the historical narrative found in Scripture, and specifically in the New Testament Gospels, a record of what really happened? And is that a question worth asking? Given the fact that the faith of Scripture is necessarily and uniquely grounded in history, these are issues which demand to be considered. *Testimonies to the Truth* makes the very compelling case that the veracity of the Gospel narratives is indeed important and demonstrable. Marshalling arguments which have been long neglected by Bible believers but which are well recognized in the worlds of historiographical research and evidentiary canons, McGrew demonstrates that the New Testament Gospels deserve to be acknowledged and embraced as an accurate record of what actually happened in the life of Jesus of Nazareth. Reflecting the meticulously careful reasoning of an analytical philosopher, based upon a delightfully close reading of the Gospels, written in an engagingly conversational and accessible style, enhanced by the techniques of a seasoned master teacher, and laser-focused on an issue of the greatest moment in today's evangelical world, this book deserves to be read—and carefully pondered—by every thinking Christian, especially by those committed to raising up another generation whose minds are shaped and governed by the written Word of God.

Douglas Bookman
Professor of Bible Exposition
Shepherds Theological Seminary

Contemporary trends in biblical studies have put a spin on historical reliability that would lead many I serve away from the Bible. In *Testimonies to the Truth,* Dr. McGrew presents a well-researched, readable alternative for laypeople and students alike, that convincingly supports the Gospels' truthfulness. The chapter summaries and questions are excellent for personal and small group engagement. I could not recommend this book more for anyone who is interested in the historicity and reliability of the Bible.

Donald Brooks
Co-Founder of Northern Discovery Academy
Pastor and former Regional Director at Ratio Christi

Lydia McGrew is one of the most important thinkers in New Testament scholarship today. In *Testimonies to the Truth: Why You Can Trust the Gospels*, Dr. McGrew offers a survey of various categories of evidence that confirm the Gospels as historical reportage. Though this book's primary target audience is the popular level and though it is more general in scope than her previous three books, being accessible to a lay audience, the book contains various insights that are not found in her previous published work. In addition to reprising the argument from undesigned coincidences (the focus of a previous book, *Hidden in Plain View*), McGrew covers a plethora of extrabiblical confirmations of the gospels. Indeed, some of the connections McGrew highlights I had not previously observed. She also covers various lines of evidence that are scarcely discussed in contemporary apologetics literature. For example, McGrew devotes two entire chapters to the unified personalities found in the gospels that are so artless, casual and subtle that they contribute to the evidential case for the robust reliability of the Gospel accounts. McGrew also discusses alleged discrepancies between the Gospels, turning the argument on its head by underscoring how reconcilable variations in fact support narrative independence and thereby tend to confirm the reliability of the accounts. She also covers other marks of verisimilitude including unexplained allusions and unnecessary details, as well as casual references to difficult local knowledge relating to geography, customs, and culture.

Whether you are an interested layperson, a pastor, a student, or a scholar, this book contains important and valuable insights that you have probably not hitherto encountered. In addition, the discussion questions that accompany each chapter (with answers included at the back of the book) are an excellent resource for small group studies and family devotions.

Jonathan McLatchie
Discovery Institute Fellow
Director of TalkAboutDoubts.com

It is often the case that a curious person, wondering about the truth of the New Testament and the historical Jesus, reaches for some piece of writing (or viewing) only to be told either that "truth" and "history" are beside the point, or that they are decidedly not qualities that the New Testament or Jesus enjoy. The effect is that Jesus and the New Testament are shrunk down to a size too small to contemplate. But this isn't all there is to say! Thankfully, to the cavalcade of sometimes-obscure and often-less-known volumes adequately *affirming* the historical quality of the New Testament, Lydia McGrew adds her voice yet again. With *Testimonies to the Truth*, we get a readable and useful summation of McGrew's academic and trade publications on the reliability of the New

Testament (and Gospels especially), with the same analytic and educated force of her other published works.

The early chapters treating external corroboration should put a stone in the path of anyone who has dismissed the Gospels as non-historical, and the remainder of the book—looking broadly at various kinds of internal connections—may well make the case for unreliability begin to seem a little foolish. (The Gospels that emerge from such a survey don't really look like what we'd expect to find if they were whatever their detractors accuse them of being.) The whole book, but the latter chapters especially and the important concepts they introduce, will benefit good faith readers who simply want to sit with an open Bible and an open mind and think hard about the nature of the Gospels in a fresh way (*no expertise required*).

Chapter summaries, study questions and answers, and discussion questions, all make *Testimonies to the Truth* an excellent place to learn about (and remember, and learn to speak about) the case for the reliability of the Gospels, and perhaps for some to begin to ask the more pressing, more personal question: "What if they were true?"

Nathan Nadeau
Ph.D. Candidate, McMaster Divinity College

In *Testimonies to the Truth*, Lydia McGrew has given a fresh, enjoyable, and eminently readable investigation of the historical reliability of the Gospels so that we may know the painstaking accuracy of what they recorded. From geography and customs, from undesigned coincidences to unexpected harmonies, to consistent character portrayals, chiefly the extraordinary figure of Jesus Himself, again and again, the authors of the Gospels get the facts right. And as Lydia points out, they aren't even trying to get this intricate labyrinth of details to agree. They are just telling the truth! In addition, Lydia has filled this wonderful book with stimulating insights concerning Jesus' words, deeds, and personality and how they connect in unexpected and marvelous ways across the Gospels. Many of these splendid truths about Jesus will inspire awe and worship. *Testimonies to the Truth* will bring new understandings (and ideas for fresh studies in the Gospels) to biblical scholars. It provides penetrating study/discussion questions for personal devotions and small groups, and it presents a compelling case that the Gospels are authentic historical records to the truth, *the* Truth (John 14.6).

Justin W. Bass
Author of *The Bedrock of Christianity:
The Unalterable Facts of Jesus' Death and Resurrection*

In *Testimonies to the Truth: Why You Can Trust the Gospels,* Christian apologist Lydia McGrew offers fascinating, rarely noticed evidences that what the Gospel writers have handed down to us are not "cleverly devised stories" but reliable eyewitness testimony of true historical happenings in the life of Jesus (2 Peter 1.16). McGrew's awareness of critical scholarship is obvious, and her dismissal of it is well-reasoned and swift. Rather than lengthy debate with detractors, she wisely chooses to give her readers commonsense reasons for not being misled and proof upon proof for why they can trust the Gospels.

This volume will prove valuable to the seasoned Bible student as well as newcomers to the Gospel records. After fifty-plus years as a Bible reader and thirty-plus years as a pastor and seminary professor, I learned much and was amazed at things I had missed in my previous reading of the Gospels. Added value is found in the Summaries, Individual Study Questions, Group Discussion Questions, and Suggested Resources that end each chapter. Pastors, Bible study leaders, home school parents, Christian school teachers, individual believers, and honest seekers will all find much to praise in this newest offering from Dr. McGrew. It is both scholarly and accessible. May God give it wide circulation is my prayer.

Jim Kinnebrew
Professor of Theology, Luther Rice Seminary (retired)
Campground Pastor, www.campingoutwithgod.com

The Gospels claim to be the testimony of people who were in a position to know what Jesus said and did, including his dying on a cross and rising from the dead. *If* they are reliable historical sources, their reader may come to *know* (not just believe) those most important truths about Jesus. In her wonderful new little book, *Testimonies to the Truth,* Lydia McGrew gives us a thoroughly convincing defense of that big "if." She very effectively describes what reliable witness accounts look like and shows that the Gospels fit those patterns time and time again. Lydia makes good on her ministry slogan that claims to "make common sense rigorous." Her careful thinking is indeed connecting the Gospel accounts to our modern-day, reasonable intuitions of how truthful witnesses sound like in the real world, and reading her making those powerful connections had me mumbling, "Oh…, that makes so much sense!" at just about every chapter.

Years ago, when I read the Gospels as an adult atheist, they challenged my unbelief partly because they struck me as having the ring of truth, even though I couldn't explain immediately what I saw that made them so truthful. But Lydia *can* and does explain it all: external confirmations, unexplained allusions, undesigned coincidences, unnecessary details, unified personalities—her excellent book carefully breaks down those intuitive markers of truth we find in the Gospels, and thereby not only provides solid justification for Christian belief, but also trains the lay person to become the apologist. What a gift.

Guillaume Bignon
Philosopher, apologist, and author
of *Confessions of a French Atheist*

Skepticism of the Bible runs rampant through Western culture. Sadly, most Christians are ill-equipped to deal with the intellectual challenges. The result? Over time, their confidence in scripture slowly erodes and the authority they once gave to the Bible disappears. This is why Lydia's book is so important. She provides a thorough yet accessible recounting of multiple lines of evidence for the historical reliability of the Gospels. In doing so, she offers a powerful case that 21st Century readers are getting actual history from the pages of scripture. As a result, Lydia shows how all human history is centered on the work of God through the person of Christ. You don't have to be a scholar to defend the Bible or trust its message; you just need to read this book.

Brett Kunkle
Founder and President of MAVEN
co-author of *A Practical Guide to Culture:
Helping the Next Generation Navigate Today's World*

Lydia McGrew's latest work is a brief, practical summary of the evidence for treating the Gospel accounts in the New Testament as factual, non-mythological, trustworthy material. For those who may find Richard Bauckham's *Jesus and the Eyewitnesses* intimidating, and for pastors, Christian workers, and Bible school students looking for instructional assistance at the centre of the apologetic task, this book is ideal.

John Warwick Montgomery, Ph.D. (Chicago),
D.Théol. (Strasbourg). LL.D. (Cardiff),
Professor Emeritus of Law and Humanities,
University of Bedfordshire (UK),
Director, International Academy of Apologetics,
Evangelism and Human Rights (Strasbourg, France)

In *Testimonies to the Truth*, Lydia McGrew builds on the already formidable case for the historical reliability of the Gospels that she developed in her previous apologetic masterpieces *Hidden in Plain View* and *The Eye of the*

Beholder. In *Testimonies*, she demonstrates convincingly that the Gospels describe real-life events recounted by real people. In addition to the presence of unintended but complementary testimony from multiple sources about incidental details (what she calls "undesigned coincidences"), she shows that the Gospels exhibit numerous other marks of historical reliability including, for example, accurate descriptions of obscure first-century Roman and Judean places and customs, unnecessary but credible details about important events, and a consistency and coherence in the portrayal of the key figures, especially the portrayal of the central figure of the Gospels, Jesus Christ. McGrew shows that these features are associated with accurate historical narrative. Thus, she argues convincingly that these features anchor all four accounts securely in the place, time, and culture they describe. They contain historical truth about the historical Jesus. *Testimonies to the Truth* is clearly written, rigorously argued, and devastatingly persuasive.

Stephen C. Meyer
Author of *The Return of the God Hypothesis*

Absolutely fascinating! This book is a delightful look at intriguing Gospel details that don't necessarily jump off the page to readers. Yet, discovering these insights will help you savor the Gospels in a whole new way and better understand the remarkable—and critically important—qualities of the texts as "testimonies to the truth."

Natasha Crain
Speaker, podcaster, and author of
four books including *Faithfully Different*

Lydia McGrew offers a fresh and powerful case for the reliability of the Gospels. Resurrecting some classic arguments and yet offering some unique insights, *Testimonies to the Truth* deserves to be read by skeptics and believers alike. This is one of the top books I will now be recommending on why the Gospels can be trusted.

Sean McDowell
Associate Professor of Christian Apologetics,
Talbot School of Theology, Biola University
Author of numerous books, including *The Fate of the Apostles*

TESTIMONIES TO THE TRUTH

Testimonies to the Truth

Why You Can Trust the Gospels

Lydia McGrew

Testimonies to the Truth: Why You Can Trust the Gospels
© 2023 by DeWard Publishing Company, Ltd.
P.O. Box 290696, Tampa, FL 33687
www.deward.com

All rights reserved. No portion of this book may be reproduced in any form without written permission from the publisher.

Cover by nvoke design.

Unless otherwise noted, Scripture quotations are taken from the New American Standard Bible®,Copyright © 1960, 1962, 1963, 1968, 1971, 1972, 1973, 1975, 1977, 1995 by The Lockman Foundation Used by permission (www.Lockman.org).

Reasonable care has been taken to trace original sources for any excerpts and quotations appearing in this book and to document such information. For material not in the public domain, fair use standards and practices were followed. Should any attribution be found to be incorrect or incomplete, the publisher welcomes written documentation supporting correction for subsequent printing.

Printed in the United States of America.

ISBN: 978-1-947929-23-4 (print)
       978-1-947929-26-5 (digital)

To
Benjamin McGrew

and in loving memory of
Marjorie McGrew

*whose quiet and faithful lives
have borne living testimony to the truth*

Contents

Preface vii

Acknowledgements xi

1. Location, Location, Location 1

2. Customs and Culture 20

3. Undesigned Coincidences 50

4. Unnecessary Details 83

5. Unexplained Allusions 114

6. Unexpected Harmonies 134

7. Unified Personalities 163

8. Unmistakable Jesus 184

Study Guide Answers 220

Endnotes 239

Index 247

Preface

This book has two intertwined purposes—historical and devotional. The historical purpose is to provide a representative sample of the evidence for the literal, factual reliability of the Gospels: Matthew, Mark, Luke, and John. This evidence is so vast that a relatively short book like this can give only a part of it, and this book is intended as a briefer version of arguments I have made at more length in three earlier works, *Hidden in Plain View*, *The Mirror or the Mask*, and *The Eye of the Beholder*. In some places I have added new points that I became aware of more recently. I encourage interested readers to explore the resources for further study listed at the end of each chapter.

Study and discussion questions are provided at the end of each chapter, and suggested answers can be found at the end of the book. Also, I use here a system meant to offer something both to readers who prefer footnotes and to those who prefer endnotes. Content notes are located at the bottom of the page, marked with daggers, while notes containing only references are grouped by chapter at the end of the book.

The arguments in this book divide fairly neatly into what are known as "external" and "internal" evidences. Chapters 1 and 2 concern the former, while Chapters 3–8 concern the latter. Briefly, external evidences use information from outside the canonical books of the Bible to support factual statements made within the biblical books. These include information about geography, archaeology, customs, and rulers. Internal evidences may sometimes use external sources to provide backdrop, but for the most part they concern ways in which the books look truthful by corresponding to what we know about how truthful people talk and write. These include undesigned coincidences, unnecessary details, unexplained allusions, reconcilable variation, and unity of personalities, all of which are explained and illustrated in the relevant chapters. In all eight chapters, especially in those covering internal evidences, I expect that even Christian readers will find arguments and information that they have never heard before. In some cases I am reviving arguments that were made by older authors but have fallen out of style in the scholarly world.

If you are a Christian reader, the historical argument is a powerful case-making tool that will equip you to engage skeptics more effectively. If you are a skeptical reader, it is meant as a challenge: If the Gospels are defensible as historical documents, might Christianity be true after all? If, for example, the resurrection stories in the Gospels are *not* gradually embellished tales but rather represent the testimony of those in a position to know, attested under circumstances of great personal danger, what does this mean about whether the bodily resurrection of Jesus really happened?

This question begets another. If Jesus rose from the dead, what implications does this have for us personally? Even a person who has committed himself to Jesus as Lord and affirms the basic tenets of Christianity may grow detached in his Christian walk, so used to certain passages of Scripture that they no longer kindle the old devotional fire. This is especially a danger for those who have grown up in church, reading the Gospels many times over and hearing countless sermons. It is possible to accept the Gospels as historically true without being personally struck by their truth-likeness or knowing how to defend their historicity to a skeptical outsider. Some Christians may even think that they should *not* give such a defense, on the grounds that the Bible should be accepted on faith alone.

It is my contention that in Christianity, faith and reason are indissolubly joined. By choosing to become incarnate, God declared that it was not his purpose that history and theology should be separated by an unbridgeable chasm. By holding the Gospels up to standards that are applicable to other ancient works, I hope to display them in a light that may never have explicitly occurred to readers before—as works that can bear historical scrutiny and come through with flying colors. I hope to show by a multitude of examples how to engage our historical imagination and thereby understand the Gospels as robustly factual documents. This reportage model, which I have defined and defended in my earlier books, is in one sense the intuitive default for conservative Christians. The goal of this work is to make that commonsense intuition rigorous while presenting it to a lay audience.

To those who are not Christians, it no doubt seems the stuff of legend to say that one man, born in one time and place, holds the answers to life's most urgent questions and can help us through our hardest times. But that is precisely what Christianity affirms as fact. God the Son was incarnate by the Holy Ghost of the virgin Mary and was made man, a specific man, Jesus of Nazareth, who died for man's sins two thousand years ago, rose again physically, and offers eternal life in the present to all who come to him. The four canonical Gospels are our best original source documents for the life, death, and resurrection of Jesus. The question, then, is vital: Can we trust them? Are they embellished or corrupted by non-historical material? That question lies at the heart of Christianity, because Jesus himself is the heart of Christianity. How can we know him if we know very little, factually, about him?

In 2022 it is hardly a cliché to say that our world becomes more dark, more dangerous, and more full of despair. The feeling that we are swinging over an abyss may arise from wars and rumors of wars, from a worldwide pandemic, from the descent of a society into totalitarianism, or from the increasing embrace of anti-human and perverse ideologies. Or it may come from personal tragedy, from physical pain, mental illness, loss of livelihood, death of a loved one, or loneliness. It is at the point where things seems worst and most hopeless that we must have truth to hold onto, assuring us that there is ultimate meaning even in suffering and loss.

Christianity offers this hope through its doctrines—the forgiveness of sins, the love of God, the resurrection of the body, and the expectation of eternal union with God in which all our sorrows will be redeemed. But is it true? We should not believe something simply because it satisfies a felt need. This is where works like this book come in. By showing that there are strong historical reasons to believe, this book affirms that Christianity is not merely one more evolutionary variant on man's search for God. It is the consummation of God's search for man.

Christians who prepare themselves to defend the historicity of the Gospels are making themselves able witnesses to that truth. This will stand them in good stead both in their own times of pain and tragedy and in those moments when they are called upon to give "a reason for the hope that is in them." By offering the world a faith founded on fact, we point them to the one Person who is able to catch us and keep us from falling into the abyss. I pray that this book will be used of God to that end.

Lydia McGrew
Kalamazoo, MI, 2022

Acknowledgements

This book has been written during a time of significant physical pain and illness. I could not have kept going on the project without the love of the Body of Christ. Special thanks to John Evans, Kristor Lawson, Cody Nelson, and Richard Porter for prayer and personal encouragement in my work. Thanks to Erik Manning and David Yuen for encouragement and help in making my work available in multiple media outlets. There are more people to thank than I could possibly name, including many who have prayed for me.

Thanks to Sarah Enterline, Don Brooks, and Nathan Nadeau for very helpful comments and for suggesting some of the study and discussion questions. Thanks to Tony Costa for help proof-reading. Thanks to Bethel McGrew for help on the preface and for proof-reading the manuscript. Thanks to Nathan Ward of DeWard Publishing for his patience and hard work on this project.

Thanks are due beyond what I can express to Tim McGrew for his constant kindness, love, and help as well as for introducing me to so many of the topics covered in this book.

1

Location, Location, Location

1. Locations are tough

Specific locations are hard on hoaxers. If you wanted to make up a fictional story and pass it off as literally true, it wouldn't be wise to put it in a highly specific location unless you were prepared to do a lot of research to make sure that you weren't making mistakes. Of course, invented details or inaccuracies wouldn't matter much if you were presenting your story as fiction. Nobody expects to find a real 221B Baker Street in London, because everyone knows that Sherlock Holmes is just a fictional character. But Matthew, Mark, Luke, and John clearly want their readers to believe that they are telling true stories, and they often use very specific settings and details. If they were making things up, they often risked getting it wrong.

As it turns out, the evangelists obviously know a lot about both the geography and the specific locations where Jesus ministered. While this may seem like no big deal to us, we have to remember that they had no Google nor even paper atlases, newspapers, or reference books at a local library where they could look these things up. If the authors didn't really know what they were talking about, it would be hard for them to find out.

The evangelists know when you go "down" to get somewhere, who ruled in what obscure territory, what specific spots in Jerusalem were like, and much more. These facts are usually woven into their stories in such a way that their knowledge confirms the stories in which they crop up. It's important to remember that the highly detailed, highly realistic historical novel didn't even exist at the time that the Gospels were written. (There was fiction, but it tended to be crudely written and melodramatic.) And in the highly unlikely event that a Gospel author decided to invent the detailed historical novel (which then disappeared again after his time), he would have found it practically speaking impossible to gather the many facts that the Gospels get right without living in a highly specific time and place.

When people look for external confirmation of the Bible, they often look in a place that wouldn't provide the strongest confirmation. They will ask, "Are there other historians who talk about Jesus?" "Do we have any place outside of Christian writings that tells about Jesus' miracles or his resurrection?" And so forth. The concern is that skeptics will say that the Bible is a biased source; people therefore tend to seek confirmation of the events in the Bible from non-biblical sources. When it comes to miracles, this notion of requiring non-Christian sources is especially misguided. If someone came to believe in Jesus' miracles, he would have been likely to become a Christian!

A non-biblical author's mention just of (say) Jesus' existence would confirm only that Jesus existed, which isn't saying very much. Or take external records of extremely famous people of the time mentioned in the Bible, like Herod the Great or Caesar Augustus. Even if the Gospels were made up, we might expect them to mention such well-known people. Mentioning Herod the Great all by itself doesn't confirm a document very much,

Location, Location, Location | 3

any more than a novel is confirmed by setting its events at the time of Queen Elizabeth I.

What confirms the Gospels much better is the interlocking between their details and *obscure* facts about geography, culture, place names, and more. What we should be looking for are multiple confirmations from facts that are *hard to get right*. This chapter and the next one will show what that looks like. In these chapters I will be giving *just some* of the many historical confirmations of the Gospels that we get from outside of the Bible—from archaeology, other ancient historians, rabbinic debates, inscriptions, and more.

This chapter will focus on places—regions, geographical details, place names, rulers, and specific locations in Jerusalem. The Gospel of John, even more than Matthew, Mark, and Luke (these latter three are often called the Synoptic Gospels), abounds in such place details. For that reason, I'm going to start this chapter with confirmations of places mentioned in the Synoptics and then talk about those in John.

2. Luke 3.1–2—Look at all those names!

Throughout this book, I will often emphasize casualness and subtlety. So often, a story will mention a detail just in passing, and then we will be able to confirm that detail. But the following verses in Luke are, admittedly, neither casual nor subtle. Luke is clearly placing the ministry of John the Baptist quite explicitly with reference to historical rulers, both sacred and secular, from the emperor on down. But what these verses lack in subtlety, they more than make up for in accuracy. The confirmations they provide for Luke's knowledge and care are impressive indeed:

> Now in the fifteenth year of the reign of Tiberius Caesar, when Pontius Pilate was governor of Judea, and Herod was tetrarch of

Galilee, and his brother Philip was tetrarch of the region of Ituraea and Trachonitis, and Lysanias was tetrarch of Abilene, in the high priesthood of Annas and Caiaphas, the word of God came to John, the son of Zacharias, in the wilderness. (Luke 3.1–2)[1]

I mentioned before that just bringing in the name of a big-name ruler, such as the Emperor Tiberius, does not provide very much in the way of evidence. Here Luke does far more than that. He starts with Tiberius and then runs through a list of other rulers, including the Jewish priests Annas and Caiaphas, and says that John the Baptist's ministry began when *all* of these people were ruling their respective regions simultaneously.

As it turns out, we can independently confirm (from sources outside of the Bible) the overlap in these names. Pilate was governor of Judea at the same time that Herod Antipas (a son of Herod the Great) was tetrarch of Galilee, which was also at the same time that Herod's brother Philip was tetrarch of a region called Trachonitis. Those times also overlapped with the high priesthood of Caiaphas. These overlaps are only partial, so Luke is designating a highly specific time period. The intersection of *all* of these rulers of *all* of these locations, *all* named by Luke, is remarkably strong evidence for Luke's care in figuring out when John the Baptist began his ministry.

I won't bother saying much about Tiberius Caesar or even Pontius Pilate, though Pilate wouldn't really be famous now if it weren't for his connection with Jesus. But there's so much else to mention that I'll just leave it at the fact that non-biblical history tells us about Pilate and tells us that he did rule this region under Tiberius.[2] That Herod Antipas, who comes up repeatedly in the Gospels, was in charge in Galilee is attested by the ancient Jewish historian Josephus,[3] and in a later section of this chapter I'll be talking about a fascinating coincidence concerning the other nearby region he was given to rule, known as Perea. Josephus also tells us about Caiaphas and his high priesthood at this time.[4] Those, you might say, are the easy ones.

Luke brings in three more obscure place names here—Iturea, Trachonitis, and Abilene. None of these regions are going to feature in his Gospel. He apparently brings them up just to nail down yet further the time of which he is speaking. It turns out that Josephus also confirms that Philip, called Philip the tetrarch by modern historians, the brother of Herod Antipas, was indeed given Trachonitis to rule after their father, Herod the Great, had died.[5] Philip's rule of Iturea (the Itureans were Arabs) is not otherwise mentioned by historians, but if anything, this just shows that Luke wasn't written by someone copying information from Josephus. Luke is an historical source in his own right. Are all these place names and ruler names making your head whirl yet? Just think how hard it would be to get all of them right! And there's more.

What about Abilene, ruled by Lysanias? This is perhaps the best one of all, because it is the hardest. For a long time scholars couldn't place the Lysanias mentioned by Luke. It goes without saying that some skeptics thought that Luke made a mistake. It seemed all the more likely that Luke was mistaken because (based on Josephus) a ruler named Lysanias did exist but couldn't have been *this* Lysanias, since the Lysanias mentioned in Josephus was executed before Jesus was born.[6] It made matters even worse for Luke (or so it seemed) because that earlier Lysanias did rule Abilene, a region in Syria. Surely it would be too much of a coincidence for there to be *two* rulers named Lysanias who ruled the same region within a period of about a hundred years! Luke must have been trying to show off by bringing in the name "Lysanias, tetrarch of Abilene" and just placed him at a time when he didn't really live. Right?

Not so fast! Later on, an inscription now known as the Abila inscription was discovered in the Syrian region of Abilene. The inscription was written by a freedman of the tetrarch Lysanias. Nymphaeus, the freedman, specifically named Lysanias in the inscription. He wanted everyone to know that he built a street and a temple and planted some orchards at his own expense; he dedicated this building project to the health of the "Augusti." The reference to the "Augusti" is good evidence that the street was built in the time of Tiberius Caesar and his mother, Livia. The emperor would have been known as "Augustus," and Livia went by the title of "Augusta" and was highly influential during the reign of her son. So apparently there *was indeed* a tetrarch of Abilene named Lysanias in the time of Tiberius Caesar, just when Luke places him.[7]

When doing history, it's always important to remember that there can be more than one person with the same name and that this isn't even a far-fetched conjecture. Nor does it have to be just a coincidence. In this case, the second Lysanias could have been the son of the earlier Lysanias and could have received the rulership of the same region. It would be absurd to think that Luke went and found Nymphaeus's street inscription in Syria and decided to incorporate this Lysanias into a non-historical account of John the Baptist. Luke just knew, from living and traveling in that region not long afterwards, that Lysanias ruled in Abilene at the same time when all these other people were ruling. So Luke decided to throw in a reference to him along with the others.

3. Jesus' ministry in Perea

Luke's Gospel tells about how Jesus was traveling on his way to Jerusalem when some Pharisees came and warned him that Herod (this, again, is Herod Antipas) would kill him if he didn't leave the region. Jesus is not impressed with this "warning," which was probably more of a taunt. He says that he must journey on to Jerusalem to die. He calls Herod a "fox" and says, almost bitterly, that it cannot be that a prophet should perish outside of Jerusalem (Luke 13.31–35).

This passage occurs in a large portion of Luke's Gospel that is famously difficult to put in chronological order. It's pretty clear that from Luke 9.51 to about 18.35 Luke is telling about a variety of sayings and incidents in Jesus' life for which he is not sure of the *exact* timing. In this section Luke apparently records material that various people told him about, for which he wasn't able to nail down exact times. Luke repeatedly mentions in these chapters that Jesus was on his way to Jerusalem, but it isn't clear that he even means us to think that this is all the same journey to Jerusalem.

The way that Luke tells the events in these chapters is what I've called elsewhere achronological narration—meaning narrating without intending to indicate a time ordering. It's very important not to mistake this for *changing* the order of events in a non-factual way, "making" something happen at a time when the author knows that it didn't happen. That would be misleading, and Luke doesn't do that. But sometimes he just "chunks things in."

All that being said, Luke 9.51 pretty clearly indicates that that verse, at least, is referring to the beginning of a journey from Galilee to Jerusalem toward the end of Jesus' life. I think it is probable that Luke 9.51 refers to Jesus' departure from Galilee for the last time before his death, and I am inclined to say that it corresponds to his journey to Jerusalem for the Feast of Tabernacles, recorded in John 7. That would have been in the autumn, about six months before Jesus died.

I think we can say that the incident in Luke 13.31–35, the Pharisees' insincere "warning" about Herod, does not *seem* to occur in Galilee. Jesus seems to have left Galilee and to be nearing the end of his life. Why is this important? It's important because, when Luke tells about Herod Antipas, he repeatedly emphasizes that he was the tetrarch of Galilee. We saw that already in Luke 3.1–2. (Luke mentions it again in Luke 23.5–12.) But if Jesus is no longer in Galilee in Luke 13.31, why do the Pharisees speak as they do? Doesn't he need to be in Herod's jurisdiction for the threat that Herod will kill him to make sense?

But there's something else about Herod Antipas that Luke doesn't mention: According to Josephus, Herod Antipas was tetrarch not only of Galilee but also of the region of Perea,[8] a strip of land east of the Jordan River. *All three* of the other Gospels confirm that, shortly before his death, Jesus spent time east of the Jordan River in Perea, though they don't use that name. (See Matt. 19.1, Mark 10.1, John 10.40–41, John 11.54.) Though Luke doesn't locate the "warning" of the Pharisees geographically, the coincidence with the other Gospels and the external information that Herod Antipas was tetrarch of Perea makes a lot of sense. In fact, it's a particularly lovely combination of facts that confirms Luke's Gospel. It's possible that Luke hadn't even picked up on the fact that Antipas was tetrarch of Perea as well as Galilee. If he knew it, he doesn't mention it. Nonetheless, he includes Jesus' dialogue with the Pharisees in 13.31 because (presumably) that was what his own sources told him. Since, it turns out, Herod ruled the region east of the Jordan River where, the other Gospels tell us, Jesus spent time in the last months before his death, everything fits together! †

---

† In Chapter 3 I will refer to this kind of fitting as an undesigned coincidence; I'm including it here because it includes the external connection with the fact that Herod Antipas was tetrarch of Perea.

4. The meaning of "Gethsemane"

Before I turn to location confirmations unique to John's Gospel, here is a beautiful little confirmation given by New Testament scholar Peter J. Williams.[9] All four Gospels talk about the place where Jesus was arrested before his crucifixion. Matthew and Mark name this garden as Gethsemane (Matt. 26.36, Mark 14.32). Luke and Mark both state explicitly that it was on the Mount of Olives (Mark 14.26, Luke 22.39), and John even describes the route to reach it, across the Kidron wadi, where the "winter flowing" Kidron (as John calls it) may or may not have been running in that spring season (John 18.1).

Williams tells us that the word "Gethsemane" means "oil press." That the Gospels describe the location of this place, with this name, on the Mount of Olives means that the name fits perfectly, but none of the Gospels emphasize this connection at all.[†]

5. Cana

We now turn to locations that are unique to the Gospel of John. John is especially rich in locations. He seems to be preoccupied with where Jesus is all the time, both geographically (what region or town) and more specifically within a city (e.g., *where* in Jerusalem).

The little town of Cana is mentioned nowhere else in the Bible and was by no means famous, but John mentions it more than once. There are several possibilities for the location of Cana, discovered by archaeologists, all within a small region in Galilee. Khirbet Qana is perhaps the most probable of these.[10] That John knew about the town at all and refers to it casually shows

---

[†]Williams also mentions that the meaning of the name "Golgotha," where Jesus was crucified, is confirmed by other Aramaic texts (*Can We Trust the Gospels?* p. 61). The word does mean "skull," though other texts usually have an extra letter L—"golgoltha" or "gulgultha." As Williams emphasizes, it is quite normal in a language like Aramaic for such an L to get "swallowed," producing a variant spelling.

a familiarity with the region. As I will remind readers repeatedly throughout this book, John's Gospel was probably first published far away in Asia Minor. He was certainly not trying to impress his first audience by mentioning little Cana, of which most of them had probably never heard.

But John knows more than just that Cana exists. He casually mentions the way that one travels from Cana in the hills to the larger, seaside town of Capernaum—by going downhill. The Sea of Galilee is even *lower* than ordinary sea level.[11] John uses the phrase "going down" to refer to this walk three times in his Gospel, as a natural part of his narrative (John 2.12, 4.49, 4.51).

But that's not all: Archaeologists have discovered a location where stone water pots were manufactured in the vicinity of the suggested locations for Cana.[12] John particularly mentions the fact that the water pots at the marriage at Cana were made of stone; like the archaeologists, he connects these jars with Jewish purification rituals (John 2.6). Stone, though heavy, is non-porous and more difficult to make ritually impure. It is also easier to clean thoroughly than other materials.

6. Bethesda

The Pool of Bethesda, where Jesus healed a paralyzed man on the Sabbath (John 5.1–14), provides another illustration of John's accuracy as well as a cautionary tale about far-fetched symbolic theories. John says that the Pool of Bethesda had five porticoes (John 5.2). In the early 20th century, a liberal French critic named Alfred Loisy suggested that this was an invented allegorical detail. The five porticoes, thought Loisy, represented the five books of the Law of Moses, and the story of the miracle (which he thought was made up) illustrated Jesus' superiority to the Old Testament law. It should have caused significant embarrassment for all such critics when excavations later in the same century found the remains of the pool itself. Archaeologists could tell that it had been bounded by four porticoes around it and one across the middle.[13] So as it turns out, John doesn't invent these things. He knew that the pool was there and mentioned, simply and casually as a fact, that it had five porticoes.

Here it's worth noting that these structures were broken down when Jerusalem was destroyed by the Romans in AD 70. After that it would have been much harder to describe them accurately unless one really had been there and remembered.

7. The Sea of Galilee

John is comfortable with and knowledgeable about the Sea of Galilee, which makes sense if he was John the son of Zebedee, a fisherman. In both John 6.1 and 21.1 he notes explicitly that it has two different names, both the Sea of Galilee and the Sea of Tiberias. Josephus tells us that Herod Antipas founded a new town near the Sea of Galilee and named it Tiberias in honor of the Emperor Tiberius,[14] and he occasionally refers to it by this second (and newer) name.[15]

John also takes note of a specific detail in the story of Jesus walking on the water. He says that they had rowed about "twenty-five or thirty stadia" (about three or four miles, John 6.19) in the storm when they saw Jesus coming toward them on the water. Mark 6.47 says that Jesus was on land when they were "in the middle of the sea."[†] John's familiarity with the Sea of Galilee is evident in his taking note of about how far they had rowed even under these circumstances.

[†] While it is true that the Sea of Galilee is about seven miles across at its widest point, John may not be implying that width here, since the disciples were probably not trying to row across at the widest point and had doubtless been blown off course anyway in the storm.

8. The Pool of Siloam

The Pool of Siloam is mentioned only by John in the Bible. It is where Jesus sends the man born blind to wash after putting mud on his eyes (John 9.7). John glosses the name of the pool as meaning "sent," probably taken from the Hebrew "shalach" meaning "to send."[16] It could be that John is here implying a theological connection, since Jesus is the one sent from God. On the other hand, he may merely be noting the meaning of the name casually. Or it may be that the connection comes to his mind since Jesus sent the blind man to wash in the pool.

But the name is not even the most interesting thing about this pool. Archaeologists have actually *found* the Pool of Siloam in Jerusalem, as recently as 2004. Fed by the Gihon spring (compare 2 Kings 20.20), its living waters and its size could even have made it suitable as a mikveh, or place for ritual bathing for purification.[17] It was also used for a water pouring ceremony that we will discuss in Chapter 2.

9. Solomon's Porch

In John 10.22–23 we're told that Jesus was in Jerusalem in the winter, at the Feast of the Dedication—what we know today as Hanukkah. In the verses that follow, Jesus talks about being the Good Shepherd and about how no one can snatch his sheep from his hand (10.27–29). Then he utters the shocking words, "I and the Father are one" (10.30). This is one of those unique sayings in the Gospel of John where Jesus points quite explicitly to his deity. The people are so outraged that they try to stone Jesus (10.31). Not surprisingly, critical scholars question the historicity of this saying, since it is more explicit than any claim of Jesus' deity found in the Synoptic Gospels.[18]

It is just here, in the context of this theological declaration, that John is absolutely explicit about the historically literal nature of the scene. Not only does he state *when* this discussion took place; he says exactly *where* it took place: "It was winter, and Jesus was walking in the Temple in the portico of Solomon" (10.23). Josephus tells us about this portico. It was a roofed cloister on the east side of the Temple that was believed to have been built by Solomon—hence the name.[19] Regardless of whether or not it was built by Solomon, it would have been an appropriate place for Jesus to teach in the winter months, providing some shelter from the elements. John, seeing again in memory a scene that he probably witnessed, tells when and where Jesus was walking when he spoke these words.

10. Bethany: distance from Jerusalem

In John 11.18, John mentions briefly that Bethany was near Jerusalem, being about fifteen stadia away. In modern terms this translates to about three kilometers, which is just under two miles. John mentions this fact in the most natural way possible, as an explanation for the fact that so many friends have come to keep Mary and Martha company in their period of mourning over their brother Lazarus, who has just died.

As it turns out, Al-Eizariya, the modern town located in the traditional place of Bethany, is indeed about three kilometers from Jerusalem, just as John says.[20] But it would be ridiculous to imagine John as dropping this bit of information in here in the hopes that someone in his audience would go and verify that Bethany was, in fact, about that far from Jerusalem and be impressed by the realism of his story. John is just getting on with his story.

The approximate distance of Bethany from Jerusalem also fits well with the other Gospel accounts of Jesus' final week. Mark mentions that Jesus went back to Bethany from Jerusalem more than once in the evening during Passion week (Mark 11.11–12,

14.3). In fact, the night of the Last Supper may have been the first night in that week when Jesus did not go back to Bethany to eat the evening meal and sleep, and that of course was when he was arrested. So the other Gospels make it clear that Bethany was close to Jerusalem, but they are not as explicit as John about just how close. John, with his mind for details, estimates and remembers the distance.

11. Unidentified locations

It's important to remember that there is a random element to what locations we are able to verify now, 2,000 years later. The Gospel authors couldn't possibly have predicted which locations much later critics or readers would know about, and that isn't on their minds. This point becomes especially clear when we see that the authors sometimes mention places that we haven't been able to identify, but they seem to know quite well what they are talking about. Mark 8.10, for example, says that Jesus and his disciples went to the area near Dalmanutha after the feeding of the 4,000, but modern archaeologists have been unable positively to identify this town. (A location near Magdala has been excavated, but there is only weak conjectural evidence that it is Dalmanutha.[21]) Mark wasn't thinking about that one way or another, he was just mentioning where they went.

This confidence both about sites that have (now) been identified and about those that have not is especially noticeable in John. John is deeply interested in location, and many of his sites have been identified archaeologically or confirmed from other historians. But John's mention of sites that we have been able to identify is no different in style or manner from his mention of those that we haven't been able to identify. He mentions all of his locations in the same confident yet offhand fashion.

For example, John 1.26–27 tells how John the Baptist attested to the coming of one greater than himself, whose sandal he was not worthy to unlatch. The narrator then states that this occurred in Bethany beyond Jordan, where he was baptizing. While there is a place on the east side of the Jordan River that is shown to tourists as this Bethany beyond the Jordan, the ruins there are Byzantine, and it is no more than a guess as to whether this was the location.[22] But notice this: John the evangelist does talk about Bethany on the Mount of Olives, as we discussed above. He knows that it is located not far from Jerusalem and was the home of Mary, Martha, and Lazarus. When he talks about John the Baptist, he apparently realizes that there was (at the time of Jesus) more than one place called Bethany, so he points out that this was the one *beyond* the Jordan, which always in the Gospels means east of the Jordan. John speaks with precision because that's how his mind works.

Similarly, John mentions Aenon near Salim (John 3.23) as another place where John the Baptist baptized people, because "there was an abundance of water there." The word "aenon" means "spring," so wherever it was there was presumably lots of water. But there are now multiple identification suggestions for this location. The point is that John is not confused about the location. He has a specific place of springs in mind and is mentioning it because he knows it is true that this is where John the Baptist was during this part of his ministry.

Commentators have differed for a long time about the location of Ephraim, mentioned in John 11.54. John says that Jesus went there to get away from "walking publicly." It was, he says, a town near the wilderness. Jesus stayed there with his disciples between the raising of Lazarus and his final entrance into Jerusalem.

It would make no sense to suppose that John made up these locations (or that Mark or Peter made up Dalmanutha) and randomly inserted them into their stories, when their stories are otherwise so firmly placed in specific, real locations large and small, famous and obscure. What we have here is reportage from people close up to the facts, who knew what they were talking about, coupled with the chances and changes of this mortal life that cause us, 2,000 years later, to be able to find many of the places but not others.

The evangelists, calmly unconcerned with the critical spirit of a later age, tell their stories accurately down to small details, because that was how things happened and because they have the facts at their disposal. We come along and, if we are wise, recognize and respect their casually correct information.

Chapter Summary

- The Gospels show detailed knowledge of places and rulers of those places.
- These pieces of accurate information are not just about famous people but also about obscure rulers, geography, and specific locations in Jerusalem.
- It would be difficult or impossible to find out these items of information by looking them up in books at the time.
- These facts are evidence in favor of the truth of the stories in which they occur.

Study Questions

1. Why would it be difficult for the authors of the Gospels to fake their geographical knowledge?

2. What kind of confirmation should we be looking for from outside sources regarding the accuracy of the Gospel accounts?

Location, Location, Location | 17

3. What is one possible explanation for multiple historical figures having the same name as each other? How does this fit with Luke's mention of Lysanias as ruling at the time of John the Baptist and Jesus?

4. Explain what achronological narration is. Why is it not a deception on the part of the author?

5. Matthew, Mark, and John all state clearly that toward the end of his life on earth, Jesus had a ministry across the Jordan in an area that we know independently was called Perea. What hint do we find in Luke of this Perean ministry?

6. What does the word "Gethsemane" mean? Why is this significant?

7. Why does John use the phrase "going down" when he mentions travel from Cana to Capernaum?

8. Why do critical scholars question the historicity of Jesus' famous saying at Solomon's Porch?

9. Describe a place where John accurately recorded the distance from one place to another.

10. Name two highly specific locations that John recorded that were confirmed by the findings of archaeologists or outside mention.

For Discussion

1. Why is the casual mention of correct information especially valuable as evidence? Describe a way in which you might refer casually to a correct, specific location in your own town, showing that you live there and are familiar with the area.

2. Give two or three of your favorite examples of correct locations or rulers of locations from this chapter that you could use in a discussion with someone who thinks the Gospels are just made-up stories.

3. Sometimes skeptics use something they call the Spiderman objection. They will point out that the Spiderman stories are set in New York City but that the fact that New York is a real city doesn't mean that the stories are true. How could you answer this objection when it comes to the Gospels' use of locations?

4. What would skeptics say if the Gospels got these kinds of location and ruler details *wrong*? What does this mean about the fact that they get them *right*?

5. Do you think that it is a bigger deal evidentially for someone to get a tiny geographical detail right or to get it wrong? For example, if someone gets such an obscure detail *wrong*, is that just as much of an argument *against* his reliability as it is evidence *for* his reliability if he gets it right?

Resources for Further Study

A note on these resources: The resources suggested at the end of each chapter are meant to help those who want to dig deeper into the issues discussed in the chapter. When a resource is legally free on-line, as in the case of a video, blog post, or book that is no longer in copyright, I have included links. I am not always endorsing every position taken in the works referred to here, especially when the reference is to an entire book. I sometimes include the same resource more than once, since it is relevant to more than one chapter. In the case of my own books, which are often included here, I attempt to refer the reader to the sections most closely connected with the contents of the chapter. I have included the names of sections so that those with the Kindle versions can find the sections easily. Page numbers apply to the physical copy.

Richard Bauckham, "Historiographical Characteristics of the Gospel of John," *New Testament Studies* 53 (2007), pp. 17–36.

E. M. Blaiklock, *The Century of the New Testament* (London: Intervarsity Fellowship, 1962).

E.M. Blaiklock *The Compact Handbook of New Testament Life* (Minneapolis, MN: Bethany House Publishers, 1979), <https://tinyurl.com/Blaiklockhandbook>, also titled *The World of the New Testament* (London: Ark Publishing, 1981).

D. A. Carson, "Historical Tradition in the Fourth Gospel: After Dodd, What?" R. T. France and David Wenham, eds., *Gospel Perspectives*, vol. 2, *Studies of History and Tradition in the Four Gospels* (Sheffield: JSOT Press, 1981), pp. 83–145, <https://tinyurl.com/CarsonTradition>.

Lydia McGrew, *The Eye of the Beholder: The Gospel of John as Historical Reportage* (Tampa, FL: DeWard Publishing, 2021), Chapter III, "John as Historical Reportage: A First Positive Case," pp. 47–92.

Leon Morris, *Studies in the Fourth Gospel* (Grand Rapids, MI: Eerdmans Publishing Company, 1969), Chapters 2–4.

Peter J. Williams, *Can We Trust the Gospels?* (Wheaton, IL: Crossway Books, 2018).

2

Customs and Culture

1. Customs are tough

Imagine a world without the Internet or Google. Some of us, of course, can remember such a world. But now go further back: Imagine a world without reliable encyclopedias, atlases, or reference books from which you can find out accurate information about places and cultures other than your own. Imagine, too, that travel is dangerous, difficult, and expensive and that you go most places by walking. Imagine that, in this world with restricted movement, places that aren't even all that far away from one another have very different customs and cultures. Even people that follow the same religion and have the same ethnicity have strong regional differences, making it quite easy to make blunders if you merely guess about how things "probably" are in another part of the world. Now imagine trying to write a credible fictional book or story set in some other region.

In the 19th century, a historian named George Rawlinson emphasized the social and political complexity of the time of Christ and the unstrained accuracy the evangelists demonstrate. His words are worth quoting at length:

The political condition of Palestine at the time to which the New Testament narrative properly belongs, was one curiously complicated and anomalous; it underwent frequent changes, but retained through all of them certain peculiarities, which made the position of the country unique among the dependencies of Rome.... A mixture, and to some extent an alternation, of Roman with native power resulted from this arrangement, and a consequent complication in the political status, which must have made it very difficult to be thoroughly understood by any one who was not a native and a contemporary. The chief representative of the Roman power in the East—the President of Syria, the local governor, whether a Herod or a Roman Procurator, and the High Priest, had each and all certain rights and a certain authority in the country. A double system of taxation, a double administration of justice, and even in some degree a double military command, were the natural consequence; while Jewish and Roman customs, Jewish and Roman words, were simultaneously in use, and a condition of things existed full of harsh contrasts, strange mixtures, and abrupt transitions....These facts we know from Josephus and other writers, who, though less accurate, on the whole confirm his statements; they render the civil history of Judaea during the period one very difficult to master and remember; the frequent changes, supervening upon the original complication, are a fertile source of confusion....The New Testament narrative, however, falls into no error in treating of the period....[A]t every turn it shows, even in such little measures as verbal expressions, the coexistence of Jewish with Roman ideas and practices in the country—a coexistence which (it must be remembered) came to an end within forty years of our Lord's crucifixion.[1]

In such a time and place it would have been so easy for the Gospel authors to get wrong the complex interrelationships among the Jews, the Romans, and intermediate rulers (such as the tetrarchs) whom the Romans installed. Instead of stumbling, the evangelists move effortlessly and naturally through matters of fact, language, and culture, taking them into account in passing without being showy, just as a person does when he refers to the way things are in his own experience. Here Rawlinson is saying something similar to a point that I emphasized in the previous chapter: This whole taped-together political arrangement came to a crashing end in AD 70, when the Romans destroyed Jerusalem and all pretense of self-rule on the part of the Jews.

In this chapter we'll see just some of the ways in which customs and culture support the Gospels.

2. The high priests

In the last chapter I quoted Luke 3.1–2, in which Luke refers to "the high priesthood of Annas and Caiaphas," but I didn't explain there how this phrase supports the Gospels' accuracy. Luke's phrase seems strange at first, since it seems to imply that two people were high priest at the same time. John seems to imply this as well, using the same names (Annas and Caiaphas). In John 18.19, John refers to the high priest, and he must be using the term there to mean Annas, since in 18.13 he stated that this was the person to whom Jesus was taken first, and in 18.24 he says that Annas sent Jesus to Caiaphas. But in 18.24, John calls Caiaphas the high priest. Moreover, in John 11.49 and John 18.13, John says that Caiaphas was "high priest that year," giving the impression that someone might be high priest in one year but not in another.

This is all rather odd and confusing, since Old Testament verses like Numbers 35.25 and 28 and Joshua 20.6 seem to imply that the office of high priest was held for life. These references by Luke and John to multiple living high priests at the same time and John's use of the phrase "high priest that year" might seem like exactly the opposite of effortless accuracy; they might seem like blunders. Needless to say, skeptics have said exactly that. 19th-century skeptic Robert Taylor scoffed at these verses in both Gospels as instances of the "falsehood of Gospel statistics," saying that "any person acquainted with the history and polity of the Jews, must have known that there never was but one high-priest at a time, any more than among ourselves there is never but one Archbishop of Canterbury" and that "no Jew could have been ignorant that the high-priest's office was not annual, but for life...."[2]

But as in several of the cases discussed in the previous chapter, it turns out that the Gospel authors know their stuff better than modern critics. The Romans fully understood that the office of high priest was politically influential, and under Roman rule, it became at least as much a political as a religious position. The Romans considered themselves licensed to change the high priesthood as they wished, though they tried to choose men who had some sort of genealogical claim to the position and who were not too much hated by the people. Sometimes they even made changes fairly rapidly within a short period of time. At the time of Jesus, Caiaphas had been high priest for some years; Annas (who according to John 18.13 was his father-in-law) was still alive, having been deposed by the Romans. Caiaphas himself did not remain high priest for very long after Jesus' death. He was replaced by the Romans in his turn in AD 36.[3] John's expression "high priest that year" is very likely an allusion to the fact that the Romans did at times change the high priest, and it may well allude to the fact that just a few years later Caiaphas himself was no longer high priest. The fact that Annas had been an influential high priest at an earlier period (which is independently confirmed), combined with the family relationship that John mentions, could easily result in his retaining influence at the time of Jesus and acting in practice as a kind of "joint high priest" along with Caiaphas.

But there's even more. Joseph Lightfoot, a 19th-century scholar and bishop who ably defended the historicity of the Gospel of John, draws our attention to a passage in Josephus that uses the phrase "high priest" and "high priests" in very much the same way that Luke and John do.[4] In the 60s, the Romans had again made multiple changes of the high priest. A former high priest named Ananias (probably the one who presided at a hostile hearing of the Apostle Paul in Acts 23.2) was still a force to be reckoned with, even though a new high priest named Jesus (Joshua) had been put in place by the Romans. According to Josephus, Ananias corrupted the newer high priest by bribery to turn a blind eye when Ananias's servants went around like gang enforcers raiding the threshing floors where the tithes were kept that were supposed to supply all the priests. The result was that some of the poorer priests went hungry. In this passage Josephus uses the term "high priest" both for Ananias and for Jesus, just as Luke and John do for Annas and Caiaphas, and in a very similar situation—cooperation between a former high priest who was still living and a current one appointed by the Romans.[5]

It's important to remember that John and Luke are writing separate documents. For evidential purposes, we shouldn't think of them as belonging to one book called "the Bible." It's extremely improbable that John put in these subtle references to Annas and Caiaphas as both being high priest and to Caiaphas as "high priest that year" in order to fit together with Luke's statement that John the Baptist began preaching in the high priesthood of Annas and Caiaphas. So just from Luke and John we have multiple confirmations that "high priest" could refer to more than one living man. Josephus then provides confirmation from entirely outside any biblical books showing that indeed, people who lived in this time period did use the term "high priest" in this way.

3. Those dumb Galileans

When I was a child growing up in Chicago in the 1970s, for some reason "Polack jokes" were all the rage. I realize that all ethnic jokes are now considered to be politically incorrect, and these were certainly insensitive. Some at least had a little cleverness to them, like this one:

> A Polish man went to the eye doctor and was told to read the bottom line of the chart, which said ZXCGYK. "Can you read the bottom line?" said the doctor. "Read it?" said the patient. "I know the guy!"

That, at least, has some connection to the idea that Polish names are oddly spelled (from an American's perspective), though if you didn't happen to know that, you wouldn't get the joke. Far more common among kids were the ones in which "Polack" just meant "stupid person," as in, "How many Polacks does it take to change a light bulb?" and so forth. We never stopped to ask ourselves why we used the Poles as exemplars of stupidity. We weren't self-reflective. My own guess is that such jokes were especially popular in urban centers like Chicago that did have a large ethnic Polish presence.

It should come as no surprise that the ancient world had its stereotypes as well, and one of these is reflected in the Gospels—namely, the prejudice in Judea against those from the northern region of Galilee. We see this regional prejudice in a couple of verses in John's Gospel and to a lesser extent in the Synoptics.

When Philip tells Nathanael that they have found the Messiah, Jesus of Nazareth, Nathanael sniffs, "Can any good thing come out of Nazareth?" (John 1.44–46). When the people in

Jerusalem are debating about Jesus, some of them say, "Surely the Christ is not going to come from Galilee, is he?" (John 7.41). This might mean simply that they think that the Messiah should be born in Bethlehem; they don't know that Jesus was, in fact, born in Bethlehem, though he grew up in Galilee. They refer to this concern in the next verse (7.42). But the regional bigotry becomes clear among the religious leaders just a little further on in the chapter. The religious leaders are displeased when Nicodemus, one of their own group, tries to defend Jesus mildly by suggesting that they should give him a chance to speak for himself rather than condemning him out of hand. Their reply betrays an obvious regional prejudice. "You are not also from Galilee, are you? Search and see, that no prophet arises out of Galilee" (John 7.52) The first sentence is an unmistakable sneer: "Oh, what are you, one of those *Galileans*?"

We find a hint of the same bias in the stories of how Peter denies Jesus. Those in the high priest's courtyard take note of Peter's accent and pick him out as a follower of Jesus in this way: "Surely you too are one of them, for the way you talk gives you away" (Matt. 26.73).

I might have put all of this thus far into the category of "unexplained allusions," which I discuss in Chapter 5. The references in John, especially, are cryptic without further cultural background. They give us no idea why speakers like Nathanael sneer at Galileans. We might well wonder, "What's the deal with Galileans?" John takes no trouble to explain, even though his hearers in Asia Minor probably would have found this as incomprehensible as a young Michigander in 2022 would if I started a joke with, "Did you hear about the Polack who…?"

But sometimes a piece of evidence can fall into more than one category, and so it is here. For, as Bishop Lightfoot points out,[6] we can confirm the Judean prejudice against Galileans from Talmudic sources. While the anti-Galilean slurs are unexplained within John for his own audience, we can find out more about the prejudice by research. One whole Talmudic passage makes fun of the Galilean dialect, telling (no doubt fictional) stories about "foolish Galileans" who could not make themselves understood because their speech did not distinguish different words. One story is about a woman complaining to a judge about some men who have stolen a wooden board. Because of her accent, the Galilean woman appears to be saying that the thieves stole the judge instead of stealing the board. Probably these would be funnier to one who spoke the relevant language. In contrast, the passage says that Judeans are clever in their speech.[7]

Another story of a rabbi who lived around or just after the time of Jesus claims that he grumbled that the Galileans "hate the law." Why? Because he lived in Galilee for many years and allegedly had only two cases brought to him to adjudicate.[8] The point of this story is supposed to be that the Galileans are not properly concerned with following the finer points of Jewish law.

All of this paints a pretty clear picture: To the Judeans, and especially to the learned among them, the Galileans were what we would call hicks. They had a funny accent, they didn't live in the cultural and religious center of Jewish life, and they supposedly didn't care enough about how things were supposed to be done. It is quite likely that Acts 4.13 reflects this same set of attitudes. Peter and John refuse boldly to be silenced in preaching about Jesus. The leaders marvel at their confidence. They perceive that they are untrained (there's that Galilean accent again), and they recognize that they have been with Jesus. Why? Because, despite their "hick" way of speaking and their lack of formal rabbinic education, they, like Jesus, are confident in what they stand for and are not overawed by the fact that the Jerusalem leaders are their "betters."

But who could have made this up in the Gospels (and this verse in Acts), working it so effortlessly and naturally into different stories—the calling of Nathanael, the sneers of the Jerusalem leaders, the denials of Peter?

4. Jesus and the widow of Nain

Only Luke tells us about how Jesus raised the son of the widow of Nain from the dead (Luke 7.11–17). Nain is a town in lower Galilee, about ten miles south of Nazareth.[9] When Jesus and his disciples are approaching the city gate, they see a funeral procession coming out. Jesus has compassion on the mother of the dead young man, approaches her, and says, "Do not weep" (7.13). There is something moving in the simplicity of this. Jesus could certainly speak harshly when it was called for (see Chapter 8 on the unified personality of Jesus in the Gospels), but his heart is touched with our grief. Here he speaks simply to the mother: "Don't cry." Verse 14 says that he then went up and approached the bier and touched it and raised the young man to life by his word.

Besides the existence of the town of Nain itself, what external confirmation could there be for this passage? New Testament scholar Craig Blomberg tells us.[10] The Talmudic sages, in discussing the words of Ecclesiastes 12.5 about the mourners who go about in the streets, say both that you should live thinking about what you want the mourners to say about you while walking *behind* your bier and that you should think about what you want them to say about you while walking *before* your bier. The Talmud reconciles these by pointing out that in Judea the custom is for the mourners (or "eulogizers") to walk behind the bier in the funeral procession while in Galilee the custom is for them to walk in front.¹¹ Since Jesus and his disciples were approaching the gate of the town, it is reasonable to picture the funeral procession as coming out of the gate in order, with the mother and other mourners walking ahead of the men carrying the body. Jesus thus approaches the mother first and speaks gently to her, then approaches the bier and stops it.

While we can't be certain that Jesus spoke to the mother first because she was walking ahead of the body, it is a very natural picture, and all the more so when we know that the mother would have been doing that according to the Galilean custom. But what an obscure piece of information! This is not at all the kind of thing that someone would easily find out who didn't already know. Who would think that such a custom would differ in two regions as relatively near to one another as Galilee and Judea? (The Talmud is full of such references to differing customs.) This little detail looks like witness testimony and probably means that Luke had the story from someone who was actually present.

5. The fish and the stater

In Matt. 17.24–27 we find the story of the Temple tax and the coin in the fish's mouth. The collectors of the two-drachma tax for the Temple come to Peter and ask if his master pays the tax. Peter answers that he does. When he enters the house in Capernaum where Jesus is staying, Jesus implies that they should not have to pay the tax. But he then tells Peter to go and throw a hook into the sea. Jesus predicts that Peter will find a coin in the fish's mouth and tells him to use it to pay the tax for the two of them. While the story doesn't actually say that this happened—that is, it does not narrate Peter's going to the sea and catching the fish—it seems fairly obvious that Matthew is implying that that actually is what happened.

External evidence confirms one of the specifics of this story, namely, the specific coin that Jesus said Peter would find in the fish's mouth. The Temple tax, as already mentioned, was two drachmas per person and is literally called the "two-drachma tax" in the Greek (Matt. 17.24). The specific word that Jesus uses for the coin that Peter will find in the fish's mouth is "stater." And as it turns out, the word "stater" had indeed come to be used for a coin worth four drachmae.[12] In other words, Jesus doesn't tell Peter to find just "a coin." Rather, he predicts that Peter will find a coin of just exactly the right denomination to pay the tax for the two of them and instructs him to use it for that purpose so as not to offend the officials. This fits with the fact that the officials asked Peter not, "Do you pay the tax?" but "Does your master pay the tax?" One can guess that if Peter showed up with the money to pay the tax for just himself or for just Jesus, they would bring up the other person and ask for payment again. Once again, we have a place where the author shows casual accuracy about the customs of the time—the amount of the Temple tax and the coin that would pay that tax for exactly two people.

An extra argument that this story is true is the very fact that it is unfinished. We would not expect an inventor to be so restrained. If this story were a fictional embellishment or a legend that grew up around Jesus, why not go on and tell about how Peter found the coin? Matthew tells his story briefly and moves on.

6. A denarius for a day's wage

Jesus tells a parable, recorded in Matthew 20.1–16, about laborers hired to work in a vineyard. The landowner and the laborers agree on the pay for a day's work. The parable then goes on to describe the jealousy of those workers when the boss pays those hired much later in the day the same amount, even though those hired later did not work through the heat of the day. Some translations give the day's pay as a penny, which is quite confusing to modern readers. In fact, the word is "denarius," and it shows the accuracy of Matthew's record of what Jesus said.

We find in the Roman historian Tacitus that lowlier Roman soldiers in about AD 14 were paid 10/16 of a Roman denarius per day. Some soldiers were better off. These were the ones who negotiated ahead of time (before enlisting) for a full denarius a day. The Praetorian guards were better off still; they were paid two denarii per day. In Tacitus, an agitator tells the soldiers that they are being treated badly, both because they don't even get a denarius per day and because of the brutal working conditions.[13] The value of a denarius remained approximately the same until the time of Nero.[14]

So the landowner's offer of one denarius per day to laborers in the story was a good offer but not exorbitant. It was about what a Roman soldier would receive if he negotiated a somewhat more favorable contract than the pay of the lowliest recruit. Just think how hard it would be now to guess (without looking it up) what pay was typical and reasonable for a certain kind of work in, say, the 1980s. Matthew's account of Jesus' parable includes the kind of knowledge that would have been difficult to fake.

7. Touchy Samaritans

In Luke 9.51, Jesus leaves Galilee to go to Jerusalem. This is, by my estimate, probably at the time of the Feast of Tabernacles described in John 7. Luke 9.52–53 says that Jesus sent messengers ahead of him to a town in Samaria. One common way of getting from Galilee to Jerusalem was to travel through Samaria. But the people in the village they chose refused to have him stay there. Luke says that it was because "he was journeying with his face toward Jerusalem." What's that all about? Why should the Samaritans care what direction he was going?†

In Josephus we learn that the Samaritans did not like the fact that the Jewish pilgrims from Galilee and parts to the north frequently passed through their region on the way to Jerusalem for the various feasts. In fact, some years later the Samaritans even killed a pilgrim under these circumstances, setting off a fight with the Galileans and a complicated dispute about whether the murder was properly prosecuted and who was more in the wrong.[15]

No doubt part of the tension surrounding the Jewish pilgrims arose from the fact that, as the woman at the well mentions to Jesus in John 4.20, the Samaritans worshiped in Mt. Gerizim. The Samaritans claimed that they worshiped the same God as the Jews and that they were doing so properly, but the Jews insisted that the only proper place to sacrifice to Yahweh was in Jerusalem itself. The repeated journeys to the Jewish feasts emphasized this theological disagreement as well as the ethnic differences between the groups. The large numbers of Jewish pilgrims traveling through the Samarians' land were probably not particularly sensitive to local feelings, especially since they despised the Samaritans. If indeed Jesus was traveling at the time of a feast in Luke 9.51–53, the Samaritans probably felt unfriendly for that reason, and those in this village apparently told his disciples to "go pound sand" rather than providing lodging for another traveling party.

Here a bit of further conjecture may add even more point to the external confirmation: If this was indeed the same journey described in John 7.2–11, we can see that Jesus went to that feast later than other travelers. His brothers taunted him, telling him

---

†We might notice how different this is from Jesus' reception by the Samaritans in John 4.3–42. Of course that may have been a different Samaritan village, and it was several years earlier. Still it may have made a difference that in that case Jesus was traveling away from Jerusalem rather than toward it, and probably at a less "touchy" time of year.

to go to the feast and reveal himself. Jesus told them to go ahead themselves. He then went a bit later with his disciples. Plausibly, then, the Samaritans had already had various parties of Jews passing through their villages. Their patience, never very great at these times, would have already worn thin, and group tensions would have already begun to show. This could provide further explanation for the refusal to receive Jesus and his disciples in the Samaritan village.†

8. Circumcision and the Sabbath

After Jesus heals a lame man in John 5.1–16 at the Pool of Bethesda, the Jerusalem religious leaders are angry, both because he healed on the Sabbath and because he told the healed man to carry his pallet on the Sabbath. In Chapter 8 I will be talking about how Jesus' discussion of this Sabbath controversy fits a pattern in the way that he taught and thought—specifically, his witty use of words to make a point about misplaced priorities. Here I want to highlight the way that external evidence confirms John's report in 7.22–23.

In John 7.22–23, Jesus refers to the healing and the controversy narrated in John 5. He says that his opponents will circumcise

---

† A further conjecture, which I do not insist upon, would be that the healing of the ten lepers described in Luke 17.11–19 actually occurred at this earlier point in time when Jesus had just been rejected in Samaria. Luke 9.56 says merely that they went to another village, not where the village was. Luke may not have been told exactly when the healing of the ten lepers occurred, merely that it was on Jesus' way to Jerusalem. Luke does not specify the time precisely. Much of the narration in this section of Luke is what I call achronological—that is, the author does not appear to be trying to specify a time ordering. The geography of the ten lepers story would fit with the incident in Luke 9. The location specified in 17.11 is probably the Jezreel Valley. Jesus could have gone east through that valley after the Samaritan village refused him, crossed the Jordan, and journeyed south that way, along a less busy route to Jerusalem. For this geographical location, though not this suggestion about chronology, see John Wenham, *Redating Matthew, Mark, and Luke: A Fresh Assault on the Synoptic Problem* (Downers Grove, IL: Intervarsity Press, 1992), p. 211.

a male child on the Sabbath day so that the law of Moses will not be broken, and he contrasts this with their rigid opposition to his healing on the Sabbath. It may be difficult for modern Gentile Christians to appreciate these legal questions, but there was an issue that could understandably arise under Jewish law: Did circumcising a baby boy count as "work"? If so, how did this fit with the commandment to circumcise on the eighth day? What if a baby boy's eighth day happened to fall on the Sabbath? How could they keep all of God's commandments?

As it turns out, Jesus' comments reflect not just a hypothetical worry that Jews of the time might have had but a real discussion that they *did* have. We have external evidence of this. Because it was possible for the two commandments—to keep the Sabbath and to circumcise on the eighth day—to appear to be in conflict, there were rabbinic rulings as to which one took precedence.[16] And just as Jesus says, it was ruled that the command to circumcise on the eighth day took precedence. Circumcision of a baby boy did not count as forbidden "work" unless the circumcision was being carried out at some non-standard time. For example, if a circumcision had already been delayed past the eighth day for some other reason, there would be no need to do it on the Sabbath. But in the more usual case, circumcision was to take place even if the boy's eighth day was the Sabbath.

Jesus goes on to make the point that it should have been equally legitimate for him to heal a man on the Sabbath. John portrays Jesus as reasoning in a typically rabbinic fashion, showing a knowledge of law and precedent and applying them in a novel way to the specific question of (miraculous) healing on the Sabbath. This is just another example of how the Gospels are rooted in the highly specific time and place where their stories occur.

9. Rivers of living water

At the end of the Feast of Tabernacles in John 7, we find this:

> Now on the last day, the great day of the feast, Jesus stood and cried out, saying, "If anyone is thirsty, let him come to Me and drink. He who believes in Me, as the Scripture said, 'From his innermost being will flow rivers of living water.'" But this He spoke of the Spirit, whom those who believed in Him were to receive; for the Spirit was not yet given, because Jesus was not yet glorified. (John 7.37–39)

These three verses alone contain no fewer than *three* confirmations of John's historical care. In Chapter 5, I'll discuss the "unexplained allusion" to "the Scripture" about living water flowing from one's innermost being.

Why is there such an emphasis in these verses upon the last day of the feast? The feast in question is the Feast of Tabernacles, sometimes called the Feast of Booths (Sukkot). At the time of Jesus there was a water-drawing ceremony during the feast, probably each day. Water was carried from the Pool of Siloam and poured over the altar in the Temple. There was also a special ceremony of lights, in which many candelabra were lit, which appears to have been associated with the water pouring on the seventh day of the feast.[17] While it is unclear whether the "great day" refers to the seventh or the eighth day, the water-drawing ceremony from the living waters of Siloam would have been in the minds of those attending the feast. The Talmud says, referring to these ceremonies, "One who did not see the Celebration of the Place of the Drawing of the Water never saw celebration in his days."[18]

We have to keep remembering that this ended in AD 70, with the destruction of Jerusalem. Though some scholars argue that John's Gospel was written before the fall of Jerusalem, I take the view that seems to fit better with the evidence of the church fathers, namely, that it was written in John's old age, after the fall of Jerusalem. By that time there would have been no water drawing from Siloam and no altar in the Temple on which to pour the living water.

Jesus' dramatic call to those who are thirsty to come to him and drink and receive a spiritual river of living water makes sense in the light of the customs of the time. Yet it's almost impossible to picture a fictionalizing author "putting" such an allusion into Jesus' mouth without referring in any clearer way to the ceremony. If John made up what Jesus said here, why not describe the ceremony to make the connection clearer? It is unlikely that everyone in his own audience would think of the water-pouring and lights ceremonies, especially Gentiles and any Jews who were too young to remember the original ceremony. Within the Gospel of John, Jesus' choice of this metaphor and the association with the last day of the Feast of Tabernacles is unexplained, subtle, and not literary at all. John writes like someone recording events, not like a literary craftsman who invents to further his own themes.

Another confirmation of historicity here lies in the fact that the narrator puts his own gloss on Jesus' words—namely, that Jesus was referring to the Holy Spirit—but he scrupulously separates his own explanation from what Jesus historically said. What John *doesn't* do is put his own interpretation into Jesus' mouth. Unfortunately, many New Testament scholars assume that the evangelists, John especially, thought that they were allowed to put words into Jesus' mouth. The theory is that John thought that, as long as he was giving a correct *interpretation* of what Jesus taught elsewhere, it was okay for him to invent a setting and a saying that didn't recognizably happen at all. For example, on this theory, John thought that it was legitimate for him to invent Jesus' saying, "I and the Father are one" in

Jerusalem (John 10.30) because Jesus' deity is implied by his statement that he has authority to forgive sins in Mark 2.10, in a completely different story that occurs in Galilee. But that is not *at all* what we find in John. Instead, when John has some interpretation to give his readers, he carefully distinguishes his own interpretation from what Jesus actually says.[†]

10. Tithing dill and cumin

Have you ever wondered whether the Gospels' portrayal of the Pharisees might be just a bit over-the-top? Exaggerated? Were there really religious teachers out there who even bothered to think about the rules that Jesus attributes to them? In this section we'll see again the accuracy of the Gospels in portraying both Jesus' words and the cultural background that his words suggest.

Matthew 23.23 is part of a section sometimes called the "woes to the Pharisees." Jesus really gets on a roll, telling off the Pharisees as blind guides:

> "Woe to you, scribes and Pharisees, hypocrites! For you tithe mint and dill and cummin and have neglected the weightier provisions of the law: justice and mercy and faithfulness; but these are the things you should have done without neglecting the others. You blind guides, who strain out a gnat and swallow a camel!" (Matt. 23.23–24)

Jesus portrays the religious leaders as literally trying to tithe herbs. How would you even do that? Just think of the spices you buy in the store—the little bottles of fennel seeds, dill seeds, or dried, crumbled oregano leaves, with an amount written on the bottle like ".5 oz." Imagine having to figure out how much of some herb you had in order to give one tenth of it to God! With some of them perhaps you could literally count ("one dill seed,

---
[†] See also John 2.21–22, 13.11, and 18.8–9 for more of these "asides."

two dill seeds, three, four"). Others you would probably have to weigh on a small scale and then compute a tenth.

But did anyone really go that far? Yes, indeed. New Testament scholar Peter J. Williams[19] points us to passages in the Talmud that discuss precisely which plants (including herbs) did and didn't need to be tithed, what part of the plant needed to be tithed, and under what circumstances. To get a sense for the kind of thing Jesus had in mind, here is a quotation from one of the sections Williams cites:

> He who husks barley may husk each [grain] singly and eat [without tithing], but if he husked and put them into his hand, he is liable [to tithe]. He who rubs parched ears of wheat may blow out [the chaff] from hand to hand and eat, but if he blows and puts the grain in his lap he is liable. If coriander was sown for the sake of the seed, the plant is exempt [from tithe]. But if sown for the sake of the plant then both the seed and the plant must be tithed. R[abbi] Eliezer said: As for dill, tithe must be given from the seed and the plant and the pods. But the sages, however, say: Both the seeds and plant are tithed only in the case of pepperwort and Eruca.[20]

Another ancient passage mentions a divergence of opinion between two rabbinic schools of thought concerning the tithing of black cumin, which was apparently related to whether it was regarded as "clean" or "unclean."[21]

So Jesus wasn't exaggerating, and Matthew wasn't exaggerating either when he reported that Jesus said this! Notice here something I will come back to in Chapter 8—Jesus' love of plays on words when exposing hypocrisy. Here he talks about mint, dill, and cumin, which are lightweight, and he portrays the Pharisees as carefully tithing them. But, he says, they have neglected the far *weightier matters* of the Old Testament law. What are those? Justice, mercy, and faithfulness.

11. The quaternion

The author of John claims to have been an eyewitness of the events he tells, and he especially emphasizes having witnessed Jesus' crucifixion in John 19.35. (See also John 21.24.) He saw it. He bore record. His record is true. We can see this eyewitness testimony confirmed in the little details, dropped here and there. He tells what he knows.

Consider the dicing soldiers, dividing up Jesus' garments.

> The soldiers therefore, when they had crucified Jesus, took His outer garments and made four parts, a part to every soldier and also the tunic; now the tunic was seamless, woven in one piece. They said therefore to one another, "Let us not tear it, but cast lots for it, to decide whose it shall be"; that the Scripture might be fulfilled, "They divided my outer garments among them and for my clothing they cast lots." (John 19.23–24)

This little passage gives rise to several incidental external confirmations. First of all, it actually was a practice under Roman law for the executioner(s) to keep the clothing and small personal items that a prisoner had on him at the time of death.[22] The soldiers callously strip Jesus naked and decide among themselves how to distribute his clothes.

Second, a tunic woven in a single piece of cloth, with a hole cut for the head, appears to have been unusual. The more usual tunic of the time would be made out of two pieces of cloth sewn together.[23] The soldiers therefore had multiple reasons for throwing dice for the tunic rather than tearing it. To tear it would ruin its usefulness as an item of clothing, and a somewhat unusual and hence valuable item of clothing at that.

But what I want to emphasize here most of all is a third confirmation: Notice how casually John implies that there were four soldiers involved in Jesus' crucifixion. He doesn't even say it explicitly. It follows from his statement that they made four piles of his clothing, one for each soldier. Why is this important? We have independent evidence that a group of four soldiers was considered a guard in the Roman army. Among other non-biblical sources, the historian Polybius, describing how a Roman camp is set up, pauses to say explicitly, "A guard consists of four men."[24] Acts 12.4 also confirms this. When Peter is put in prison, he is guarded by four squads of soldiers; the Greek means literally "four sets of four." This may mean that each quaternion was on duty for six hours of the day.

John is not in any way parading his knowledge that there were four soldiers. It is woven right into the story. Clearly the last thing on his mind is implying that there were four soldiers so that people familiar with the Roman military system will be impressed. Even though he strongly emphasizes his eyewitness status in verse 35 (describing the blood and water that came from Jesus' side when the soldier pierced it), the facts surrounding the soldiers' dividing Jesus' clothes are told simply and straightforwardly. It comes out quite naturally that the usual Roman guard, a quaternion (group of four), carried out the crucifixion.

The scene is vivid, and it would have been even more so to those living in an age when crucifixions actually took place. The soldiers strip their victims (Jesus and the two thieves), nail them up, and then sit down under the crosses to cast dice for the tunic. As Matthew says, "And sitting down, they began to keep watch over Him there" (Matt 27.36).

12. Name statistics and "last" names

Do you know what the most popular girls' or boys' name was in your part of the country in the year when you were born? No Googling now! No using a baby names book published at the time. I would bet that most of us could not answer that question correctly, despite the fact that it concerns our own region and time period. All the more so, if you were to write a fictional story about a time and place other than your own, you would be wise to do careful research in order to give names to your characters that fit the context.

At the time of Jesus, the Jews lived in many different parts of the Roman empire. And contrary to what one might think, they didn't give their children the same names in all of those places. In Egypt, for example, in the time of Christ, Sabbataius was a very popular male name, which it most certainly was not in Jerusalem. Scholars of Jewish history have investigated these name statistics for different eras by using written documents, inscriptions, and names carved on ossuaries (burial boxes). It is fascinating research and has important ramifications for the reliability of the Gospels.

It turns out that there is an interesting correlation between the names that we find most frequently in the Gospels (and Acts) and the names that were actually the most popular names in Jesus' time and place. The name Simon is a good example here. It was the most popular male name in Palestine in Jesus' time and is also the most frequent male New Testament name.[25] Mary was the most popular female name in that time and place, and sure enough, despite the relatively small number of female names in the Gospels, we find that it is the most common name in the Gospels as well.[26]

The statistical correlation is not exact for all of the Gospel names, and we wouldn't expect it to be. Any small sample is going to be only partially similar to the larger group of which it is a part. So we find for example that there is only one real person named Lazarus in the Gospels and one person in a parable, though Lazarus was the third most popular male Jewish name at that place and time. Again, this is an expected result of working with a small sample.

When we combine rankings and stick to male names we see quite a striking similarity. About 15.6% of men in Palestine at the time had one or the other of the top two male names. In the Gospels and Acts, we find 18.2% that fall into that category. When we combine the top nine male names the correlation is even closer: 41.5% and 40.3%.[27]

To go along with this correlation in name statistics we find another *very* exciting piece of evidence—the evidence of "extra" names to distinguish between different people by the same name. In the modern world, we use last names for this purpose; we may also use nicknames or other descriptions. If you know five people named Bob, and if you mention "Bob" to a mutual friend who also knows several people by this first name, he may ask, "Which Bob?" If you know the last name of the Bob you have in mind, you might tell him that. Or you'll give a description: "You know, Bob the sound guy at church."

In the time and place of the Gospels, there were no last names. Instead, if someone had a common name, people would use a description to distinguish him from others of the same name. This might be his father's name, the town he was from, his occupation, or some striking characteristic for which he was known. (Many of our modern last names came originally from occupations as well—Smith, Waggoner, Brewer, etc. Some came from "the son of"—e.g., Johnson.)

In the Gospels, we find that the people who have the most common names also have these extra names, which scholars call disambiguators. So we have Simon Peter, Simon the leper, Simon the tanner (in Acts), and so forth. John (Yohanan) was a popular male name, and so we have John the son of Zebedee distinguished from John the Baptist. For the popular Jewish female name Mary (Miriam) we have Mary the mother of Jesus, Mary the mother of James and Joses (Mark 15.40), and Mary Magdalene.

A fascinating exercise, suggested by Peter J. Williams, is examining the list of the twelve disciples in Matthew 10.2–4.[28] Notice the names that do have disambiguators and those that don't. The name Judas was #4 on the charts at the time, and so Judas Iscariot gets a disambiguator. (Scholars differ on whether "Iscariot" refers to a town or is a modified version of some other word). Notice that in John 14.22 when another Judas among the twelve asks a question, John carefully tells us that he was "not Iscariot." In fact, based on a comparison of the lists of the twelve in Luke and in Matthew, it looks like the Greek name Thaddeus, which was uncommon in Palestine at the time, was another name for Judas, not Iscariot. Calling him "not Iscariot" would have been awkward in daily practice. If he was also known by the name "Thaddeus" (possibly because of a similarity of sound between the Greek name and the Aramaic "Judah"), he might well have preferred to go by Thaddeus, especially after Judas Iscariot betrayed Jesus.[29] Thaddeus didn't require any further phrase. Similarly, Bartholomew was in 50th place among male Palestinian names, and there is no further phrase describing him in the lists of the twelve.

This practice of adding extra names to avoid ambiguity has a special application to the name Jesus. Although we don't find a lot of characters in the New Testament named Jesus, it's clear that the people in the stories do know multiple people by that name. How can you tell? Because Jesus' name is almost always given with some extra description. Most commonly this is the phrase "the Nazarene" or "of Nazareth." But he's also called "the son of Joseph," "the son of the carpenter," "Jesus who is called the Christ

(Messiah)." (Notice that this is different from just saying "Jesus Christ," which was a later Christian development).

The narrators of the Gospels are thinking of only one person named Jesus. So the narrator just says "Jesus." (In John 1.17 the narrator says "Jesus Christ.") But the people of the time who speak in the stories almost always use a disambiguator. There are almost no exceptions.†

While all of this may sound like a welter of confusing details, it has a very important point: The Gospel authors, all four of them, portray names very naturally and accurately both in their own story telling and in the words that people say in the stories. Evidence that their name assignments are uncannily accurate for the time period is evidence for the truth of their stories. After all, who is Mary Magdalene? She is the woman who comes to the tomb on Easter Sunday morning and finds it empty, one of the first to see Jesus alive. The people are embedded in the stories, and the names are attached to the people.

Similarly, if the authors were trying to make Jesus in their own image, to make him address their own interests and concerns, why do they so naturally and correctly show how people of the time referred to him—as Jesus of Nazareth or Jesus the son of the carpenter? Among themselves the Christians in the AD 50s and 60s almost certainly did not speak of him that way. If the evangelists were turning Jesus into their own mouthpiece to say the things that they, as Christians, wanted him to say, and to do the things that they wanted him to do, it is much less likely that they would so casually portray people of the time calling him by such specific, un-theological names. "Jesus the son of the

---

†The man born blind in John 9.11 says "the man who is called Jesus" without indicating any further which Jesus. But he is one of the few people in the Gospels whom Jesus spontaneously approaches to offer a miracle. The idea is that he has had very little time to find out anything about this stranger who restored his sight, so the story hangs together very well.

carpenter" had no theological significance. It was merely a way of saying which Jesus you were talking about.

This, by the way, helps to explain why Bartimaeus in Jericho gets so excited (Mark 10.47) when the people tell him that Jesus of Nazareth is passing by. He has heard of *that* Jesus and probably has heard of his healing the man born blind, though that miracle occurs in John's Gospel. As Williams points out, just hearing that someone named Jesus was passing by wouldn't have been exciting in itself. But Bartimaeus knows that Jesus of Nazareth is someone special.[30]

We can see this point about names even better if we contrast the real Gospels with the fake, later Gnostic "Gospels." As Williams points out, they have nothing like the name accuracy that we find in the canonical Gospels.[31] The author of the second-century so-called "Gospel of Mary" apparently didn't even know that there would be many women named Mary in that time and place. So he doesn't even say which Mary the Gospel is about. Jesus is spoken of simply as "the Savior," not even as Jesus, much less Jesus of Nazareth. Similarly the "Gospel of Judas" introduces a host of names arising from a mishmash of the Greek Bible and Greek mysticism. These include Nebro, Saklas, and Yaldabaoth. Obviously this is not accurate history.

Who would have thought that the little things described in this chapter could have so much evidential power? They have this power precisely because the Gospel authors aren't even trying. From the four soldiers dividing Jesus' clothes to the many women named Mary to the two men called "high priest"—again and again the evangelists get it right. They don't do this by way of arduous research. They do it by knowing what really happened. Outside facts about culture and customs confirm the Gospels because truth hangs together.

Chapter Summary

- The Gospels get hard things right about the customs and culture of the highly specific time and place in which Jesus ministered.

- These obscure facts concern a wide variety of issues—prejudices of the time, Jewish rabbis' debates, the names that were common, and more.

- The confirmation of these details in the Gospels shows us that the authors were not making up their stories. They really knew what they were talking about.

Study Questions

1. According to Rawlinson, which two cultures coexisted in Palestine at the time the Gospel stories took place? How did this make the situation complicated?

2. Discuss why the naming of both Annas and Caiaphas as high priest at the same time in Luke and in John is not an error.

3. When Nathanael asks if any good thing can come out of Nazareth, what cultural fact of the time does this reflect? Name some other allusions in the Gospels to this same cultural fact.

4. How does Jesus' reference in John 7 to circumcision show that the story is embedded in the real Jewish situation of the time? Describe another reference that Jesus made to real rabbinical discussions.

5. When the narrator in John 7 pauses to explain that Jesus was referring to the Holy Spirit when he mentioned rivers of living water, how does this confirm the historical truthfulness of the Gospel of John?

6. What is a quaternion? How does John indirectly show accurate information about the soldiers who crucified Jesus?

7. How does the Gospels' use of "extra" names show a casual accuracy in telling their stories?

8. How does the name "Jesus" illustrate the point in the previous question?

For Discussion

1. Give examples of some obscure cultural facts in your own background or current cultural context that a truthful reporter might casually mention in a true story.

2. Discuss what it was like to gather information about other cultures before the advent of the Internet and after the advent of the Internet. Contrast both of these with the time of the Gospels.

3. Choose two or three favorite obscure facts from this chapter to have available in discussions of Gospel reliability.

4. It has been argued that Matthew couldn't really have had both the name "Levi" as Mark gives it (in the story about Matthew's calling to be a disciple) and "Matthew" as Matthew's Gospel gives it. The argument is that, in the name statistics we have gathered from the time, it is uncommon to find two relatively common Hebrew names used for the same person. Even though these name statistics are important for arguing that the Gospels are reliable, they should not be used in a wooden way. Give examples from your own experience where people have unusual combinations of names—e.g., an Irish first name and a Hebrew middle name.

5. Explain in your own words the point of the exercise in the chapter where we went through the names of the Twelve and found out which ones have "extra" names attached and which ones don't. Did the result of this exercise surprise you?

6. Do you know of other examples either in our own time or in history where there have been complex political relationships between different levels of government that would be hard for an outsider to weave into a story without making mistakes?

Resources for Further Study

Richard Bauckham, *Jesus and the Eyewitnesses*, 2nd ed. (Grand Rapids, MI: Eerdmans, 2017), Chapters 3–5, pp. 39–113.

E.M. Blaiklock *The Compact Handbook of New Testament Life* (Minneapolis, MN: Bethany House Publishers, 1979), <https://tinyurl.com/Blaiklockhandbook>; also titled *The World of the New Testament* (London: Ark Publishing, 1981).

Craig L. Blomberg, *The Historical Reliability of the Gospels* (Downers Grove, IL: IVP Academic, 2007).

Lydia McGrew, "The Annotated Rawlinson," *Extra Thoughts*, April 29, 2015, <https://tinyurl.com/McGrewRawlinson>.

Lydia McGrew, *The Mirror or the Mask: Liberating the Gospels from Literary Devices* (Tampa, FL: DeWard Publishing, 2019), Chapter XI, "Evidence and the Artless Author," sections 6–9, pp. 278–298.

Leon Morris, *Studies in the Fourth Gospel* (Grand Rapids, MI: Eerdmans Publishing Company, 1969), Chapters 2–4.

George Rawlinson, *The Historical Evidences of the Truth of the Scripture Records: Stated Anew* (Boston: Gould and Lincoln, 1860), <https://tinyurl.com/GeorgeRawl>.

Peter J. Williams, *Can We Trust the Gospels?* (Wheaton, IL: Crossway Books, 2018).

3

Undesigned Coincidences

1. What is an undesigned coincidence?

One of the most exciting arguments for the reliability of the Gospels to make a comeback in the early 21st century is the argument from undesigned coincidences. I say "make a comeback," because this argument is so old that it's new again. The phrase "undesigned coincidences" was coined by the 18th-century Christian scholar William Paley, who wrote extensively about it in connection with the way that the letters of Paul dovetail with each other and with the book of Acts. Paley also suggested that this type of evidence supports the Gospels. During the 19th century a number of other scholars, especially the clergyman J. J. Blunt, wrote at more length about how the argument could be applied to the Gospels. Due to the rise of liberal higher criticism and other social factors, it fell out of style and out of mind, but it was never refuted.

In the early 21st century, three different authors working largely independently revived the argument—New Testament scholar Peter J. Williams, cold-case detective and popular apologist J. Warner Wallace, and philosopher Timothy McGrew. After I learned of the argument from Timothy McGrew (my husband) and studied it in the work of Paley and Blunt, I devoted a whole book to it—*Hidden in Plain View: Undesigned Coincidences in the Gospels and Acts*, published in 2017.

So what does the phrase "undesigned coincidences" mean? One response I often hear when I first introduce the phrase is, "Isn't a coincidence automatically undesigned?" Sometimes this is said humorously. How could something be a designed coincidence, anyway? But if you understand the meaning of the word "coincidence" as Paley used it, you'll realize that the phrase isn't redundant at all. Paley used the word to mean co-incidence—coming together. So in an undesigned coincidence, two or more things come together, they fit with each other, they coincide, but without the authors trying to make it happen that way. An undesigned coincidence is a casual interlocking that points to truth.

The concept of an undesigned coincidence is best understood by examples, and I often find that beginning with a modern hypothetical example works best. Suppose that the police get a phone call that a bank robbery has occurred. They go to the scene of the alleged robbery and start questioning people who claim to have witnessed it. Now imagine two alleged witnesses whose testimony fits together in the form of a question and answer. One says that the bank robber was wearing tennis shoes and that one of them was untied. The other says that when the robber ran out of the bank, he tripped and almost fell. But note: The person who mentions the tripping doesn't mention the untied shoelace, and the person who mentions the untied shoelace doesn't mention the tripping. This is an example of an undesigned coincidence. The untied shoelace could easily explain the tripping. It answers the question, "Why did the robber trip?" The two statements fit together like pieces of a puzzle. Each witness seems to be describing one part of the larger picture of what happened. Since reality fits together, the statements fit together.

Here we need to think a bit about witness separation. Witness separation is a "gold standard" in investigating a crime. Ideally, the hope is to make sure that the witnesses (or alleged witnesses) couldn't be influencing each other *at all*. Police try to separate the witnesses and take their statements before they have any chance to talk with each other. If you can really make absolutely sure of that, then even when they do affirm the very same thing (such as the color of a car), you can take them to be stating it just because that's what they remember and not at all because they are being influenced by each other. When witnesses overhear each other or talk with each other before making their statements, the concern arises that one person's memory might be influencing the other's. But sometimes we can't tell if two people have talked to each other. Or maybe we know that they *have* been talking to each other. What then? Should we just discard the second person's evidence? That would be an extreme reaction, since both people had opportunity to know about the facts. We shouldn't just *assume* that the second person has nothing factual to add. One way to deal with witnesses who did have a chance to hear each other's testimony is to look for signs that they are trying to tell their own stories, not just copying. Such signs can include varying details or even apparent contradictions.

In the case of an undesigned coincidence, absolute witness separation isn't strictly necessary (though it would be nice to have), because the connection between the two details seems to arise unintentionally. The fact that one person's testimony raises a question and the other provides the answer is in and of itself a variation and hence a sign of factual independence. Even if the two witnesses did overhear each other's testimony, it doesn't appear that they are trying to corroborate each other. The co-incidence (coming together) of their statements appears undesigned because it is casual. It's hard to imagine one witness thinking to himself, "I didn't notice him trip, but that person did. I'll bet the reason why he tripped is that his shoe was untied. When that police officer comes to talk to me, I'll mention that his shoe was untied, but I *won't* mention that this is connected with the tripping." It is even harder to imagine this if one person is lying. In that case the second witness would have to be thinking, "I'll *say* that his shoe was untied, even though I didn't see that at all. That will fit with the fact that that other guy said he tripped. Then the police will believe me." This is a psychologically implausible thought process to attribute to a liar. What if the police don't notice the connection? We should take seriously the evidential value of the witnesses' apparent casualness and the way that these varying statements just happen to fit together, one explaining the other. This is evidence that both witnesses saw what really happened and that both are telling the truth.

2. Undesigned coincidences, the Gospels, and the Synoptic problem

How does the concept of undesigned coincidences apply to the Gospels? The Gospels present themselves as truthful, historical records of the life and teaching of Jesus. There are four of them, and they all have differences. Some stories are told in multiple Gospels, some only in one Gospel. Sometimes the different Gospels' stories of the same events will tell different details. Sometimes they might even seem to contradict each other, though often these claimed contradictions are drummed up by critics and skeptics and are unimpressive when we look at them rigorously.

These variations can be a good thing. Like witness statements about the bank robbery, Gospel accounts that contain differences give us different perspectives and additional facts. The fact that they aren't exactly the same gives us reason to think that they haven't simply been copied from one another or from a common source. Just as we would expect if they really were written by four different people who all had their own access to the facts, we often find that they complement one another. The differences in the accounts are often fruitful, fitting together in incidental interlockings that point to truth. These are undesigned coincidences in the Gospels.

Here, though, I must say something about what is known as the Synoptic problem, because if you make the argument from undesigned coincidences, you may be told that somehow this Synoptic problem undermines the argument. The Synoptic Gospels are Matthew, Mark, and Luke. It's easy to see just by reading them that these three Gospels resemble each other more than any of them resemble John. For one thing, there is much more overlap in which stories they tell. But the resemblance goes farther than that. Often we find that the wording in the stories is similar, too. These facts have led to an enormous amount of scholarship arguing over which one was written first and how, exactly, they are connected. It seems like there is some literary dependence somewhere, but exactly what is it? One of the most popular theories among scholars is that Mark was written first and that both Matthew and Luke used Mark for much of their material. Then, so goes the theory, Matthew and Luke also used another (hypothesized) document which we don't have, which is often just called "Q" by scholars. Again, this is a conjectured document. Maybe it existed and maybe it didn't. If it did, we are to a large extent guessing what it contained. Stories and sayings that are common to Matthew and Luke but aren't found in Mark are often called "Q material." The view that Matthew and Luke are based on Mark and "Q" together with other material unique to each of them is referred to as "the two-source hypothesis." Sometimes the phrase "Markan priority" (meaning that Mark wrote first) is used as a kind of shorthand for this whole two-source hypothesis. Another view is that Matthew wrote first and that both Luke and Mark used Matthew. The late John Wenham has given this minority view a good run for its money.[1]

I've stated these theories so far in their most minimal form, but it's important to realize that, unfortunately, sometimes a scholar's use of the two-source hypothesis comes with extra "baggage" that doesn't at all follow from a boring proposition like, "Mark wrote first, and Matthew made some use of Mark." The additional "baggage" that often slips in without additional argument goes approximately like this: "If Matthew's or Luke's wording in some story is similar to Mark's, then as far as facts go they were *only* using Mark for that story. They didn't have any additional information about what really happened. So if we see wording changed or some different material included in a story that is found in Mark as well as in Matthew or Luke, we should assume that Matthew or Luke just *made up* the additional details without any good reason for believing they were true."

These assumptions are highly dubious. Yet they are often stated confidently as if they follow deductively from the idea that Matthew used Mark. Scholars will often say things like, "We can see here how Matthew used Mark," referring to such alleged invention. This far more questionable version of "the two-source hypothesis" means that Matthew and Luke are *erased* as separate factual sources about what happened whenever they appear similar to Mark. It imports a picture of Matthew and Luke as having no hesitation about changing or making up facts, and it treats them as though they can't know anything more about a given story than what they allegedly got from Mark.

At the most, an argument from similar wording might lead us to conclude that Matthew or Luke borrowed some wording from Mark. But does it follow that they had no additional factual information about what happened in that incident? Not even close. In fact, since Matthew was a disciple and Mark wasn't, it would be very strange to assume that, if Matthew tells a story found in Mark, he doesn't have any other information. Yes, Mark's Gospel may well have been based on the memories of Peter, but why think that Matthew had no memories *apart from* those of Peter? This exaggerated version of the "two-source hypothesis" goes far beyond the evidence and should be rejected, no matter how popular it happens to be among scholars.

But, it might be urged, doesn't the presence of similar wording mean that these Gospels can't possibly be giving us independent factual accounts of what happened? No, it doesn't mean that, unless you assume that the only kind of independence that can exist is absolute independence in which one source doesn't know what the other source says. But as we've already discussed, testimony isn't "all or nothing" like that. If we activate our real-world imagination—that indispensable tool of historical investigation—we can easily imagine something like this: Suppose that Mark wrote before Matthew, but that Matthew doesn't want to reinvent the wheel. There are no concerns about plagiarism in that time. It's perfectly fine for him to borrow some of Mark's wording. Mark has, let's suppose, already written a Gospel in Greek based on the memories of Peter, and Matthew decides to use it. It can help with parts of Jesus' ministry before he was personally called as a disciple. It can prompt his memory, and it can give him convenient wording to use, though of course he reserves the right to use his own words as well. So, he starts. But he finds in various places that he remembers or knows something that varies from the story as it is told in Mark. In these places he feels entirely free to supplement Mark from his own memories or from the memories of other people whom he spoke to about the events.

Something similar could happen with Luke. Luke was not personally a disciple, but he seems to have spoken with various witnesses of the events. In fact, he is the only Gospel author to mention Joanna; we'll see in this chapter how she comes up in an undesigned coincidence. In Chapter 7, I discuss the very real possibility that Luke had his own access to Peter, which allowed him to include details and stories not found in Mark. So Luke definitely was not confined to just one source of information. He probably had many. Let's suppose, then, that Luke had Mark, but he also had "Q," if that was a real document. Maybe he had Matthew. (Or maybe "Q" was an earlier version of Matthew written in Hebrew or Aramaic, and Luke had that but not our Greek Matthew, which Matthew himself may have written later.[2]) Luke also, let's say, has conversations with many other people, and probably he has notes on those conversations.

When he brings all of this together in writing his Gospel, he finds that he sometimes follows Mark's selection of material and sometimes even uses some of Mark's wording. But like Matthew, Luke considers himself completely entitled to add known details to those stories. So, for example, in both Mark and Luke we learn that Jesus healed a man with a withered hand, but only Luke 6.6 tells us that it was his right hand. Should we assume that Luke just made that bit up? Why think a thing like that? Couldn't Luke have had both Mark and other witness testimony about what happened? Of course he could, and he probably did.

These theories would mean that Luke and Matthew were partly dependent on Mark but also partly independent. That is, they had their own separate information about what happened.

Remember: Dependence isn't a yes-no thing. Nor am I suggesting the idea of partial dependence and partial independence out of the blue. It is supported by the facts themselves: Namely, in some stories the story is the same between two Gospels and even some of the wording is the same, but there is also some variation of wording and some differences in what is reported.

Just here, undesigned coincidences come on the scene, even among the three Synoptic Gospels. As we'll see, there are places where a rigid critic might say that Matthew or Luke "got the story from Mark" and that anything different in Luke's or Matthew's version must be a non-factual invention. But we find in some of those very places that the different details are confirmed by undesigned coincidences. This is exciting evidence for just what I have been suggesting.

As the chapter on reconcilable variation (Chapter 6) will show, even alleged contradictions between the Synoptic Gospels support this same point. After all, if Luke or Matthew were *merely* trying to copy Mark and add an embellishment here or there, couldn't he at least have made sure not to contradict him? I've written about this very issue in a secular philosophy journal, analyzing the probability of this kind of scenario.[3] If there's one thing that apparent contradictions between accounts show, it's that literary theories where one person is poring over the other person's story and making all his changes deliberately are probably false. If he were doing that, he could have easily avoided any apparent contradictions.

I'm bringing all of this up to say this: If you hear anybody saying that undesigned coincidences don't make sense because they have to assume that the Synoptic Gospels are totally independent of each other, that's not correct. And if you're told vaguely that the Synoptic problem disproves undesigned coincidences, that's not true either.

Undesigned Coincidences | 59

With all of this in place, let's look at some specific examples of undesigned coincidences in the Gospels. We will be able to discuss only a few in this chapter, compared to the large number that there are. See *Hidden in Plain View* for many more. You'll also find other undesigned coincidences occasionally cropping up in other chapters of this book. For example, in Chapter 1, I discussed an undesigned coincidence about Jesus' ministry in Perea, on the eastern side of the Jordan River, in the last six months of his life. There I connected the fact that Herod Antipas was ruler of Perea with a conversation that Jesus had with some religious leaders in Luke and with statements made in Matthew, Mark, and John about where Jesus was between the fall and following spring of his last year of ministry.

One more thing: It's important to recognize that the argument from undesigned coincidences is cumulative. Different people will be struck by different coincidences, and some are stronger evidence than others. This is one reason why it was important to write a whole book about them. Here I can give only a sampling, hoping that you will be interested enough to read more elsewhere.

3. Joanna and what Herod said to his servants

Since we have just discussed the supposed problem posed by the Synoptic Gospels for undesigned coincidences, it makes sense to start with an example where Matthew adds a detail to a story that otherwise sounds a lot like Mark. Matthew's additional details turns out to be confirmed by an undesigned coincidence.

In Matthew 14.1–2, we learn what Herod Antipas thought about Jesus when he heard of his miracles. Matthew says, as does Mark 6.14, that Herod initially thought Jesus was John the Baptist risen from the dead. Both Gospels then launch into a flashback story about how Herod had John the Baptist beheaded. Apparently, Herod was somewhat superstitious due to his guilty conscience, causing him to theorize that this might be who Jesus was. The wording of the passages, all the way through the story of the beheading of John the Baptist in both Matthew and Mark, is fairly similar.

If you accept the theory that Mark's Gospel came first and that Matthew might have used it as a literary source, this passage is a plausible candidate for a place where he did that. But remember: That wouldn't mean that Mark is Matthew's only *factual* source. Here is an interesting little factual addition in Matthew's Gospel: Matthew 14.2 says that when Herod speculated that Jesus might be John the Baptist come back to life, he said it "to his servants." No other Gospel mentions this.

If we were to think that the Gospel authors made things up, this detail might seem like a place where Matthew did that. After all, we might wonder, how could Matthew possibly know what Herod was saying to his servants? Was Matthew there? Obviously not. Maybe Matthew made this up to make the passage more vivid.

But not so fast! If we look at Luke 8.1–3 we find a plausible way in which Matthew could have heard what Herod was saying to his servants. This passage in Luke, I want to stress, is not about the beheading of John the Baptist nor about Herod. Luke is talking about a completely different topic, namely, a group of women who followed Jesus in Galilee and gave money to his ministry. Among those in the list is Joanna, the wife of Chuza, Herod's steward. Here we find Luke mentioning a high-ranking servant of Herod whose wife was involved in the new movement following Jesus. It seems like a reasonable assumption that Chuza himself was also sympathetic to Jesus, and Joanna's discipleship provides an entirely natural way in which Jesus' male disciples, such as Matthew, could have learned what Herod said to his servants.

Clearly Luke did not mention Joanna in 8.1–3 with the intention of explaining Matthew. Luke doesn't mention Joanna or Chuza at all when he tells about Herod beheading John the Baptist in Luke 9.7–9. It looks like Luke mentions Joanna as a follower of Jesus just because he knew about her and the other women he names. Luke may have known Joanna personally. He is the only evangelist who mentions her, and he brings her name up again in Luke 24.10, where he lists her as one of the women who went to the tomb. Luke is also the only one to mention that Herod was eager to see Jesus (Luke 9.9) and hoped to see him perform a miracle (Luke 23.8). He is the only one to mention that Pilate sent Jesus to Herod, that Herod's soldiers mocked Jesus, and that Pilate and Herod formed a new friendship after that time (Luke 23.7–12). It's possible that Luke also received those additional pieces of information about Herod from Joanna, though if so, he doesn't say so anywhere. He never mentions Joanna at all in connection with any stories *about* Herod. He just says, when he lists her name among the other women who ministered to Jesus, that Chuza, Herod's steward, was her husband. Luke's mention of Joanna while listing the women who contributed to Jesus' ministry casually and unintentionally confirms Matthew's small additional detail—namely, that Herod was speaking to his servants when speculating about Jesus' identity.

4. Why ask Philip?

The feeding of the five thousand is the only miracle (not counting Jesus' resurrection) described in all four Gospels. This presents an opportunity for a wealth of undesigned coincidences surrounding this incident, and the accounts provide them. I've discussed these in other books.[4] In this chapter we'll have space for just one of these; it is one of the most interesting, because it involves little clues from multiple passages.

This coincidence begins with the Gospel of John. According to the Synoptic Gospels (e.g., Matt. 14.14), on the day of the feeding of the five thousand, Jesus was with the crowd all day, healing and teaching. Perhaps later in the day he and his disciples slipped away up the mountain for a little break. But eventually some in the crowd caught sight of them, as a crowd might catch sight of the performers after a concert or of a celebrity in a crowded restaurant. As the crowd approaches, Jesus turns to one of his disciples with a question:

> Therefore Jesus, lifting up His eyes and seeing that a large crowd was coming to Him, said to Philip, "Where are we to buy bread, so that these may eat?" This He was saying to test him, for He Himself knew what He was intending to do. (John 6.5–6)

Reading the story quickly, one might not stop to wonder about this, but the detail is worth questioning: Why Philip, specifically? Philip is not one of the *most* prominent disciples. Aside from the lists of the disciples in the Synoptic Gospels, Philip is mentioned only a few times in the Gospels, all of them in John. He is not one of the "inner three"—Peter, James, and John, who come up in story after story. He is not the treasurer of the group, who might have been concerned with doling out money for purchasing food. That was Judas Iscariot. There is no apparent reason for Jesus' selection of Philip for this question.

It's possible that there *was* no special reason. Maybe Philip just happened to be standing near Jesus at that moment. But a connection among three different passages provides a more satisfactory answer. Look next at Luke 9.10, where we hear that the feeding of the five thousand took place near the town of Bethsaida, which was likely near the northeastern shore of the Sea of Galilee. Well, all right, you may wonder, so what? What does that have to do with Philip?

But now look at John 1.43–44 and John 12.20–21. Those passages are completely unrelated to the feeding of the five thousand. One of them is about Jesus' decision to go north to Galilee. He asks Philip to go with him. John mentions in passing that Philip was from Bethsaida. In John 12, some Greeks approach Philip, asking to see Jesus, and John mentions the same thing about where Philip was from, though he doesn't explain (and we can only guess) what this has to do with the Greeks and their request.

Think about how all of this fits together. Luke says that the feeding of the five thousand took place near Bethsaida. John says, in telling about the feeding, that Jesus asked Philip where they could buy bread, but he says nothing at all about where all of this was taking place. And in two unrelated passages, John casually mentions that Philip was from Bethsaida. Jesus is in essence saying, "Philip, you're from around here. Where can we get bread for all these people?"

To be clear, I am not saying that Jesus was seriously proposing buying bread for the multitude! John, in fact, expressly says (vs. 6) that he was testing Philip, knowing himself that he planned to feed the people miraculously. That is the way in which Jesus interacted with his disciples. He would often say cryptic things or ask them questions merely to draw out their responses. One can even picture Jesus asking the question in a slightly teasing manner. The fact that Philip was from that vicinity makes the question (and the humor) more pointed.

This coincidence is especially beautiful, since one needs three different passages to put it together. A question is raised by John's account of the feeding; it is answered only by putting together an apparently unrelated statement in Luke with an entirely different and otherwise unrelated passage in John—a complex and interesting coincidence and one that makes any hypothesis of design on the part of John extremely unlikely. If John had made up the detail that Jesus asked Philip, intending it to fit together with the location of the miracle, it is highly improbable that he would have left out any mention of Philip's home town *and* any mention of the location of the feeding. If he did that, he would be leaving the reader to find *both* of these facts for himself in other places and put it all together just to see John's cleverness! The same is true if John knew the Gospel of Luke. Even if John did know Luke, he doesn't appear to have this aspect of Luke in mind (that the feeding took place near Bethsaida). If the mention of Bethsaida was influencing John's account, he would have been much more likely to mention the *town* than to invent a question to *Philip*. It would be extremely indirect to mention a question to Philip *because* Philip was from Bethsaida without saying anything about the town at all. And of course all of this would be even more improbable if John invented Philip's connection to Bethsaida in the other parts of his own Gospel.

Another point here is related to what I call "reconcilable variation" in Chapter 6. John himself doesn't make *any attempt whatsoever* to harmonize his account of the feeding of the five thousand with the accounts in the Synoptic Gospels. On the contrary, he leaves rather striking loose ends. For example, he does not mention that Jesus taught and healed the people all day (as the Synoptics say). If all that we had were John, we might get the impression that Jesus fed them almost immediately upon seeing them. Here is another difference: John tells about Jesus going up the mountain later on to escape the people, who wanted to make him king (John 6.15) and only after that (vs. 16) mentions that the disciples came down in the evening and embarked in a boat. One might get the impression from this that they didn't even start down to the shore until after Jesus went up the mountain. But in Mark 6.45–46 we learn that Jesus sent them away in the boat while he himself dismissed the crowd. This variation doesn't present any irreconcilable contradiction. Different parts of the story can be taking place at once. Jesus, for example, may have "sent" the disciples in the sense of telling them to leave right away, when all of them were some distance from the shore. It could then have taken them some time to make their way through the crowd (who may have tried to detain them or talk to them) to the boat, while Jesus was dismissing the crowd and eventually (as John would have learned from Jesus himself) going up the mountain. With these events taking place at about the same time, each author has to tell about them in some order or other, and Mark does not have to mean that the disciples actually sailed away before Jesus dismissed the crowd. But the independence is quite obvious. John is not tailoring his account to fit in subtle ways with the Synoptics. He's telling his own story as he knows it.

So we can take it that, when John's account of this event does fit together in casual detail with the Synoptic Gospels, it is *not* a result of design at all. The clear independence of the accounts makes these subtle interlockings valuable indeed as evidence of truthful testimony.

5. How did Bartimaeus know?

One of the most interesting facts about undesigned coincidences in the Gospels is their tendency to confirm the historicity of John. This is a little unexpected, because John doesn't tell many of the same stories that are told in the other three Gospels. In fact, it often seems that John is going his own way deliberately, filling in material that was untold in the Synoptic Gospels. We might expect that we'd have fewer undesigned coincidences that involve John, since that Gospel isn't telling a lot of the same stories, but the exact opposite is true. The more that John tells us, the more he has a chance to be confirmed. Some of these coincidences arise from the few stories that do overlap between John and the Synoptics, such as the feeding of the five thousand (as we saw in the last section). But sometimes details from completely different stories dovetail, making it all the more obvious that the authors weren't trying to fit them together.

All three of the Synoptic Gospels tell about how Jesus healed a blind man (Matthew clarifies that there were two blind men) in Jericho, shortly before his death. According to Mark, one of these men was named Bartimaeus (Matt. 20.29–34, Mark 10.46–52, Luke 18.35–43). It's possible that Mark mentions only this blind man because he was the only one whose name Mark learned. Or perhaps Peter, who informed Mark, remembered this particular man. In all three stories, this blind man hears the crowd passing by and asks what is going on. When he hears that Jesus of Nazareth is coming, he begins to call out, calling Jesus the son of David, and asking him to have mercy. At first the crowd tries to hush him, but Jesus says to bring him over. Jesus asks what he wants, and of course he asks to receive his sight, a request Jesus grants.

We are so used to thinking of Jesus as a healer that we don't always stop to think about geography. While all three other Gospels mention Jesus healing the blind before this time (Matt. 9.27–31, Mark 8.22–25, Luke 7.21), these healings happened up in the Galilee region, several days' walk (at least) north of Jericho. In fact, hard as it is to believe, none of the Synoptic Gospels record *any* healing miracles as far south as Jericho prior to this story. Since Jesus' ministry had been going on for several years, one can guess that stories of his healing power had filtered down south and that the blind men in Jericho had heard of him, but their response to his name is immediate and unequivocal. This is a person whom they confidently believe is able to cause the blind to see. Is there a better explanation for their confidence than travelers' tales from Galilee making their way south over the years?

I think there is. In John 9, Jesus heals a man born blind in Jerusalem, much closer to Jericho. This miracle probably occurred just six months or so before the healing in Jericho. Jesus had gone to Jerusalem for the Feast of Booths (John 7.2, 10), and the healing of the man born blind in John 9 probably happened after that, since John seems to be ordering his stories chronologically in these chapters. In fact, we have another reason to believe that this miracle was fresh in the minds of people in the area. The raising of Lazarus took place even closer to the time of Jesus' death, and in John 11.27, the friends of Mary and Martha in Bethany wonder among themselves why Jesus didn't come and heal Lazarus rather than showing up only after he was dead. If he could heal a man born blind, they wonder, why didn't he heal Lazarus? This particular miracle had clearly made quite a stir.

While we cannot be absolutely sure, it is entirely reasonable to guess that Bartimaeus and his friend had also heard of this miracle, which occurred only about fifteen miles away in Jerusalem and fairly recently. This is a better explanation of their confidence in Jesus than their having heard of earlier healings of the blind much farther away in Galilee. Thus they instantly recognize Jesus' name when they hear that he is passing by, and they cry out, "Son of David, have mercy on us!"

This undesigned coincidence connects two completely different stories, one of which (the healing of the man born blind) is found only in John—the Gospel that is the "odd man out." For exactly that reason, John provides extra information that explains what happens in the other three.

6. "May it never be!"

For this undesigned coincidence we return to the relationship among the three Synoptic Gospels and to a bit of unique material found in Matthew's Gospel in a story that New Testament scholars would probably say he "got from Mark." Once again, when scholars say that, they are often tempted to ignore the possibility that Matthew had pieces of his own to add to the picture. Mark 12.1–12, Matthew 21.33–46, and Luke 20.9–19 all record a parable that Jesus told during the last days before his crucifixion that angered the Jewish leaders. This is the parable of the wicked tenants of the vineyard. In broad outline, the parable tells of a group of tenants, representing the leaders of Israel at Jesus' time, who refuse to pay the due rent from the fruits of the vineyard. They kill the servants, and finally the son, of the rightful owner.

There are various differences in the exact wording of the parable among the three Gospels. But by the time Jesus finishes, all three Gospels indicate that it was clear to the leaders that he was speaking of them and was foretelling that power would be taken away from them and given to others. Just *how* this was made clear is one of the things that is reported a little differently. Mark 9.9 says that Jesus asked what the owner would do and then answered his own question: He will destroy the wicked tenants and give the vineyard to others. Luke 20.15–16 says the same. Luke 20.16 adds that the people immediately said, "May it never be!"

When you stop to think about it, the account in Luke raises an interesting question. Since at this point Jesus is still speaking in terms of the story, talking about the wicked tenants and the master, why would the people in the audience be so quick to sympathize with the bad guys? Of course, we may guess that they *assumed* that the wicked tenants represented themselves, or their leaders, or the Jewish nation as a whole. But even if they realized that Jesus was making a dire prediction in the form of a story, the response, "May it never be!" seems a little odd. It doesn't even sound (in itself) like this audience was angry at Jesus. Taken by itself, Luke's account might give the impression that the audience standing around immediately identified themselves with the villains of the story and were far more overwhelmed with horror at the thought of punishment than they were angry at Jesus for comparing them to wicked murderers. One might expect them at least to wait for the point to be made more explicit before sympathizing with the fate of the wicked tenants.

As it turns out, Matthew says that's exactly what *did* happen—Jesus did make the point explicit. Matt. 21.43 reports that Jesus said, "Therefore I say to you, the kingdom of God will be taken away from you, and be given to a nation producing the fruit of it." Matthew does not report that the people said, "May it never be!" Luke mentions that they burst out with this exclamation, but Luke does not report that Jesus made the point of the parable explicit. That is found only in Matthew. When we put the two together, we have a more complete picture. We can well imagine that it was after Jesus told them that the kingdom would be taken away and given to others that some in the crowd exclaimed, "May it never be!" Only by fitting the two versions together do we see this.†

---

†There are remaining differences in the order of Jesus' words in these passages, but this simply illustrates the normal variation that we find among witness testimonies. Also, Matthew mentions that Jesus asks what the owner will do and that some in the audience (appearing quite naturally to side with the owner while the story is taking place) say that he will destroy the tenants and give the vineyard to others, whereupon Jesus applies the story to them. Luke and Mark mention Jesus' question and show him answering his own question. But of course these differences are quite reconcilable. People often speak at the same time, or Jesus could have affirmed what some in the crowd said: "That's right!" For further discussion see Lydia McGrew, *The Mirror or the Mask: Liberating the Gospels from Literary Devices* (Tampa, FL: DeWard Publishing, 2019), pp. 264–268.

Here is an undesigned coincidence right in the small variations of a story told in all three Synoptic Gospels, between two small details that Matthew and Luke have that are not found in Mark at all. This is why we should never assume that, just because a story appears in somewhat similar words in these three Gospels, there is no factual independence. Often it is precisely in those small departures from identical wording that we find evidence that the authors really were talking to different people who were present. When they tell things in slightly different ways and those different ways explain one another, that is evidence not only that they have their own ways of writing but that they have their own accurate information.

7. "I am among you as the one who serves."

There are a couple of places in the Gospels where Luke explains John and, in the same passage, John explains Luke. The accounts of the Last Supper provide one of these. Both Luke and John tell about the Last Supper that Jesus had with his disciples. But neither of them gives a complete account of everything Jesus did and said on that night. When it comes to the place where Jesus washes the disciples' feet, Luke explains John. How can that be, since Luke never even mentions the foot washing? That's right, he doesn't. But Luke says that there was a dispute among the disciples about who would be the greatest and that Jesus taught the disciples on that occasion that they must be willing to be humble and to serve one another (Luke 22.24–27). The dispute and Jesus' desire to illustrate humility, which Luke alone tells about, provide the occasion for the foot-washing, which only John tells about. John says nothing about the bickering, and Luke says nothing about Jesus washing their feet, but the two fit together like pieces of a jigsaw puzzle.

Luke and John contain a coincidence in the opposite direction, too, so that John explains Luke. This is what Jesus says in Luke when he rebukes his disciples for fighting:

> And He said to them, "The kings of the Gentiles lord it over them; and those who have authority over them are called 'Benefactors.' But it is not this way with you, but the one who is the greatest among you must become like the youngest, and the leader like the servant. For who is greater, the one who reclines at the table or the one who serves? Is it not the one who reclines at the table? But I am among you as the one who serves." (Luke 22.25–27)

Here is Jesus' teaching after the foot washing as recorded in John:

> When he had washed their feet and put on his outer garments and resumed his place, he said to them, "Do you understand what I have done to you? You call me Teacher and Lord, and you are right, for so I am. If I then, your Lord and Teacher, have washed your feet, you also ought to wash one another's feet. For I have given you an example, that you also should do just as I have done to you. Truly, truly, I say to you, a servant is not greater than his master, nor is a messenger greater than the one who sent him. If you know these things, blessed are you if you do them...." (John 13.12–17)

John does not mention Jesus' statement, "I am among you as the one who serves." And John does not give the rhetorical questions and answers that Jesus uses in Luke: Who is greater, the one who reclines at table or the one who serves? In one sense, the earthly sense, the one who reclines at the table is greater than a mere servant, but Jesus is teaching that the one who serves is, in the eyes of heaven, greater than the one who is served. He illustrates this spiritual teaching by the fact that he, their teacher and master, takes the part of the one who serves.

Luke leaves something unclear about the statement, "I am among you as the one who serves." To what, specifically, does that statement refer in Luke? It's so common for us to hear sermons on servant leadership that it may never occur to us to ask. We think of Jesus as just generally being servant-like all the time. Actually, he is very authoritative with his disciples and often rebukes them. This statement would, I think, have seemed much odder to the disciples than it does to us, if Jesus had not done anything specific at that time that was servant-like. In Luke's account alone, we don't hear about anything like that, so how is he among them as the one who serves? It might look especially strange for Jesus to say this, since according to Luke 22.14, Jesus is indeed reclining at the table right along with them. So why does he make that particular contrast, as if he is serving *instead of* reclining at the table?

John's account of the foot-washing fills in this gap: When Jesus said, "I am among you as the one who serves," he was not merely making some generic statement about his being a servant-like leader. He was referring to his concrete act of having taken on the role of a servant, washing their feet. John's description is vivid:

> Jesus, knowing that the Father had given all things into His hands, and that He had come forth from God and was going back to God, got up from supper, and laid aside His garments; and taking a towel, He girded Himself. Then He poured water into the basin, and began to wash the disciples' feet and to wipe them with the towel with which He was girded. (John 13.3–5)

No doubt it was because of the symbolism of this act, in which Jesus left his place reclining at the table and was "among them as the one who serves" that Peter objected to Jesus' washing his feet (John 13.8). It is after this concrete demonstration of humility, in which Jesus takes upon himself the form of a servant (just as the Apostle Paul says in Philippians 2.7), that Jesus teaches the disciples that they ought to do likewise.

This is great evidence for the truth of both stories. John could not, of course, have arranged matters so that Luke's earlier account would leave this gap for him to fill in. The oddity of Jesus' words, without the foot washing, seems to arise from the way that Luke heard the story from his human source, probably one of the disciples. It seems quite plausible that Luke's human source didn't mention the foot washing. Whether he knew about it or not, we shouldn't think that Luke slyly included (or invented) Jesus' saying to allude to it without *quite* coming out and mentioning it. Why do a thing like that?

On the other hand, if John *made up* the foot-washing to explain what Jesus meant by "I am among you as one who serves," why not include the saying itself? If John were influenced to *invent* the foot-washing scene by access to Luke (or to stories similar to Luke's), why did John leave out the disciples' dispute that fits so well with the foot-washing?

The apparent casualness of the connection leads to the reasonable conclusion that neither author was trying to make his story fit with the other's. The co-incidence appears undesigned, and we must never lose sight of the evidential value of apparent casualness. If indeed John was a disciple himself and told what he remembered, and if Luke's sources told truthfully what they remembered, exactly this sort of situation could arise in which partial accounts fit together and explain each other.

There is an interesting point here, too, concerning Luke's independence from Mark and Matthew. As it happens, Luke 22.24–26 is, in part, similar in wording to Mark 10.42–44 and Matthew 20.25–28. But those passages are about an entirely different story in which the mother of the sons of Zebedee (James and John) comes to ask if her sons may sit on Jesus' right and left hands in the kingdom. The other ten disciples resent the request, and Jesus rebukes the disciples for this spirit of competition. Biblical critics jump on these sorts of similarities to say that for some reason of his own Luke merely copied these sayings from Mark into a scene that is quite different. The critical theory is that Luke has *moved* what Jesus said about servanthood and competition to a completely different setting—the night of the Last Supper. In other words, that theory says that Jesus didn't really say this at that time at all. That obviously would not be good news for Luke's reliability. It would mean that he's trying to make it look like Jesus said things on a very specific occasion while knowing full-well that Jesus didn't do that. Luke (on this critical theory) was writing in a way that would be practically guaranteed to mislead everyone but the clever modern scholars who have supposedly figured out what he was doing.[5]

The undesigned coincidence is evidence against this critical theory that Luke "made" Jesus say something when he didn't really say it. From the point where Jesus says, "For who is the greater, one who reclines at table or one who serves?" Luke's wording is actually unique, and it is precisely in that uniqueness that Luke's verses are confirmed by the foot-washing account in John. For it is only at the Last Supper that Jesus becomes, literally, the one who serves. The point that Jesus is making, beginning by contrasting the social structures of the Gentiles with the behavior he expects from his own disciples, leads seamlessly into the unique verses in Luke.

Any of us who are parents know quite well how often our children bicker over the same grievances. It's not at all implausible that the request of James and John rankled with the other disciples and burst out yet again in childish squabbling about who would be the greatest. Since Luke tells us that they did argue about that very topic, why should we not think that Jesus rebuked them in similar terms on more than one occasion? We parents have often said to our children, "How many times do I have to tell you…?" and then repeated the same lecture that we gave just last week. It happens all the time. This sort of real-world imagination allows us to see more clearly, while critical theories about nonfactual editing and moving create confusion.

These questions and answers, these gaps and the details that fill them in, fit together not as literary tales, not as redaction of earlier sources, not as legends. They fit together as eyewitness testimony fits together.

8. "So you're a king? No problem!"

In Luke's account of Jesus' trial before Pilate, the sequence of events raises a question:

> Then the whole body of them got up and brought Him before Pilate. And they began to accuse Him, saying, "We found this man misleading our nation and forbidding to pay taxes to Caesar, and saying that He Himself is Christ, a King." So Pilate asked Him, saying, "Are You the King of the Jews?" And He answered him and said, "It is as you say." Then Pilate said to the chief priests and the crowds, "I find no guilt in this man." (Luke 23.1–4)

Here in Luke the crowd accuses Jesus of sedition, a very serious crime from the perspective of Rome. Pilate, the Roman governor, is obliged to take this seriously, so he naturally asks Jesus, "Are you the King of the Jews?" But what follows is quite surprising. Jesus does not reject the charge. His answer is translated differently in different English versions. The New American Standard Bible (NASB) translates his answer, "It is as you say." If this is right, his phrase "you have said so" (the literal translation) is rather like the emphatic American expression, "You said it," meaning, "Yes." Or his answer could be an ambiguous refusal to answer the charge: "Well, *you* say so." Such ambiguity by itself would be cheeky, at a minimum, in response to an accusation that put his life at risk. Interestingly, Jesus' similar expression in another context (the trial before the Sanhedrin) definitely seems to mean "yes."[†]

Whether Pilate took Jesus to mean, "You said it! I'm a king!" or just "Hey, you said it, I didn't," there is no good explanation in Luke for Pilate's going back to the crowd and stating that he finds Jesus innocent. Why didn't he at least question Jesus further? Why did he seem so unfazed by Jesus' reply? Why go so far as to declare Jesus free of all guilt concerning the charge of sedition?

The explanation is found in John's account of the same scene:

> Therefore Pilate entered again into the Praetorium, and summoned Jesus and said to Him, "Are You the King of the Jews?" Jesus answered, "Are you saying this on your own initiative, or did others tell you about Me?" Pilate answered, "I am not a Jew, am I? Your own nation and the chief priests delivered You to me; what have You done?" Jesus answered, "My kingdom is not of this world. If My kingdom were of this world, then My servants would be fighting so that I would not be handed over to the Jews; but as it is, My kingdom is not of this realm." Therefore Pilate said to Him, "So You are a king?" Jesus answered, "You say correctly that I am a king. For this I have been born, and for this I have come into the world, to testify to the truth. Everyone who is of the truth hears My voice." Pilate said to Him, "What is truth?" And when he had said this, he went out again to the Jews and said to them, "I find no guilt in Him. (John 18.33–38)

[†] Compare Matt. 26.64, where the literal wording in the Greek is, "You have said so," which is very similar to what Jesus says in the scene before Pilate, with Mark 14.62, which reports what appears to be the same answer with the literal affirmative, "I am."

John gives the rest of the dialogue that Luke gives only partially. As John shows, Jesus does affirm that he was born to be a king. But he makes it clear that his kingdom is not of this world and that he is not encouraging the use of physical force to achieve his aims. Pilate evidently concludes that he is a harmless religious crank, and that is why he tells the Jewish leaders that he finds no guilt in Jesus.

Together these accounts present a complete picture—an accusation of sedition, Pilate's question, Jesus' answer that he is a king, but not a king of this world, and Pilate's conclusion that he is not guilty in the eyes of Roman law.

How tempting it would be for a skeptic to claim that the differences between John's and Luke's versions are contradictions. Notice that in John 18.29–30, Pilate asks the Jewish leaders what accusation they bring against Jesus, and they don't give a straight answer. If we had only John's account, we might think that they sullenly refused to answer, merely saying that if Jesus were not an evildoer they would not have brought him to Pilate and leaving it at that. (Though John doesn't actually say that.) But that assumption would make John's account itself odd, because in verse 33, Pilate asks Jesus if he is the king of the Jews. If they made no accusation at all, why would Pilate ask Jesus if he is the king of the Jews? Here, too, the two accounts complement each other, since Luke tells about the accusation of sedition.

In the larger picture, here is the way it may have gone: The accusers said at first that if he were not a "bad guy," they would not have brought him. When (John 19.31) it became clear that Pilate preferred not to be involved and hoped that this was merely some matter of Jewish law in which they could judge and punish Jesus on their own, they came out clearly with the accusation of sedition (as told in Luke), requiring death, which was Pilate's business to judge and punish. The independence of the accounts is certainly clear from the differences in what Luke and John include, but so far from being contradictory, the two partial accounts are complementary.

This is an important lesson in the limitations of the argument from silence in history. Just because one account doesn't tell about something, that doesn't mean that it didn't happen. This is why harmonization (putting accounts together and using reasonable historical imagination) is so fundamental to historical inquiry—because different accounts supply different information. I'll have a lot more to say about harmonization in Chapter 6.

Since Luke himself was probably not a disciple, we don't know who his source or sources would have been for this scene, but it appears that they were not the same as John's, since the two accounts represent different reported material. It isn't that Luke had access to the version of the story found in John and merely selected parts of it to tell, nor vice versa. Rather, each account includes things that the other doesn't, which gives the impression that they come from different people who remembered or were struck by different parts of what happened. It is even possible that the author of the Gospel of Luke got his information from Mary, the mother of Jesus. (The earliest chapters of the Gospel of Luke seem to show Mary's perspective.) If the author of the Gospel of John was the Beloved Disciple John himself, then it may be that John is his own source and reports the scene as a witness, as he remembers it, with his own emphases and details.

This chapter provides just a sampling of the undesigned coincidences that confirm the truth of the Gospels. There are many more! This type of evidence would be especially hard to fake, and thus it gives us reason to think that the Gospel authors didn't fake things. They reported the facts as they knew them. Undesigned coincidences encourage us to think in a "real-world" way, asking natural questions that arise: Why did this happen? What did he mean by that? How did this person know that? Even if we don't get answers to all of these questions, they make sense in the context of reality, where these people really existed and really said and did what the Gospels report. The ultimate "source" that lies behind these stories is not an elaborate literary construct but reality itself. Undesigned coincidences help manifest that reality in its many-faceted complexity.

Chapter Summary

- Undesigned coincidences are incidental interlockings between aspects of different accounts that point to the truth of the accounts.

- Undesigned coincidences work because reality is consistent and because different aspects of reality explain each other.

- The "Synoptic problem" does not mean that there cannot be undesigned coincidences in the Gospels, even between the Synoptic Gospels (Matthew, Mark, and Luke).

- The fact that different accounts use similar wording does not mean that they have no factual independence.

- John is confirmed by many undesigned coincidences with the other Gospels even though he tells many stories that are not found elsewhere.

Study Questions

1. Briefly explain the concept of an undesigned coincidence.

2. Which Gospels are called the Synoptic Gospels? How do critical scholars use the puzzle about the Synoptic Gospels to undermine the reliability of Matthew and Luke?

3. How could Matthew have learned what Herod Antipas was saying to his servants?

4. How could Bartimaeus have found out that Jesus healed the blind? How is geography important to this question?

5. When Jesus said, "I am among you as the one who serves" in Luke, what was he probably referring to?

6. Jesus' rebuke to the disciples in Luke, when they have been arguing about who is going to be the greatest, has some overlap with his rebuke to them in Mark on the same topic. Is this the same event? Why or why not?

7. Why did Pilate decide that Jesus was not guilty even though Jesus apparently admitted that he was the king of the Jews?

For Discussion

1. If you have noticed or can think of an undesigned coincidence in your own life or in a story you have heard of, explain how it went. If not, make up an example of a modern undesigned coincidence similar to the illustration given at the beginning of the chapter.

2 Why is it good for Christian laymen to know something about the theories of scholars that would undermine the reliability of the Gospels?

3. Why is it an important part of an undesigned coincidence that only one part of the undesigned coincidence is mentioned in each passage? Would it mean that the account was not true if an author said, "This happened because that happened," mentioning both the question and the answer together?

4. How would the point discussed in the previous question help you to answer a skeptic who dismissed undesigned coincidences by saying that an author like John might have read an author like Luke and might have built on Luke's story by making up something that fit with what Luke said?

5. Explain in your own words the difference discussed in the chapter between verbal dependence and factual dependence. Do you have examples in your own experience where one person used some language that he was remembering from someone else but also shared additional facts about what happened?

6. Choose one or two favorite undesigned coincidences either from this chapter or (if you have access to it) from the book *Hidden in Plain View*, and be prepared to explain them to someone who has never heard of undesigned coincidences.

Resources for Further Study

John James Blunt, *Undesigned Coincidences in the Writing Both of the Old and the New Testament: An Argument of Their Veracity* (London: John Murray, 1850), <https://tinyurl.com/JJBlunt>.

Lydia McGrew, *Hidden in Plain View: Undesigned Coincidences in the Gospels and Acts* (Chillicothe: OH: DeWard Publishing, 2017), Introduction and Chapters I-IV, pp. 11–130.

Lydia McGrew, *The Mirror or the Mask: Liberating the Gospels From Literary Devices* (Tampa, FL: DeWard Publishing, 2019), Chapter XI, "Evidence and the Artless Author," sections 1–5, pp. 255–277.

Lydia McGrew, "What I Think About the Synoptic Problem," *Lydia McGrew YouTube Channel*, September 19, 2021, <https://tinyurl.com/McGrewSynoptic>.

John Wenham, *Redating Matthew, Mark, and Luke: A Fresh Assault on the Synoptic Problem* (Downers Grove, IL: Intervarsity Press, 1992).

4

Unnecessary Details

1. Real people and real stories

Recently I was listening to an interview with country music great Jimmy Fortune. Fortune was telling the story of how he began singing with the Statler Brothers. He described his trip to Nashville for an audition (during which he nearly missed the plane) and then said, "The bus driver for the Statler Brothers, Dale Harman, picked me up at the airport in a Lincoln Continental." There was nothing else in the story that hinged on the make and model of the car in which Jimmy Fortune was picked up at the airport. Nor did the identity of the driver feature in the story. Jimmy apparently just likes cars and mentioned these details because he remembered it that way.

Think for a minute about how real people you know tell real stories. Of course, a lot depends on context. Are you just trying to get the facts across quickly, or do you have leisure to tell the story at more length? I'm thinking here more of the second situation. What's that like?

Each person is different. But if you think about it, many people include at least *some* true details that aren't necessary to the story. Why is that? Well, when you cast your mind back over what happened, you remember more of it than is necessary to any bigger point you are trying to make. You remember what clothes someone was wearing, what month of the year it was, how the timing of the event related to other events, where (specifically) it occurred, and much more. Sometimes, too, the point is just to tell the story at leisure. People enjoy telling about things. It's not as though every detail *needs* to relate to some bigger point.

The Gospels are no different. While some Gospels are more detailed than others, they all show to some degree that tendency of witnesses to include unnecessary details. This is in and of itself a mark of truth.

In this book I'm not spending a lot of time on alternative theories and objections. (I did that a lot more in my longer books on the reliability of the Gospels, which provide additional resources.) But in this chapter, it's important to pause and address one type of objection that is going to come up: Liars also include unnecessary details. I know that well. I'm sure we've all known or heard of someone who makes up stories and throws in all sorts of fake details just to make people think he's telling the truth. Maybe some of us have had a "creative" child who does this. So the skeptic will immediately ridicule this chapter's claim that unnecessary details are a mark of truth. "Ha! Just because there are extra details in a story, that doesn't mean it's true. The authors could have just made up all that stuff and included it. How do you know they didn't?" And you may be wondering about that yourself. You should be prepared to answer that objection if you are going to use the information in this chapter.

One of the central purposes of this book is to help readers recognize the *texture* of the Gospels as memoirs of the life of Jesus, told by people who actually knew him. Recognizing the texture of true reports is a difficult thing to teach. One might say that in the end, either you see it or you don't. It can, however, help to listen to people tell true stories with which they were personally acquainted, trying consciously to notice what special qualities those stories have. That is how I happened to notice the unnecessary details in Jimmy Fortune's interview.

Skeptics (and unfortunately some Christians, too, if their minds have been made rigid by a certain kind of scholarship) tend to have a very hard time seeing the gritty, real-life texture of testimony in the Gospels. Here are just a few points about unnecessary details that can help to answer the "liars do it too" or "fiction authors do it too" objection.

First, *why* do liars add unnecessary details to their accounts? Because that makes the accounts look true! But that is, all by itself, an admission that such details *do* make the accounts look true. At that point we put together the fact that the Gospels contain these details with the other evidence of truth and of the authors' sincerity, where so many things (including details) are confirmed. The simplest explanation is that an evangelist says the grass was green (Mark 6.39) because the grass was green, not because he is making it up.

Second, we've seen in earlier chapters (and we will see in this chapter as well) that many unnecessary details in the Gospels have extra confirmation. Not all of them, but enough to guide us away from the hypothesis of fakery. Sometimes details are confirmed by external information, as discussed in Chapters 1 and 2. Sometimes they are confirmed by undesigned coincidences, as discussed in Chapter 3. In this chapter, I will try to flag those details that have specific confirmation.

Third, the Gospels present themselves as true, repeatedly. This is not only implicit in the narratives but is sometimes explicitly stated. One obvious example is Luke 1.1–4, where Luke assures

Theophilus, the person to whom he was sending the book, that he has followed everything carefully from the beginning and wants to give him a true account. Another is John 19.35, where the Beloved Disciple tells readers that he saw the crucifixion and gives a true record of what happened. (See also John 21.24.) We also know that the earliest church fathers took the Gospels to be historically truthful and were very interested in knowing historical facts.[1]

Why is this point important? It forces those who think the evangelists made things up into a dilemma: Either the evangelists didn't make things up, or they were hoaxing. Any attempt to avoid this dilemma by talking about a so-called "genre" that allowed them to make things up without being misleading is doomed to failure. That is not how the authors present their work, nor is it how their work was taken by early readers. The arguments that the Gospels are in such a genre fail repeatedly. (See *The Mirror or the Mask: Liberating the Gospels from Literary Devices* for more on this point.) This means that these unnecessary details would have been taken literally by the audience. If either stories or details were invented, the authors were highly deceptive, since they make the stories look real.

Fourth, suppose that someone tries to make an analogy between the Gospels and historically realistic modern fiction. We should be prepared to point out that comparisons between the evangelists and talented historical novelists who use realism to make better stories are anachronistic. While there was fiction at the time of the Gospels, there was no hyper-realistic fiction of the kind that we are familiar with in our own day and time, fiction that brings in subtle, vivid details without being over-the-top.[†]

[†] The ancient novel *Callirhoe* by the Greek Chariton is not at all like the Gospels, nor for that matter like modern fiction. It is a romance, complete with melodramatic description, and with only a thin historical veneer. It is a rollicking, fun story, but if its

And fifth, as we will see in the section below on the "Goldilocks zone," the Gospels don't look like modern, realistic fiction either. They have a distinctive texture that sometimes includes details and sometimes doesn't. Chapter 5 on unexplained allusions makes this same point, since unexplained allusions are confusing details that are left dangling. They interrupt the narrative rather than keeping the reader's attention.

In what follows, I'm going to give just some of the interesting, unnecessary details that illustrate this texture in the Gospels, using three broad categories: Brief details in the Synoptic Gospels (Matthew, Mark, and Luke), brief details in John, and longer scenes in John. It was necessary to include the final category, because John includes fewer stories in his Gospels and takes more space for each. This allows him to go into more detail and gives his scenes a quality of longer memoir realism that is neither rhetorical nor novelistic.

2. Some unnecessary details in the Synoptic Gospels

In this section, I'm going to tell you in a rapid-fire fashion about some unnecessary details in Matthew, Mark, and Luke. I won't discuss them at length. The goal is just to show you that the Gospels do contain these otherwise pointless details that, like the make of the car and the name of the driver in Jimmy Fortune's story, are marks of eyewitness memory. I'll put the details in roughly chronological order in Jesus' ministry, following the order of stories in Mark where that is available. If there is other information that confirms a detail, such as external evidence or an undesigned coincidence, I'll pause to mention that briefly.

Luke 6.6 says that it was a man's *right* hand that Jesus healed on the Sabbath day, annoying the religious leaders.

---

author had tried to pretend that it was historically true, the attempt would have been unconvincing. The Gospels, in contrast, are restrained and unrhetorical.

In the story of Jesus stilling the storm after being awakened by the terrified disciples, Mark specifies that he was asleep *on a cushion* in the stern of the boat (Mark 4.38).

In the story of the raising of Jairus's daughter, only Matthew mentions that there were flute players among the mourners whom Jesus dismissed from the room (Matt. 9.23). Since Matthew was not among the disciples whom Jesus took into the house (those were Peter, James, and John), Matthew presumably learned this detail from one of them. This particular detail is externally confirmed. The Jewish historian Josephus mentions pipe players as a part of mourning, and one rabbi recorded in the Talmud places an obligation on a husband to hire two flute players for his wife's death.[2]

In Chapter 3 on undesigned coincidences, we've already talked about Matthew's detail in 14.2—that Herod was speaking to his servants when he said that Jesus must be John the Baptist risen from the dead. There we saw how this detail is confirmed by the way that it dovetails with Luke's mention of Joanna, the wife of Herod's steward. Here I merely list it as another of those unnecessary details.

Luke's mention of the approximate place of the feeding of the five thousand (near Bethsaida) is confirmed by an undesigned coincidence with Jesus' question to Philip, also discussed in Chapter 3. Within the Gospel of Luke, the detail of the nearby town serves no apparent purpose. It's just there because Luke knew about it.[†]

[†] Another undesigned coincidence also confirms this location for the feeding: Jesus calls down woe upon Bethsaida for not repenting, since so many mighty works were done in that town (Luke 10.13). The feeding of the five thousand in the vicinity of Bethsaida, and the healings that Jesus did on that day, seem to be the mighty works he is referring to. But these passages are separated and give no appearance of referring to each other. Notice too that Luke 10.13 condemns Chorazin, but neither Luke nor any Gospel reports miracles done in Chorazin. Luke is not inventing miracles to go with the names of these towns.

Unnecessary Details | 89

The accounts of the feeding of the five thousand are full of unnecessary details and undesigned coincidences. Mark casually mentions that the people sat down on the green grass (Mark 6.39), and this little detail is confirmed by the equally casual detail in John 6.4 that the feeding took place around the time of Passover, when the grass would be green in that area.[3]

Only Matthew and Mark tell about another miraculous feeding, the feeding of the four thousand. Naturally, biblical critics have given in to the temptation to say that one of these is made up—something biblical scholars call a doublet. (A doublet is an alleged copy of an event or saying, told with some changes that make it look like a second event or saying. Critical biblical scholars claim that the Gospel authors created such doublets, though they would not be very reliable if that were the case. In fact, we have no reason to think the evangelists did this.) Actually, Matthew and Mark tell the two stories in ways that are casually different, indicating that these really were separate events. The Greek words that the accounts use for "basket" are different (Mark 6.43, 8.8). The word in the feeding of the four thousand probably means a larger basket, since it is the same word used in Acts 9.25 for the basket in which Paul was lowered over the walls of Damascus to escape his enemies. This fits casually with the fact that twelve (smaller) baskets of fragments were collected after the feeding of the five thousand but seven (larger) baskets after the feeding of the four thousand. The Gospels also unnecessarily note the difference in the number of loaves of bread—five vs. seven. John 6.9 mentions that the loaves in the feeding of the five thousand were barley loaves. In the feeding of the five thousand, we're told that there were only two fish, but in the feeding of the four thousand, Mark says "a few small fish" (Mark 8.7). If the Gospel authors didn't know a more specific number, they didn't make one up.

As Jesus approaches the end of his earthly ministry, we have the story of the healing of blind Bartimaeus (and, Matthew tells us, his companion) in Jericho. Here Mark (the only Gospel to tell us Bartimaeus's name) has a small, vivid detail: Mark says that when they told him to come to Jesus, "casting his cloak aside, he jumped up, and came to Jesus" (Mark 10.50).

Shortly thereafter, in Jericho, Jesus encountered Zacchaeus, made famous by a children's chorus in my childhood that went, "Zacchaeus was a wee little man, and a wee little man was he. He climbed up in a sycamore tree, for the Lord he wanted to see." This story is found in Luke only, and it is also Luke alone that tells of Jesus' saying (Luke 17.6) that if the disciples had faith like a mustard seed, they could tell a tree (translated in the NASB as a "mulberry") to be uprooted and planted in the sea. From the English translations of these two passages, you would never guess that the name of the "mulberry" tree of Luke 17.6 sounds similar in the original language to the sycamore tree that Zacchaeus climbed. The tree in Jesus' saying, in Greek, is a sycamine. "Sycamine" and "sycamore" sound a lot alike, but in fact they are different trees. Luke carefully distinguishes them, using "sycamine" in Luke 17.6 (Jesus' saying) and "sycamore" in Luke 19 (the story of Zacchaeus). To top it off, we have independent evidence that sycamore trees grew, specifically, in Jericho, just as Luke says.[4] The next time you hear someone say that the Gospel authors didn't care much about details and felt free to change them as long as they had the "gist" of the story right, bear some of these examples in mind! Luke cared about a sycamore as opposed to a sycamine.

When we get to the preparation for Jesus' Triumphal Entry into Jerusalem, Mark has some unique, wholly unnecessary details about where they found the colt: He says that when they followed Jesus' instructions, they found the colt "at the door outside in the street." While we would expect the donkey to be outside, there is no reason to mention this, much less that it was tied at a door in the street. Matthew and Luke are less specific about exactly where the colt was tied, though Matthew adds that its mother was brought to Jesus as well (Matt. 21.2).†

After Jesus' death, all four Gospels (see Matt. 27.59, for example) tell us that Jesus was wrapped in a linen cloth or cloths. Later, we will see what else John says about the grave clothes when carefully describing the scene in which Peter and John discover the empty tomb. Here, I am just noting the unnecessary detail that the cloth was linen.

After Jesus rises again, when Luke is telling about Jesus' meeting with two disciples on the road to Emmaus, he specifies that Emmaus is about seven miles from Jerusalem (Luke 24.13). It would have been enough for Luke to say "near Jerusalem" without giving a more specific distance. But evidently, since he had the information, he decided to include it.

3. Some unnecessary details in John

John is so much the evangelist of details that it can be difficult to pick out a selection to mention. The distinction between John's detailed scenes (discussed in the next section) and passing details in other parts of his Gospel is also somewhat arbitrary—more a difference of degree than of kind. In this section, like the last, I will briefly describe some of John's unnecessary details.

John likes to make note of specific numbers and times, and in his Gospel (as opposed to the Synoptics) we find references to times that are not multiples of three. It seems to have been a con-

---

†Matthew's inclusion of the mother donkey has led to rather silly skeptical claims, based on Matt. 21.7, that Matthew portrays Jesus as riding two donkeys at the same time! Of course, Matthew says nothing of the kind. The "them" on which Jesus sat, in Greek just as in the English translation, can refer to the clothes that the disciples spread out.

vention to give the hour to the nearest multiple of three, but John tries to be more precise when he can.[5] In John 1.39, for example, he mentions that it was the tenth hour (probably around 4 p.m.) when Jesus was speaking to two disciples of John the Baptist who followed Jesus to the place where he was staying.

When John tells us about the wedding at Cana, he doesn't say merely that the water pots were large; he specifies that there were six of them, made of stone, and that they each held about twenty or thirty gallons each. (See Chapter 1 for more about the stone jars.) This would not make good fiction. The reader doesn't really need to know that they contained about twenty or thirty gallons—nobody wants to have to do mental math to figure out how much wine Jesus produced at the wedding. But if you were actually there, this is how you might tell the story, estimating the size of the jars. The narrative voice is the voice of a witness.

The next unnecessary detail requires a bit of set-up. John tells of a dialogue between Jesus and the Jewish leaders after he first cleanses the Temple, in which Jesus uses the phrase, "Destroy this Temple, and in three days I will raise it up" (John 2.20). This saying of Jesus is confirmed by an undesigned coincidence. Compare Mark 14.58: What are the false witnesses at Jesus' Sanhedrin trial referring to when they say that Jesus said that he would destroy the Temple and raise it again in three days? Apparently they have in mind a garbled version of the saying recorded only in John 2.20.

The religious leaders in John 2 misunderstand and assume that Jesus is referring to the literal, physical Temple. They scoff, saying that it has taken forty-six years to build the Temple (John 2.20). This saying, too, is confirmed by comparing these forty-six years with Luke's reference to the fifteenth year of Tiberius Caesar as the beginning of the ministry of John the Baptist (Luke 3.1) and

Unnecessary Details | 93

putting all of that together with external evidence about the beginning of the building of Herod the Great's Temple.[6] Notice the specificity of the number "forty-six." It is not a round number, nor does it lend itself to symbolism. It is an unnecessary detail, included apparently because that was what the leaders said. If John were making up a number as part of an invented dialogue, why make up this number?

In the story where Jesus heals the son of a royal official, we have another of those "odd" times of day: It was the seventh hour when the fever left the man's son (John 4.52).

The crippled man whom Jesus heals at the Pool of Bethesda had been unable to walk for thirty-eight years (John 5.5). Forty would do just as well for purposes of the story, but John loves his precise numbers. Once again, don't let anyone tell you that the evangelists didn't care about specifics or that John sacrifices precision in order to make a theological point. There isn't any need for him to do so. His theological points are compatible with as much precision as he happened to remember.

Jesus, John tells us, came to the vicinity of Jerusalem (to Bethany, on the slopes of the Mount of Olives) six days before Passover (John 12.1). As I have discussed elsewhere in more detail, a comparison with verses like Mark 11.11, 19, and 14.1 allows us to count these days before Passover.[7]

I will have more to say in the next section about John's vivid recollection of the Last Supper. Here, I'll just note his careful naming of the disciple who asks Jesus a question in 14.22: "Judas, not Iscariot." We've discussed in Chapter 2 the fact that "Judas" was a very popular male name at the time, which means that this use of a disambiguating phrase is evidence of truth in itself. Consider this point as well: Why did John have to name the disciple at all? He could have just said, "The disciples asked him" or "One of them asked him." If John were the sort of author to make up dialogue, there was no need to saddle himself with a bit of dialogue involving an obscure disciple who doesn't show up anywhere else. And why name him "Judas" and then be forced to distinguish him from the infamous Judas Iscariot? The specificity of this unnecessary detail is its own mark of truth. It shows that there really was such a discussion and that Judas, not Iscariot, did ask this question.

We also have the mention of the charcoal fire in John 18.18 in the scene of Peter's denial. There isn't anything about Peter's denial that is connected in any way with the fact that the fire is made out of charcoal. John apparently just says it because he believes it's true. If the author himself was the "other disciple" who followed Jesus and his captors to the palace of the high priest, who was familiar with the household, and who convinced the door girl to let Peter in (John 18.15–16), he probably saw the charcoal fire with his own eyes.

In this same context, we should not miss the reference to the name of the man whom Peter wounded in the garden—Malchus (John 18.10)—and to the fact that it was one of his kinsmen who recognized Peter as having been with Jesus there (John 18.26). Neither of these specific facts is found in the Synoptics, but if the author was known among the servants of the high priest, he would likely have known some of their names and who was related to whom.†

---

†This familiarity of the "other" disciple, who is probably the Beloved Disciple, with the high priest's household has been used as an argument that he was not John the son of Zebedee. Supposedly a Galilean fisherman could not have been in any way acquainted with the high priest. But "known to the high priest" does not have to mean that he was close friends with the high priest, and the evidence in the text directly concerns his acquaintance with servants in the large palace. I have discussed this attempted argument in *The Eye of the Beholder* (Tampa, FL: DeWard Publishing, 2021), pp. 423–427.

4. John's scenes

John's account of the raising of Lazarus is full of specificity, including both precision and vividness. As noted in Chapter 1, John precisely mentions that Bethany was about fifteen stadia from Jerusalem (11.18–19), or about two miles. This, he implies, accounts for the many mourners who had come to keep Mary and Martha company.

It is fascinating to see how verses 28–31 combine vividness with what I can only call "clunkiness." John tells us in verse 28 that Martha, who has just had a vigorous dialogue with Jesus in keeping with her personality (see Chapter 7) went and called Mary to come and speak with Jesus. In verse 29, John says that Mary arose hastily to go to Jesus. Verse 30 pauses to inform us unnecessarily that Jesus was still outside the village where Martha had met him. Couldn't the reader be left to figure that out for himself? Verse 31 goes on to point out that this was *why* the people who had come to mourn with the sisters didn't know where Mary was going (they didn't know that Jesus had arrived, since he hadn't come to the house) and had to surmise that she was going to the grave to weep. At this point we can see everything quite clearly, but this is not the way that a smooth narrator tells a story. It is, however, the way that someone remembering tells a story. Sometimes a witness will go into too much explanation; sometimes he will leave things unexplained altogether, as we'll discuss in the next chapter. This is because he isn't engaging in a literary project but in a testimonial project—testifying to the truth as he recalls it.

When Mary meets Jesus, she falls at his feet, in keeping with her personality. We can't know for sure that Martha did *not* fall at Jesus' feet, but it isn't mentioned, and although they say the same thing ("Lord, if you had been here, my brother would not have died"), in Martha's mouth these words come across as a challenge, whereas Mary is weeping when she says them (vs. 33).

We can tell that Jesus himself is moved by Mary's emotion, since verse 33 says so explicitly and verse 35 tells us that Jesus himself wept. But there is even more than that to verse 33. The NASB translation might give the impression that the narrator is telling us about Jesus' purely private feelings, since that translation says that Jesus was "deeply moved in spirit" (John 11.33) and at the grave "deeply moved in himself" (11.38). The qualifiers "in spirit" and "in himself" are certainly there in the Greek, but we should not assume that the author merely describes what Jesus was feeling. Rather, the word translated "deeply moved" is given more literally in the King James Version as "groaned." It apparently refers to a sound that Jesus made, not just something that he felt, though perhaps the sound would have been heard only by someone nearby. New Testament scholar Leon Morris comments shrewdly on the term for the sound Jesus makes:

> The Greek verb is a very down-to-earth one and may be used, for example, of horses snorting. It is not the kind of word that one could easily imagine a pious fabricator applying to Jesus.[8]

We'll return to Martha's practical personality in Chapter 7. That personality fits with her concern about the stench if they open the grave (vs. 39). We should also reflect that she was probably right, and that John remembers that she was right. We are then to imagine a smell of death coming from the tomb when the stone is removed and clinging to the grave clothes that Jesus tells them to remove from the living Lazarus when he comes out at Jesus' loud cry, all wrapped up (vs. 44). (Compare the vivid mention of the sweet smell of the spikenard that Mary lavishly pours on Jesus in John 12.3. John, remembering, tells us that the house was filled with the fragrance.) I doubt that those who loved Lazarus hesitated when Jesus told them to unbind him and let him go, for underneath those grave clothes was no zombie but their own friend and brother, alive and well.

John's story of the night of the Last Supper is filled with too many details for it to be possible to note them all. It would be a good exercise to read chapters 13–16 of John's Gospel and, while soaking in Jesus' teaching, note the many little indications of realism. Two sections stand out in this respect—the description of the foot washing and the description of how Jesus hands the sop to Judas Iscariot, who then leaves to betray him.

John 13.2–5 shows the combination of theology and physical detail that is so characteristic of John. Verse 2 illustrates John's preoccupation with Judas Iscariot. When John thinks of the night of the Last Supper, and even of the foot washing, he thinks first of the fact that Judas Iscariot had already decided to betray Jesus. Verse 3 emphasizes the fact that Jesus knew that the Father had given all things into his hands and that he came from the Father and was returning to the Father. Suddenly in verse 4 we come to pure visual description:

> [Jesus] rose from supper, and laid aside His garments; and taking a towel, He girded Himself about. Then He poured water into the basin, and began to wash the disciples' feet, and to wipe them with the towel with which He was girded. (John 13.4–5)

Here John is "all eyes." You can tell that he is replaying Jesus' gestures in his own mind—rising from the reclining place at the table, setting aside his garment, girding himself with a towel, and so forth. Nothing is overstated. Nothing is "purple," as authors call it. He's just telling what Jesus did in carrying out this act, which was usually only performed by slaves.[9]

After the wonderful dialogue with Peter, which shows Peter's personality so clearly (see Chapter 7), John carefully tells us that Jesus put his garments back on and reclined at the table again (vs. 12) before talking to them about the meaning of what he just did. As discussed in the last chapter, the scene takes on additional meaning when we recall that, according to Luke, they had recently been arguing about which one of them would be the greatest in the kingdom, so Jesus' words here were a rebuke.

In John 13.21, Jesus tells the disciples that one of them will betray him. Verse 22 emphasizes that they began looking at one another, wondering which of them it could be. It is easy to see that uneasy, shocked look that the disciples gave each other around the table. Now they cannot trust each other. Perhaps they cannot even trust themselves! Verse 23 mentions that the disciple Jesus loved was reclining next to him. There is nothing particularly emotional about the statement that he was reclining "on Jesus' breast." Since people leaned forward to eat at the table, the one next to Jesus on one side would be able to lean back toward Jesus' shoulder to speak to him. (Remember that John 21.24 says quite clearly that this disciple for whom Jesus had a special love is the author of the book.) Simon Peter knows that this disciple has a special relationship with Jesus and also, of course, that he's ideally placed to ask Jesus a question without raising his voice. So in verse 25, Peter motions to him to ask, "Who is it?" Jesus says (vs. 26) that he will dip the bread into the bowl and give it to the one who is to betray him, and of course he gives it to Judas, saying, "What you do, do quickly."

It isn't clear that the other disciples heard Jesus' statement about giving the sop at all. (If not, Peter didn't get his wish to find out who was going to betray Jesus.) Verses 28–29 say that none of them knew what Jesus meant by telling Judas to do something quickly; they made various conjectures. But didn't the Beloved Disciple know? The statement may just mean that no one *else* knew, but it may mean that everything was happening so quickly that even the Beloved Disciple couldn't quite figure out exactly what Judas was going to do.

The scene thus far is very tense. Our imaginations can fill it out, though I note here that the author himself does *not* use emotional language. He just tells us what they said and did and a little of what they wondered and guessed. We can imagine that Jesus' eyes locked with those of Judas when he told him to get on with it quickly, though we don't know exactly what tone he used. John does not use the manner either of a modern novelist or of an ancient orator here. Yet this is one of the most vivid scenes in all of the Bible. And to top it off, there is this understated but masterful note in verse 30: "And so after receiving the morsel, he went out immediately, and it was night."

It seems that the room had no windows. While they have been eating the Passover, night has fallen outside, and this strikes the eye of the Beloved Disciple, the eye of the beholder, when Judas goes out. Here I cannot do better than to quote Christian classicist E.M. Blaiklock:

> ...Judas opened the door to leave the tense and puzzled group. An oblong of sudden darkness seen for a second stamped itself on one mind forever; and remembering, the writer comments, 'And it was night'.[10]

The chapters describing Jesus' betrayal and arrest, Peter's denials beside the charcoal fire on a cold evening, Jesus' various interrogations, and his crucifixion would yield more such scenes and sub-scenes, but we cannot discuss them all here. The Passion of our Lord in John's Gospel, all by itself, is sufficient refutation of the confused notion that John's interest in theology is at odds with physical accuracy. His interest in theology *gives rise to* his vivid memory and his interest in literal accuracy, as when he describes the blood and water that flowed from Jesus' side, which he saw with his own eyes (John 19.34–35).

Having seen that John has a great memory for physical details and especially for physical motion, consider the so-called "race to the tomb" between Peter and the Beloved Disciple on Easter morning after Mary Magdalene tells them that the tomb is open and empty:

> Peter therefore went forth, and the other disciple, and they were going to the tomb. And the two were running together; and the other disciple ran ahead faster than Peter, and came to the tomb first; and stooping and looking in, he saw the linen wrappings lying there; but he did not go in. Simon Peter therefore also came, following him, and entered the tomb; and he beheld the linen wrappings lying there, and the face-cloth, which had been on His head, not lying with the linen wrappings, but rolled up in a place by itself. So the other disciple who had first come to the tomb entered then also, and he saw and believed. (John 20.3–8)

This passage is strikingly like what we would expect from someone who was personally present. In fact, if you replace the word "they" with the word "we" and imagine it as told in the present tense, you can see the resemblance to the way that a modern person might narrate his own experience: "So Peter goes out, and so do I, and we're going to the tomb. And the two of us are running together, and I run ahead faster and get there first. And I bend down and look in, but I don't go in..." And so forth. The emphasis on physical motion is very noticeable. The two are running together; the Beloved Disciple runs ahead. He stoops down. He looks in. But he doesn't go in. Then Peter comes up behind and rushes past him, and then the Beloved Disciple follows him. As Leon Morris says, "If this is not eyewitness, it must be invention, but what is the point of inventing the race, and the hesitation, and then the belief of this disciple?"[11]

As for the grave clothes, the description here is fascinating and shows once more that sharp visual memory that we have noticed elsewhere in John.[12] Grave robbers would have no reason at all for taking off the grave clothes. To the contrary, if someone wanted to steal the body, it would be far easier to leave the wrappings on the body and carry it away wrapped up. Why take the time and trouble to unwrap it? (This is all the more obvious if the myrrh and aloes mentioned in John 19.39 were sticky, though scholars are not agreed about whether they were sticky ointments or dried herbs.[†]) The eye of the Beloved Disciple also carefully registered the separation between the cloth for the body and the face napkin neatly wrapped together by itself.

The next vivid scene in John that I want to draw attention to is the meeting between Jesus and Mary Magdalene. I fully admit that John could not have been personally present at this scene. Jesus and Mary are clearly alone. But the Gospel emphasizes (20.18) that Mary Magdalene told them what Jesus had said to her. I'm sure that she described the whole scene many times, and it is this closeness to the original facts that we find in the vividness of the scene:

> But Mary was standing outside the tomb weeping; and so, as she wept, she stooped and looked into the tomb; and she be-

---

[†] John Wenham, in his excellent *Easter Enigma: Are the Resurrection Accounts in Conflict?* (Eugene, OR: Wipf and Stock, 1992), p. 67, says that these would have been dried herbs. But I am inclined to think that the great weight of the burial spices John records is better explained if they were in the form of liquid or ointment. For a further, fascinating discussion of the grave clothes and the Greek words used for them, see pp. 92–93 of Wenham's book.

held two angels in white sitting, one at the head, and one at the feet, where the body of Jesus had been lying. And they said to her, "Woman, why are you weeping?" She said to them, "Because they have taken away my Lord, and I do not know where they have laid Him." When she had said this, she turned around, and beheld Jesus standing there, and did not know that it was Jesus. Jesus said to her, "Woman, why are you weeping? Whom are you seeking?" Supposing Him to be the gardener, she said to Him, "Sir, if you have carried Him away, tell me where you have laid Him, and I will take Him away." Jesus said to her, "Mary!" She turned and said to Him in Hebrew, "Rabboni!" (which means, Teacher). (John 20.11–16)

Notice that Mary scarcely even seems to wonder who these men are in the tomb talking to her. This is a fascinating note of realism in the scene. One might think that Mary would wonder, "Who are these people, and what are they doing inside the tomb?" The thought doesn't even seem to cross her mind. The insightful 19th-century French commentator F. L. Godet notes this point eloquently:

> Mary remains and weeps, and as one does when vainly seeking for a precious object, she looks ever anew at the place where it seems to her that He should be....Mary answers the question of the celestial visitors as simply as if she had been conversing with human beings, so completely is she preoccupied with a single idea: to recover her Master. Who could have invented this feature of the story?[13]

Mary's physical movements, like those of the Beloved Disciple earlier, are described quite precisely. Like the Beloved Disciple, she stoops down to look into the tomb. After answering the angels, the narrator says explicitly, she turns and sees Jesus behind her (vs. 14). Then she looks back again into the tomb. She knows that Jesus' body isn't there, but isn't that what we all do when we have lost something? We look again and again at the place where it *should be*. Even though the text doesn't say that she looked into the tomb again, she must have done so, because when Jesus speaks her name, the text says for the second time that she turned to him (vs. 16). Probably she turned back to look into the tomb while she was answering him, supposing him to be the gardener. Her first answer to him is much like her answer to the angels. She has only one thought in her mind—to try to find Jesus' body. Even her failure to recognize Jesus fits here. She is weeping, has turned away from him almost immediately, and has her mind set on the idea that the body has been taken away. But when he says her name, she recognizes his voice and turns back to him in astonished joy, crying out, "Rabboni!" One can picture the young John listening to Mary Magdalene telling the story herself, perhaps illustrating her narrative with gestures. And like Jesus' mother, he kept all these things and pondered them in his heart (Luke 2.19).

The last scene from John we'll discuss here is the scene by the Sea of Galilee where the disciples see Jesus early in the morning after a night of fishing. Here again we see John's interest in physical details:

> There were together Simon Peter, and Thomas called Didymus, and Nathanael of Cana in Galilee, and the sons of Zebedee, and two others of His disciples. Simon Peter said to them, "I am going fishing." They said to him, "We will also come with you." They went out, and got into the boat; and that night they caught nothing. But when the day was now breaking, Jesus stood on the beach; yet the disciples did not know that it was Jesus. Jesus therefore said to them, "Children, you do not have any fish, do you?" They answered Him, "No." And He said to them, "Cast the net on the right-hand side of the boat, and you will find a

catch." They cast therefore, and then they were not able to haul it in because of the great number of fish. That disciple therefore whom Jesus loved said to Peter, "It is the Lord." And so when Simon Peter heard that it was the Lord, he put his outer garment on (for he was stripped for work), and threw himself into the sea. But the other disciples came in the little boat, for they were not far from the land, but about one hundred yards away, dragging the net full of fish. And so when they got out upon the land, they saw a charcoal fire already laid, and fish placed on it, and bread. (John 21.2–9)

It's worth noting in passing that the willingness of the Beloved Disciple to come fishing with Peter is one argument that he was a fisherman or at least from the Galilee region, which fits well with his being John the son of Zebedee. While some scholars have suggested that the author is a well-connected resident of Jerusalem who did not accompany Jesus in his Galilean ministry, that theory hardly fits with the quickness with which he apparently agrees to go out fishing all night. The disciples don't plan to meet Jesus right after fishing; that is quite unexpected from their point of view. Such quickness to "enjoy" the experience of staying up all night fishing in a small boat on the Sea of Galilee would be unlikely in a high-class Jerusalem landlubber who has not regularly been traveling with the other disciples!

The note in verse 4 that Jesus was standing on the seashore when the day was breaking is not, strictly speaking, an unnecessary detail; it explains why the disciples did not immediately recognize him.† However, it isn't at all clear that John includes the

---

† In fact, there is only one time in the Gospels when someone fails to recognize Jesus after the resurrection that is not well explained by natural causes. The one unnatural failure of recognition occurs on the road to Emmaus. There Luke expressly notes that the eyes of the two were "held" (Luke 24.16) so that they did not recognize him, implying that the default assumption was recognition. We should question the common assumption that there was something about Jesus that looked significantly

mention of daybreak to provide this explanation. He may have been just noting the time, which is one of his preoccupations throughout the Gospel.

The Beloved Disciple recognizes Jesus in verse 6, probably by a combination of the sound of his voice and, of course, the great catch of fish in verse 5 following Jesus' somewhat playful suggestion that they cast the net on the other side of the boat.

It is, of course, Peter who impulsively flings himself into the water to swim to Jesus, not wanting to wait until the boat lands. Here we have one of my very favorite unnecessary details: Peter put *on* his outer garment before jumping in. Why? Surely it would make more sense to take *off* any clothes that one happened to be wearing that might impede swimming, rather than pausing to put something on. Upon reflection, we might think that Peter did not want to appear before Jesus naked, since (as John notes) he was stripped for work, but that is only a guess. That John would interrupt his narrative with this odd little detail about Peter's movements is a mark of truth in the story.

With his usual slightly ponderous attention to detail, John explains in verse 8 that the other disciples used a boat to drag the net to land, since they were nearby (he gives a specific distance). The word here for "little boat" is slightly different in the Greek from the word in verse 3; commentators aren't sure if John is just varying his wording for the same boat (which would not have been very big) or if he means to indicate a yet-smaller boat, normally attached to the side of the fishing boat, into which some of them shifted for purposes of dragging the net. In verse 9, we find another charcoal fire; John remembers this fire clearly, just as he remembered the fire on the night of the betrayal.

---

different after his resurrection and made him hard to recognize. In fact, it seems that Jesus was fully recognizable in a normal way by those who knew him well, as implied in Matt. 28.9 and Luke 24.36.

Verse 11 is vivid: Peter comes up streaming out of the sea and belatedly helps his friends to get the fish. (After all, this was his fishing trip to begin with.) He hauls in the laden net himself, standing on the shore. How did they know that there were 153 fish? They counted them, of course! Fishermen of your acquaintance no doubt measure their fish and tell their fish stories again and again. This number reflects the same impulse. The fish would have had to be taken out of the net by hand anyway; we can imagine the astonished, grinning faces of the men as they cast them out of the net one by one, counting, probably aloud. That no doubt happened after breakfast. Once the net was pulled up on land, they would have leisure to eat and collect their catch a bit later. John reports the number here as he portrays Peter pulling in the net.

There is, too, the little aside that the net did not break, though there were so many fish. This doubtless reflects John's memory of the catch in Luke 5.4–10, though he does not say so. In that case, the net began to break, and Peter had to call for the sons of Zebedee, his partners, to come in another boat and help out. Once again, we see the evidential value of casualness. John doesn't particularly care if his readers recognize a subtle reference to the earlier catch, which isn't even mentioned in his own Gospel. It's probably wrong even to call this a reference, as if it were a literary allusion to the other book. Rather, it is his *memory* of the earlier event itself that leads him to mention here that the net did not break. This is the way that real memory works.

Many sermons have been preached on this chapter of John. Often a sermon will focus on the subsequent dialogue between Jesus and Simon Peter, which marks Peter's formal restoration before the other disciples after his disastrous failure on a dark Thursday night more than a week earlier. I do not want to discourage any pastors who preach on Jesus' loving yet stern words to Peter, but I do want to suggest another possible focus: The vivid and unnecessary details of the passage are of evidential value. They show the eye of the beholder, so important in John's Gospel. They show us that this really happened.

5. Gospel details in the Goldilocks zone

Goldilocks, of course, is the little girl in the fairy tale of the Three Bears. Coming into the bears' house, she tries their porridge, chairs, and beds, and she keeps finding that what belongs to Baby Bear is *just right* for her. The "Goldilocks zone," then, is just right. Another way to see that the Gospels' unnecessary details reflect eyewitness testimony is to compare them to the use of details in modern fiction. When we do so, we find that they fall into that "just right" zone—enough detail to look like memoir, but not enough to look like fiction.

Pick up a favorite work of realistic modern fiction and notice how consistent the author is with details. He wants, of course, to paint a picture. The modern reader demands to be drawn in and to see just what everything was like. If a novelist is going to describe a scene, he's expected to keep up a fairly consistent level of detail all the way through it. He will be sure to tell you at multiple points what tone a speaker used, what gestures he made, what his facial expression was, and so forth.

I've already pointed out in the introduction that such modern, hyper-realistic fiction simply didn't exist at the time of the Gospels. But here I want to note that even if it had existed, the Gospels don't sound like that at all. Even in John's most vivid scenes, there is not that consistent level of detail. Indeed, often in describing John's scenes above, I have suggested details of my own, such as the way that Jesus and Judas might have looked at one another or the laughter of the disciples as they counted the fish. None of that is *in John itself*, and I was careful to make that clear. Even John, probably the most vivid of all the evangelists, is not cinematic or melodramatic, nor is he anything like a modern fiction author. If he remembers a detail, he may very well include it, as a witness will often do when calling up an event at which he was present. But his effort is not a literary one, and so there is no literary attempt to keep up a consistent level of detail.

Look, to give just one example, at the jump between John 21.13–14 and verse 15. 21.13–14 says, "Jesus came and took the bread, and gave them, and the fish likewise. This is now the third time that Jesus was manifested to the disciples, after He was raised from the dead." Wouldn't we like to know more about that breakfast? It must have taken some time to eat it. What *else* did Jesus say to them? John does not tell us any more. He wants to get on to the dialogue between Jesus and Peter. He simply begins verse 15 with, "So when they had finished breakfast..." and moves on.

Nor does he mention (though he must have known) what Luke 24.34 says—that Peter and Jesus had already had one meeting before this, presumably a private one. When John 21.14 says that this was the third time that Jesus was manifested to his disciples, it refers to group meetings. Can you imagine any modern novelist leaving out an account of the private meeting between Jesus and Peter? Of course not! A novelist would include not only the private meeting but a detailed account of Peter's thoughts by the seashore as he wondered where Jesus was going with this questioning and how he ought to answer. It must have been very uncomfortable for Peter, and his private meeting with Jesus must have been in his mind. The closest that John gets to psychology is to say in verse 17 that Peter was grieved that Jesus asked him three times if he loved him; this was probably evident in Peter's face and voice at the time, though John does not try to describe them.

The fact that Gospel details fall into this "Goldilocks zone," not too much and not too little, is also evident when we contrast the Gospels with ancient rhetoric. The rhetorical teacher Quintilian was not over-scrupulous about matters of truth and cynically advises future lawyers to play upon the emotions of the audience by a melodramatic form of scene-painting meant to prompt a response. While it isn't always clear whether Quintilian means that rhetoricians should portray the scenes in question as having really happened or merely as the kind of thing that *might* have happened, even a couple of examples of the rhetorical style he suggests are enough to distinguish it sharply from the Gospels' style. Quintilian says,

> I am complaining that a man has been murdered. Shall I not bring before my eyes all the circumstances which it is reasonable to imagine must have occurred in such a connection? Shall I not see the assassin burst suddenly from his hiding-place, the victim tremble, cry for help, beg for mercy, or turn to run? Shall I not see the fatal blow delivered and the stricken body fall? Will not the blood, the deathly pallor, the groan of agony, the death-rattle, be indelibly impressed upon my mind?[14]

Quintilian explains that the idea of such rhetoric is to move the judge, since orators were often pleading cases in the courts:

> For oratory fails of its full effect, and does not assert itself as it should, if its appeal is merely to the hearing, and if the judge merely feels that the facts on which he has to give his decision are being narrated to him, and not displayed in their living truth to the eyes of the mind.[15]

The imaginative picture of the murder scene as suggested by Quintilian is different both from modern fiction and, more importantly, from the simple restraint of the Gospels.

When we stop to think about such contrasts, it helps us to resist misguided comparisons that skeptics and (unfortunately) even some Christian scholars will make that might seem to undermine the evidential value of unnecessary details.†

6. The texture of real-world testimony

This chapter, somewhat longer than others in this book, is meant to illustrate the value of close reading of the text coupled with the use of common sense. You don't need to be a scholar to do it; in fact, certain types of scholarship can cause one to forget how real people think and speak. What you do need is the ability to dig in and pay attention to details, seeing how they contribute to the credibility of the document. What we find in these documents is a texture that is almost impossible to imitate. The Gospels are vivid but never slick, detailed but inconsistently so. They tell amazing stories of miracles, deaths, and resurrections in the manner of a witness whose only power over his readers is that of recollection. Was ever anything more like truth?

Chapter Summary

- The Gospels contain many unnecessary details that make them look like oral testimony about real things that have happened.

---

† Evangelical scholar Michael Licona has suggested that specific sensory details in the Gospels, such as Mark's mention of the green grass at the feeding of the five thousand, may be added just to make the reader feel like he is present in the scene. He cites Quintilian as if Quintilian's advice is relevant to the Gospels. But the Gospels are not exaggerated, rhetorical orations, nor are their authors careless about literal truth. "Do We Have Evidence for Jesus' Resurrection: Mike Licona Responds," S. J. Thomason, Christian-Apologist.com, February 2, 2019, minute 57:22, https://youtu.be/qcAHjxkvT5A?t=3442.

- People often throw in pointless details in a story just because they are remembering vividly what happened.
- The Gospels' use of these details does not look like either over-the-top ancient rhetoric or modern fiction.

Study Questions

1. What characteristic of real-world testimony are we discussing in this chapter?

2. Give at least two or three answers to the objection that liars or fiction authors also add unnecessary details to their stories.

3. What extra detail does Mark give in the story about how Jesus stilled the storm?

4. How does Luke show his precision by an unnecessary detail in the story about Zacchaeus?

5. When telling time, what do the Gospel authors sometimes round to? How is John a little different in this area?

6. List two or more unnecessarily specific numbers given in the Gospel of John.

7. Describe one of John's vivid scenes, giving as many details as you can remember that make the scene vivid.

8. What does it mean to say that the Gospels' use of details falls into a "Goldilocks zone"?

9. How did Quintilian's advice to ancient orators differ from what we find the Gospel authors doing?

For Discussion

1. Compare and contrast various people you know with respect to how many unnecessary details they include in their true stories.

2. As an exercise, take a true story that you or someone you know has told and try to make up symbolic meanings for unnecessary details in the story. Have fun with this exercise. The purpose is to show that such symbolic "explanations" are unnecessary if the details are actually true. People often just remember true details and include them.

3. Suppose that someone tried to argue that it's contrary to the doctrine of inspiration to say that there are any unnecessary details in the Bible, since God made sure that the authors included all the details that they do have. How could you answer this objection?

4. Select a scene from a modern work of fiction that maintains the same level of detailed narration all the way through the scene as discussed in the chapter. The modern novelist may tell all of the characters' gestures and facial expressions and sometimes even their thoughts. Notice how this differs from the Gospels' less constant use of details in all scenes and all the way through scenes.

Resources for Further Study

Lydia McGrew, *The Eye of the Beholder: The Gospel of John as Historical Reportage* (Tampa, FL: DeWard Publishing, 2021), Chapter X, "John Who Saw," pp. 320–347, Conclusion "Huckster or Historical Witness: The Johannine Dilemma," pp. 416–420.

Lydia McGrew, "Gospel Details in the Goldilocks Zone," *Lydia McGrew YouTube Channel*, May 21, 2021, <https://tinyurl.com/GospelsGoldilocks>.

Lydia McGrew, *The Mirror or the Mask: Liberating the Gospels From Literary Devices* (Tampa, FL: DeWard Publishing, 2019), Chapter XII, "Still More Evidence for the Reportage Model," section 2, pp. 306–316.

Leon Morris, *Studies in the Fourth Gospel* (Grand Rapids, MI: Eerdmans Publishing Company, 1969), Chapters 2–4.

5

Unexplained Allusions

1. What are unexplained allusions?

Wednesday was a rough day for Sue, culminating in a car accident. No one was hurt, but her own car was a write-off. Sue recently joined a new church and has been meeting with a ladies' Bible study, mostly people she doesn't know very well. After the accident, Sue took her husband's car to Bible study on Thursday night and told her new friends about her day. Explaining how she got into the accident, she said,

> I had to go to meet with Kyle's teacher yesterday to talk about his ISP for next year. When I was driving home, I was thinking about that, and I just didn't see this little car that ran a red light. I hit the other car. Nobody was hurt, thank God, and the other car just had minor damage, but my car is totaled. I need prayer that it will be fixed soon and that the insurance will pay for the repairs.

Sue probably didn't stop to ask herself if her new friends know what an ISP is. As it happened, only one of the other ladies present recognized the term. The letters mean "individualized service plan" and are used in a public-school context to refer to the educational plan for a student, often a special-needs student. Sue, busy telling about the car accident, didn't worry about whether or not most of the other ladies would understand the reference. Some of them have no children yet, some of them have never used an ISP, and some are home schoolers, so only one recognized it. Familiarity with "ISP" isn't strictly required for understanding the story, but the use of it in this context does create a loose end.

That is the very reason why Sue's use of that term lends authenticity to the rest of the story. Sue's honesty is evident in the fact that, while telling the story, she isn't worrying about the impression that she is making. She isn't carefully trying to craft her story in the way that will be best understood by the audience. She isn't pausing to explain herself or to ask if they understand. She is speaking unselfconsciously, which results in her using a phrase that most of the people in her audience don't happen to know.

Sue's reference to an ISP in this story is an unexplained allusion. A witness sometimes refers to things that the original audience, or some significant portion of it, doesn't know about. These details aren't included in a sneaky attempt to make the story look good. They don't show a lot of "audience smarts." And they don't look like well-written fiction. They are just included because the person believes or knows that they are true and because they come to mind in the course of telling the story. The Gospels contain a number of unexplained allusions; the Gospel of John is especially full of them.

I've deliberately placed this chapter after the chapters on external confirmations, undesigned coincidences, and unnecessary details, because as we will see, unexplained allusions can overlap with these other categories. An unexplained allusion is somewhat different from Mark's reference to Jesus sleeping on a pillow in the stern of the boat when the storm came up (Mark 4.38). That at least makes the scene easier to picture. But for a reader or listener who doesn't happen to know what a particular unexplained allusion refers to, it actually interrupts the flow of the narrative, introducing an unanswered question and distracting attention. It does make the story look true, but only for those who happen to think of this point—that the author appears to be unselfconscious. It confirms truth in a clumsy, negative way. No good author of realistic fiction (even if that had existed at the time of the Gospels) would do this deliberately.

It would be truly implausible to imagine Sue making up the story about the car accident and saying to herself, "I'll say that I was coming home from an ISP meeting. The homeschooling moms in the group will be impressed by that because they won't know what it is, so they'll be more likely to believe my story."

An unexplained allusion can also be one half of an undesigned coincidence or one half of an external confirmation, and when we get to some examples that could fall into those categories, I'll explain how that works. Let's start, though, with an unexplained allusion in the Gospels that doesn't fit into either of those additional categories.

2. The sons of thunder

Mark 3.17 is part of a passage in which Mark is listing the names of Jesus' disciples. When he comes to James and John, the sons of Zebedee, he says that Jesus gave them the name Boanerges, which means "the sons of thunder." That's it. There is no further explanation of this nickname. It is a parenthetical remark; some translations even put it in parentheses. If Mark had any idea why Jesus called these young men by this nickname, he doesn't tell us. Maybe he never heard why.

If Mark had been making up parts of his Gospel, we might have expected that he would tell a little "origin story" about how they came to have this name. Such a story could end, "And from that day forward, Jesus called them Boanerges, which means 'the sons of thunder.'" But we find nothing of the kind. Mark just casually drops this little detail into the list of the twelve disciples.

Some see a connection here to Luke 9.53–55, where Luke tells us that James and John suggested calling down fire upon a Samaritan village that wouldn't let Jesus pass through on his way to Jerusalem. Luke says that Jesus rebuked them for this harsh plan. While this story is a possible explanation of the name, I think it is unlikely that this story tells us where the nickname came from initially. For one thing, Jesus hardly seems to have been in a mood to give a nickname in this context. Instead, he tells James and John that they are in the wrong. For another thing, that event occurs late in Jesus' ministry. Mark's way of referring to the nickname makes somewhat more sense if Jesus gave them this name earlier.

It's possible that the story about calling down fire represents the personality of James and John that gave rise to the nickname. Maybe they were somewhat harsh toward those who didn't respect Jesus. But it's just as likely that Jesus called them by this nickname because they were loud and rambunctious. We simply don't know.

The point is that Mark tells this detail briefly and casually, without going to any trouble to be sure that his audience knows more about it. Here we see once again the evidential importance of casualness. On the face of it, it looks like Mark said it just because it was true. It is a sign of that artless honesty that we are talking about throughout this book.

3. The Galileans and those on whom the tower fell

Luke 13.1–5 gives us two unexplained allusions in the space of just five short verses. In these cases, Jesus' *own* original audience, the people he was speaking to, *did* know what he was referring to. In fact, some in the audience actually brought up the first allusion. But these are unexplained allusions in the context of the Gospel of Luke, because it seems probable that Luke's audience, especially his original reader, Theophilus (see Luke 1.1–4), would *not* have known what Jesus was talking about without further explanation. Luke doesn't give any explanation.

In these verses, Jesus is having a conversation with some in the crowd who begin talking, apparently, about recent events. Some people in the audience mention to him some Galileans whose "blood Pilate had mingled with their sacrifices." We don't know anything more about this incident from any other historian, though it fits with the character of Pilate as revealed in other incidents.[1] Apparently, there had been a violent incident in which Pilate had killed some Galileans while they were sacrificing, or perhaps on their way to sacrifice.

This would have been one small event in one somewhat outlying province of the Roman empire. There is no reason to think that it would have been familiar to Theophilus. It is not as though people in other parts of the Roman empire were reading news stories about what was happening in Judea and Galilee. This was not the information age! If Luke himself knows what happened, he doesn't bother to stop to explain it. He doesn't seem to worry about whether or not Theophilus knows it. He wants to get on to what Jesus said.

That brings us to the second unexplained allusion in this passage, which occurs in the words of Jesus. Jesus says,

> "Do you suppose that these Galileans were greater sinners than all other Galileans, because they suffered this fate? I tell you, no, but, unless you repent, you will all likewise perish. Or do you suppose that those eighteen on whom the tower in Siloam fell and killed them, were worse culprits than all the men who live

in Jerusalem? I tell you, no, but, unless you repent, you will all likewise perish." (Luke 13.2–5)

We can't be certain where the Tower of Siloam was, though some have claimed that its ruins have been found.[2] Probably it was in Jerusalem, near the Pool of Siloam. We certainly have no other report of the fall of this tower that survives in any other historian. If Luke were making up what Jesus said, there would have been no reason for him to make up a reference to an event that the first readers of his own Gospel would likely not have heard of. He might as well have referred to more generic deaths if he were making up Jesus' words: For example, "Consider the lepers who are dying outside the city. Do you think that they are greater sinners than all others who live in Jerusalem? No, but unless you repent, you will likewise perish."

Luke's purpose in this passage is not to craft a polished story with all the loose ends tied up. Rather, he wants to tell what his sources have told him about the life and teachings of Jesus. If this was the way that the conversation went between Jesus and his audience, that's what Luke wants to write. Once again, we see the straightforwardness of the Gospel author in an unexplained allusion.

Here I want to point out something else interesting: Suppose that we *did* somehow find out more about the Galileans or the fall of the tower. Suppose that we were to discover inscriptions or letters that mention these incidents. That would then turn this passage into the occasion for incidental, external confirmations like those discussed in Chapters 1 and 2. They wouldn't necessarily stop being unexplained allusions, though. The events would still be unexplained *within the text of Luke's Gospel* and would still be relatively obscure. We shouldn't assume even then that Luke was referring to them as known background facts.

The great classicist and New Testament scholar Colin Hemer tells of many confirmations of the book of Acts that we have from such sources, which do not at all indicate that these were matters of general knowledge.[3] These little references point to the type of thing that could end up counting as both an unexplained allusion (from the perspective of the first audience of the Gospel) and an external confirmation (based on our further knowledge).

4. Going down to Capernaum for a few days

John 2.12 says briefly that, after the wedding at Cana, Jesus went with his mother, brothers, and disciples down to Capernaum and stayed there for a few days. John gives no explanation for this trip to Capernaum, and the very next verse mentions Jesus' journey to Jerusalem for Passover, which is the beginning of the story about the (first) time Jesus cleansed the Temple. Verse 12, about the visit to Capernaum, is left dangling. It has no apparent narrative, theological, or thematic purpose. In fact, it interrupts the literary flow of the chapter, because it isn't part of either the story of the wedding or the story of the Passover.

We know from the Synoptic Gospels that Jesus ended up making Capernaum a regular base of operations (Matt. 4.13); that appears to be at a slightly later time in his ministry. Peter apparently lived in Capernaum with his family at about this time (Mark 1.21–29), and Peter was already following Jesus (John 1.41–42), so perhaps they stayed in Peter's home when they went to Capernaum for a few days. But John doesn't say so, nor would this explain *why* they made the trip. It isn't clear if the trip to Jerusalem occurred immediately after this trip to Capernaum; even if Capernaum were a place to stop on the way to Jerusalem, that wouldn't require staying for several days, especially since it isn't very far along the way from Cana to Jerusalem.

Unexplained Allusions | 121

Of course, there could be many reasons. Maybe Peter wanted Jesus to stay for a while and meet his wife and other friends. Maybe they were all getting along well at that time (Jesus' family didn't always approve of his ministry, as we see from Mark 3.21) and just decided to "hang out" together before going on to Jerusalem for Passover. The point is not that the short stay is improbable but rather that John tells about it in the casual, unexplained manner of a person reminiscing.

This unexplained allusion is further evidence that the author was an eyewitness of Jesus' ministry. This is not to say that it's absolutely necessary for the author to be a personal eyewitness, provided that he is knowledgeable and careful. Luke's Gospel is very reliable in that way; Luke wasn't one of Jesus' own disciples and got his information from witnesses and from earlier documents. But John 2.12 looks like it comes directly from someone who was there. If the author wasn't present and learned about these events from someone else, he would have been more likely to cut out this pointless reference to an unexplained visit to Capernaum.

Here is another great thing: This little verse is a "twofer"—it contains both an unexplained allusion and an incidental external confirmation. As already mentioned in Chapter 1, even though archaeologists aren't sure of the exact location of Cana, all of the candidates for that location are in the hill country of Galilee. You do indeed go "down" from Cana to Capernaum, because Capernaum is right next to the Sea of Galilee. John refers twice to "going down," once here and once when telling about the official who came to Jesus in Cana and asked him to heal his son who was sick in Capernaum (John 4.46–51). Jesus did not go to Capernaum; he healed from a distance. The next day, the official's servants met him and gave him an update when he was going "down," returning to Capernaum. This casual reference to the actual geography of the land is very telling, especially since John was probably first writing to people in Asia Minor who probably had never heard of Cana outside of this story and would not have recognized the accuracy of the phrase "going down" from Cana to Capernaum.

5. A dispute with a Jew about purification

John's Gospel tells about a time when Jesus' disciples baptized (see John 4.2) while John the Baptist was still alive:

> After these things Jesus and His disciples came into the land of Judea, and there He was spending time with them and baptizing. John also was baptizing in Aenon near Salim, because there was much water there; and people were coming and were being baptized—for John had not yet been thrown into prison. Therefore there arose a discussion on the part of John's disciples with a Jew about purification. And they came to John and said to him, "Rabbi, He who was with you beyond the Jordan, to whom you have testified, behold, He is baptizing and all are coming to Him." (John 3.22–26)

This passage contains an unexplained allusion: What was the dispute between John the Baptist's disciples and another Jew about purification? What about purification? Did John the Baptist agree with his own disciples or with the other person? John (the narrator) gives us no further details, and it seems unlikely that we will ever know, because when John the Baptist answers (vss. 27–30), he addresses only the issue of Jesus' superiority to himself. This leads up to his humble declaration in verse 30, "He must increase, but I must decrease."

Baptism probably was originally connected to Jewish purification rituals, but that does not tell us much about the dispute that John the Baptist's disciples asked him to resolve. John the evangelist records only their concern that Jesus' ministry was more successful than that of their own teacher. How is that complaint related to the dispute? We can only guess. Maybe Jesus' disciples carried out baptism in a different form or under a different set of ritual requirements than John the Baptist used. Maybe the person they were talking with was a follower of Jesus, and they were debating these differences with him. But that's entirely a guess and gives us no idea what the differences might have been.

The Gospel author is going somewhere else. He reports the dispute with the Jew about purification in passing, exactly as an artless witness would do, as part of the lead-in to the complaint and John the Baptist's declaration of his own subordination to Jesus.

For purposes of the story, there was no need even to *mention* the dispute. It would have been smoother to start out with the complaint that Jesus' disciples are baptizing so many; that is what sets up John the Baptist's words. The dispute with the Jew is irrelevant, when you stop to think about it. But if John the evangelist actually witnessed the scene, he may very well have told it in this way, including the unexplained and irrelevant mention of the dispute.[†]

6. "As the Scripture said"

We've already seen unexplained allusions in the teachings of Jesus about the Galileans whom Pilate killed and about the tower falling. John 7.38 contains another unexplained allusion in the words of Jesus.[‡] At the Feast of Tabernacles, Jesus stands up and cries out

---

[†] John the evangelist may have been John the Baptist's disciple first, before following Jesus. While I am not completely convinced that he is one of the two disciples of John the Baptist mentioned in John 1.35, 40, he certainly seems to have been with Jesus from very early in his ministry, and this would be explained if he was originally a disciple of John the Baptist and then followed Jesus.

[‡] Yet another one occurs in John 6.36. Jesus said that he told them before that they have seen him and still do not believe, but we have no record in any Gospel of the time that he "told them before." If John felt free to elaborate or change Jesus'

to the crowd, inviting anyone who is thirsty to come to him and drink. He then says, "He who believes in Me, as the Scripture said, 'From his innermost being will flow rivers of living water.'"

Which Scripture might that be? Nobody knows! At least, nobody knows for sure. Plenty of Old Testament verses have been suggested about water flowing, which Jesus might have had in mind, including Isaiah 44.3, Joel 2.28, and Ezekiel 47.1, but none of them says clearly what Jesus says. The late scholar Leon Morris explains how this is evidence for John's truthfulness:

> One [problem] is the notorious difficulty of knowing what passage of the Old Testament Jesus had in mind. But the very fact that the difficulty can arise is, of course, evidence for the genuineness of the passage.... It is intelligible that Jesus cited Scripture in an unusual fashion. It is not intelligible that someone who was manufacturing the incident would affirm that Jesus ascribed certain words to Scripture, but do it so badly that no one has been able to find the passage.[4]

Morris's way of putting this is especially good. Jesus could easily have been giving an *interpretation* of some *set* of Old Testament Scriptures. The effect would be similar if a modern preacher were to say, "The Bible says God will give the Holy Spirit to all who believe on Jesus." There isn't just one Scripture that says exactly what the preacher says, though of course it can be easily inferred from many different Bible verses put together.

But here's the point: John is unlikely to have *invented* such an indirect, composite Scripture citation, putting it into Jesus' mouth. If someone were to go to the trouble to *invent* Jesus' teachings, and if he invented Jesus saying, "As the Scripture says…," he would be much more likely to make Jesus cite some

---

words, he could easily have crafted an earlier scene in which Jesus told them this before, but he does not.

Old Testament verse more clearly. We know from Acts 2.17–21 that Joel 2.28–32 was popular with the apostles; Peter cites it to explain the events at Pentecost when he and the others are speaking in tongues. John even tells the readers in John 7.39 that Jesus was speaking about the Holy Spirit here when he spoke of the rivers of living water. If John were even partly making up Jesus' words here, it would have been very easy for him to make Jesus quote Joel 2.28 and 32 clearly. It could have gone like this: "If anyone is thirsty, let him come to me and drink. As the Scripture says, 'I will pour out my Spirit on all men, and whoever calls upon the name of the Lord shall be saved.'" The fact that John instead reports that Jesus said something more obscure is evidence all by itself that this is what Jesus really said.

We should be careful not to assume that everybody in John's audience was a biblical scholar, much less a mind reader, attuned to every possible obscure allusion, reference, or symbolic meaning that the author might have had in mind. New Testament scholars sometimes talk like this, saying things like, "John's ancient readers would have been aware of the symbolism John was putting into this detail…" But there isn't any reason to think this. Even those among John's readers who knew the Old Testament well would not have been able to read the mind of Jesus (or of John) to know with reasonable confidence that some *specific* Old Testament reference or references are in view. After all, modern Bible readers and scholars who are *very* familiar with the Old Testament can't do more than guess.

Just being an "ancient person" didn't give you a secret decoder ring that allowed you to see all sorts of invisible, private nuances in the minds of the evangelists, and we should question scholarly theories that imply such thought reading. Too often the implication of special "ancient" understanding, allowing one to discern hidden meaning, is used to endorse whatever theory a modern scholar himself prefers, which is quite a suspicious circumstance. In this case, there is no more reason to think that John's earliest readers or even (for that matter) John himself knew which *specific* Old Testament verse or verses Jesus had in mind. So while John is quite willing to say that he believes that Jesus is talking about the Holy Spirit (a reasonable inference), he doesn't try to give a clearer Old Testament reference. He certainly doesn't seem to think he's licensed to make Jesus say something clearer. It looks like he is just telling us truthfully what Jesus said about the rivers of living water.[†]

7. Jesus' "threat" to destroy the Temple

In this section I want to talk about an unexplained allusion that is also "one half" of an undesigned coincidence. This does sometimes happen, and it helps to illustrate the variety of unexplained allusions that we have in the Gospels.

In Mark's and Matthew's Gospels we find the following account of part of Jesus' trial before the Sanhedrin. Here is the version in Mark:

> Now the chief priests and the whole Council kept trying to obtain testimony against Jesus to put Him to death; and they were not finding any. For many were giving false testimony against Him, and yet their testimony was not consistent. And some stood up and began to give false testimony against Him, saying, "We heard Him say, 'I will destroy this temple made with hands, and in three

---

[†] Don't forget the evidence of truthfulness in this passage in the "aside," discussed in Chapter 2. John doesn't put his own interpretation of what Jesus said into the mouth of Jesus. He scrupulously distinguishes his interpretation (that Jesus was speaking of the Holy Spirit) from his record of what Jesus said in the historical situation. This goes directly contrary to the view that John thought it was okay to expand Jesus' teachings by adding his own interpretations and writing as if Jesus taught those interpretations explicitly.

days I will build another made without hands.'" And not even in this respect was their testimony consistent. (Mark 14.55–59)

As I mentioned briefly in the previous chapter, there is no account at all in any of the Synoptic Gospels of Jesus saying anything like this. You might think, "Well, no kidding! It says right there that they were giving false testimony!" It does say that, but does it really sound like it's *just* false testimony? Certainly, any prediction or threat to destroy the Temple would be highly unpopular in first-century Palestine. It would be like telling a TSA agent that you have a bomb in your bag—not a wise joke to make. But what about that part where they say that Jesus said he would raise the Temple again, not made with hands, in three days? That doesn't sound like it's made up out of whole cloth. If the witnesses were just liars, suborned by Jesus' enemies to get him in trouble, they could have left that part out altogether. They could have just elaborated on the destructive part, maybe saying that he said he would use his great power to destroy the Temple so that it would never be built again.

What this sounds most like is a garbled version of something or other that Jesus really said. If we heard a claim like this nowadays, made by someone's enemies, we would probably get on Google right away and start trying to "fact check" it, trying to find the original recording, to figure out what happened and how the original words might have been misunderstood or taken out of context. But the Synoptic Gospels provide no such information.

It's also interesting that Mark adds that even these witnesses didn't wholly agree with one another, though he doesn't elaborate on how they were inconsistent with each other. A partial explanation might come from Matthew, who gives their words as, "I am able to destroy the Temple of God and to rebuild it in three days" (Matt. 26.61). This might just be Matthew's recollection and recognizable paraphrase of Mark's account.[†] But it may reflect a variation between what different witnesses actually said. There is some difference between "I am able to destroy" and "I will destroy," and a friend of Jesus might be indignant if his enemies emphasized the latter rather than the former, seeing it as a distortion to make him look bad.

It seems that there must be more to the whole story of where this testimony came from, but either Mark doesn't know it or he doesn't tell it. If he doesn't know it, he doesn't make up a "back story" to fill in the gap. He just gets on with telling what he's heard about the trial, leaving this bit of negative testimony dangling. This is evidential in itself. Nor does he simplify matters by leaving out the part about rebuilding the Temple, to make the story flow more smoothly. He doesn't really seem to care about the unanswered questions that this passage raises. He's telling what he believes is true, even though that creates an unexplained allusion to whatever lies behind the false witnesses' testimony.

In this case, as it happens, we can find the rest of the story, but not in the Synoptic Gospels. It's found in John, almost certainly written well after Mark. In John 2.13–22 we have the story of the earlier time that Jesus cleansed the Temple. He drove out the animals, turned over the tables of the moneychangers, and condemned turning his Father's house into a house of merchandise. (He also did something similar several years later, during Holy Week.) When the Jewish leaders indignantly ask him what sign he gives of his authority to do all of this, he says, "Destroy this temple, and in three days I will raise it up" (John 2.19)—a pretty cryptic saying, and one that does not satisfy them. John pauses

---

[†]We shouldn't assume that the Gospel authors always had their own writing scrolls and source scrolls open at the same time. This would be very difficult to do given the size of scrolls. They probably worked from notes. See John Wenham, *Redating Matthew, Mark, & Luke: A Fresh Assault on the Synoptic Problem* (Downers Grove, IL: InterVarsity Press, 1992), pp. 204–206.

to explain that he was speaking about his body, predicting his own resurrection.†

There can't be much doubt that this is the explanation of the strange allegations at Jesus' trial several years later. John makes it quite clear that those asking him for a sign mistakenly believe that he's speaking of the literal Temple, and Jesus doesn't bother to set them straight. Obviously this saying of his was repeated in Jerusalem and puzzled over, and the witnesses at his trial bring it up as a charge against him. The fact that they are repeating a confused version, and the fact that it wasn't understood originally, may well have something to do with the inconsistency Mark refers to.

This is an undesigned coincidence such as I discussed in Chapter 3. I have placed it here because one half of it—the testimony of the witnesses told in Mark and Matthew—is an unexplained allusion. What are they talking about? Why would they say that Jesus said he would not only destroy the Temple but raise it up? We have the other puzzle piece in John, but John certainly didn't arrange for Matthew and Mark to leave a convenient gap for him to fill in later. Matthew and Mark may not have known or remembered anything about what Jesus said at the first Temple cleansing. (Matthew was not a disciple of Jesus yet at that time.) They don't seem to be trying to refer to the incident recorded in John. The passages therefore provide two different kinds of evidence, both an unexplained allusion and an undesigned coincidence, for the truthfulness of the accounts.

Unexplained allusions are a type of evidence for Gospel truth that doesn't get much coverage in today's scholarly or apologetic world. It runs completely contrary to the all-too-common picture of the Gospel authors as hyper-subtle overthinkers who were

---

† Notice that John does not "put" this interpretation into Jesus' mouth, apparently because Jesus did not explain what he meant. This shows again that John was careful about distinguishing his own interpretations from what Jesus actually said.

crafting their narratives with an eye to including as many unstated theological and symbolic meanings as possible.

In contrast, the artless mention of irrelevancies without explanation is a *positive* quality of the stories. It isn't simply an argument from our own ignorance. The argument from unexplained allusions comes from our knowledge of *how witnesses actually talk*. The tendency to make parenthetical digressions or to mention small details simply because they interest the speaker or occur to his mind, forgetting or not caring that the original audience won't get them, is a real quality of oral history, just as in Sue's story to her friends about the car accident. The best explanation of this quality in the Gospels is that their authors were truthful reporters, close to the facts.

Chapter Summary

- In an unexplained allusion, a speaker or an author mentions something in passing that the original audience probably wouldn't have understood. But the person telling the story is so interested in what he has to tell that he doesn't pause to explain.
- The Gospels contain quite a number of unexplained allusions. Some of these are also "one half" of an undesigned coincidence or are confirmed by external evidence.
- Unexplained allusions would make bad realistic fiction by interrupting the flow of the narrative and confusing the reader, which makes them evidence of truth.

Study Questions

1. Unexplained allusions are usually also unnecessary details. What is special about an unexplained allusion beyond being an unnecessary detail?

Unexplained Allusions | 131

2. Why would a talented modern novelist be unlikely to include a completely unexplained allusion?

3. What does it mean to say that one half of an undesigned coincidence can be an unexplained allusion?

4. What does Mark not provide when he says that Jesus called James and John Boanerges, the sons of thunder?

5. Since the people Jesus was speaking to did apparently know about the Galileans whom Pilate killed, why is this considered an unexplained allusion?

6. Why is the dispute about purification in John 3 an unexplained allusion?

7. When Jesus says, "As the Scripture said…" in John 7.38 and then doesn't quote any Scripture that we can easily identify, how is this especially good evidence that John is truthful in his Gospel?

8. What did Jesus really say that was reported at his trial as a threat to destroy the Temple? Why is this both an unexplained allusion and an undesigned coincidence?

For Discussion

1. Do you ever make unexplained allusions? Give an example of an unexplained allusion you have made or heard someone else make in real life, like the example of Sue and the ISP at the beginning of the chapter. Explain in your own words why this is a mark of truth.

2. A world-building fantasy author like J. R. R. Tolkien sometimes makes an unexplained allusion in his fiction to a backstory that

is part of his fictional "world." Usually this further aspect of his fantasy world is explained in some other part of his fictional work. Discuss why such instances are not problematic for the claim that unexplained allusions generally make poor fiction.

3. This book has mentioned several times the evidential value of John's "asides," where he says what Jesus meant by something, as in John 7.39. Other examples occur in John 2.21 and 13.11. How do they provide evidence for John's truthfulness in recording what Jesus said historically? Suppose that someone made the claim that the inspiration of the Holy Spirit made it okay for John to elaborate and put his own words in Jesus' mouth deliberately, even though he knew that he was going well beyond what Jesus historically said. How does John 14.26 provide evidence against this claim?

4. If you are very "audience conscious," there are two ways to avoid an unexplained allusion. One way is just to leave it out and to tell the story or make your point without that detail. Another way is to pause and explain it for those in your audience who might not understand it. Try to put yourself into the mindset of John in John 2.12, where he mentions the visit to Capernaum for a few days but doesn't explain the purpose of the visit. Discuss how the following factors make the unexplained allusion more likely: 1) John may have been dictating his memories aloud to a secretary. 2) There was no word processing. Once something was written down it was hard to erase or move it. 3) John was probably with Jesus at the time in his ministry when the trip to Capernaum occurred after the marriage at Cana.

5. Suppose that you were telling someone about a sermon you heard on YouTube, given several years ago by a well-known preacher. The preacher referred in the sermon to an event at the time that your own later audience might not have heard about.

What sort of factors could lead to your not pausing to explain to the audience the backstory of that event?

Resources for Further Study

Lydia McGrew, "Is Jesus John's Mouthpiece? Reconsidering Johannine Idiom," *Conspectus* 32 (2021), pp. 43–57, <https://tinyurl.com/McGrewMouthpiece>.

Lydia McGrew, *The Eye of the Beholder: The Gospel of John as Historical Reportage* (Tampa, FL: DeWard Publishing, 2021), Chapter XI, sections 1–2, pp. 349–360.

Lydia McGrew, *The Mirror or the Mask: Liberating the Gospels From Literary Devices* (Tampa, FL: DeWard Publishing, 2019), Chapter XII, "Still More Evidence for the Reportage Model," section 1, pp. 300–306.

Leon Morris, *Studies in the Fourth Gospel* (Grand Rapids, MI: Eerdmans Publishing Company, 1969), Chapters 2–4.

6

Unexpected Harmonies

1. What is reconcilable variation?

Bill's rich aunt has passed away, and the police strongly suspect foul play. Since she left Bill all of her money, the police are carefully tracing his movements on the day she died. They have narrowed down the time of death to between 3 and 3:30 p.m. Does Bill have an alibi?

Bill insists that he was at the gym all that afternoon until 3:30, and the gym is a good 45 minutes away from his aunt's house. But since the gym was mostly empty that day, there are not a lot of people who can confirm this. He says that he did see his friend Ginny briefly toward the end of his time at the gym. Ginny agrees with this; she says she said hello to Bill around 3:15. But the police know that Bill and Ginny are close friends; maybe they colluded to provide him with an alibi.

Does Bill have any other confirmation of his alibi? He tells the police that he stopped at a grocery store about ten minutes away from the gym on his way home. The police question the employees, and one of the checkout clerks recognizes Bill's picture. She says that he came through the line and bought a loaf of bread and a half gallon of milk at about 3:30.

One could argue that the checkout clerk's testimony contradicts Bill's, since he says he was at the gym until 3:30. But if he was at that grocery store at 3:30, this is an alibi in itself. Neither the clerk nor Bill has to be precise in giving times. The fact that the clerk mentions that Bill was only getting a couple of items also fits into the picture, since it would not have taken him long to pick up these two things before going through the line. Notice, too, that the clerk is almost certainly not colluding with either Bill or Ginny, since they aren't friends (that we know of). So the clerk's testimony is quite valuable and also tends to confirm Ginny's part of the alibi.

If either Ginny or the clerk had said anything much different about the time when they saw Bill, that could have been a problem for Bill. For example, if the clerk said that she saw Bill at around 2:00, that would be harder to fit with his and Ginny's accounts of his movements. There would have been plenty of time after that for him to travel to his aunt's house.

Bill's, Ginny's, and the clerk's testimonies exhibit what the 19th-century Anglican scholar T.R. Birks called reconcilable variation.[1] Reconcilable variation has some overlap with undesigned coincidences, which we talked about in Chapter 3; in fact, Birks himself included undesigned coincidences under the heading of reconcilable variation, while I'm treating the categories as related but a bit different. We have reconcilable variation between accounts when they have differences that someone might say are discrepancies, but these differences do not really amount to irreconcilable contradiction. In a reconcilable variation, the application of historical common sense works well to resolve the alleged discrepancy, while this would be harder to do if the stories were made up or erroneous. The clerk says that Bill was at the grocery store at about 3:30 while Bill says he was at the gym until 3:30. But the two locations are not far away from one another, and a little imprecision on the part of the clerk is enough to explain this minor apparent discrepancy. She isn't claiming to be precise to the minute. In the larger scheme of things, the fact that she attests to the fact that at around 3:30 Bill was on the opposite side of town from his aunt's house is far more important for confirming his alibi.

When two accounts are truthful, they are in principle reconcilable, since reality is consistent. When an account is fabricated, it is far more likely to result in an irreconcilable contradiction with some other fact or account.

The activity of seeing how stories can fit together even when there is some appearance of discrepancy is known in biblical studies as harmonization. Unfortunately, harmonization gets a bad rap in scholarly circles, because scholars tend to assume that the only reason why someone in the modern world would do it is because that person has a theological commitment to the Bible. Since scholars want to be able to say that they are just following the objective evidence, too many scholars, including some evangelicals, tend to shy away from harmonization. But as our example here shows, harmonization is not a religious activity, nor is it something you do only when you have a previous theological commitment. You don't need any religious commitment to Bill's truthfulness to see that, "I was at the gym until 3:30" and "He came through the checkout line [at a nearby store] at about 3:30" are quite easily compatible.

The Gospels exhibit reconcilable variation frequently, and this is one chapter where I am going to talk somewhat about alleged contradictions, a subject I've dealt with at much more length in *The Mirror or the Mask* and *The Eye of the Beholder*.† On the one

---

† I am *not* claiming that the alleged contradictions that I discuss in this chapter are all the ones that have been brought up! There are far too many such claims (many of them quite frivolous) for me to attempt to do that. Even in my other books, I am

hand, showing how an alleged contradiction can be reasonably resolved is a defensive move; it answers an objection that was threatening to downgrade our confidence in the Gospels' reliability. But in another sense, when we find that alleged discrepancies can be resolved repeatedly among documents telling about the same people and the same events, this reconcilable variation comes to have a positive evidential quality. The Gospel accounts hold together like the threads of a woven cloth, creating a tough fabric that doesn't give way easily. And the fact that they vary and even in some cases present an initial appearance of discrepancy gives us reason to think that the accounts come from different witnesses who had independent access to the facts. They aren't just based on each other with no further factual input.

2. Variations with no apparent discrepancy

In this section I want to discuss a few examples of Gospel variation in the accounts where there is no apparent discrepancy. This section will illustrate the importance of being willing to resist artificial claims of contradiction or invention by boldly pointing out that the passages in question, rightly considered, don't even *appear* to contradict each other. The next section will discuss the somewhat more complicated resurrection accounts and some of the alleged contradictions there as examples of reconcilable variation, when there is at least some initial appearance of discrepancy.

Far too often, if you try to reconcile Gospel passages, skeptics will scoff and call this activity "artificial." What we need to talk about even more is the artificial activity of creating contradictions where none exist. In the example in the introduction, an investigator who insisted that the store clerk was contradicting Bill's

---

able to discuss only some of the claims of contradiction that have been made. Here I am only trying to give representative examples of both extremely simple and somewhat more difficult claims of discrepancy.

alibi, rather than recognizing that she was confirming it, would not be a good investigator. If Bill were tried for murdering his aunt, and if the prosecuting attorney tried to insist that this was a contradiction and use it against Bill, he would be doing it because of his own agenda, not because this is a reasonable way to read the evidence. Similarly, many places in the Gospels are so easy to put together that we almost shouldn't even call doing so "harmonization," since there is no apparent problem to be resolved. Even if we keep that word "harmonization" in these easy cases, we *certainly* shouldn't be brow-beaten by the phrase "artificial harmonization."

One set of such easy cases concerns places where one Gospel mentions one person (or, in one story, one animal) while another Gospel mentions two. When Jesus heals the blind in Jericho, Mark mentions one blind man, named Bartimaeus (Mark 10.46–52), while Matthew mentions two blind men (Matt. 20.29–34). But this doesn't really create a problem. Why should it? There could be plenty of reasons for Mark to mention only one blind man. Perhaps Peter remembered Bartimaeus because he found out his name, so he mentioned him to Mark. Perhaps Bartimaeus was the only one who spoke. And so forth. This is not to say that Mark knew that there were two men. He may have heard about only one. But his Gospel never says, "There was *one and only one* blind man begging by the road." To state that there was one blind man isn't to *deny* that there was a second one on that occasion.

Similarly, Matthew mentions that there was a mother donkey there on the day when Jesus rode into Jerusalem while the other Gospels mention only the colt (Matt. 21.2–3, Mark 11.2–3, Luke 19.30–31, John 12.14–15). Should we therefore jump to the conclusion that Matthew invented the mother donkey? Why think a thing like that? The other evangelists don't say, "And by the way, there was *only one* donkey there." If in fact, as Jesus says in Mark 11.2, the colt had never before been ridden, it's not all that implausible that he was still fairly young and that he and his mother were tied up together. His mother could have been brought along to keep him calm, and that may have been why the owners kept them together. Again, for the other Gospels to mention the colt isn't for them to deny the mother, so there isn't even an apparent contradiction here.†

At the tomb on Easter morning, Matthew and Mark mention only one angel, while Luke 24.4 mentions two. Luke calls them "men," but this is obviously not a problem, since in the Bible stories it is quite common for angels to appear as men (Gen. 18.1–16, 19.1–6, Heb. 13.2). There isn't any contradiction here. Again, it's quite probable that only one angel actually spoke to the women, and this is why Mark and Matthew mention only one. Since there were multiple women at the tomb, Luke had a chance to get a fuller account that mentioned the second angel. We'll see more of the variations between the women's accounts in the next section.

The accounts of Jesus' crucifixion provide more examples of reconcilable variation without even the appearance of discrepancy. Different Gospels tell about different things that Jesus said on the cross. Sometimes these sayings appear to have been said at approximately the same time. But unless we are determined to find or create a contradiction, there is ample room for all of them. For example, Mark and Matthew record that Jesus cried out, "My God, my God, why have you forsaken me?" and that some of the bystanders mistook his utterance (because it was in Aramaic) for his calling for Elijah to come and rescue him (Mark 15.34–36). One of

---

† Sometimes one will hear that Matthew has a pattern of doubling up on things. But in fact there are only three places where Matthew has two of something while the other Gospels have one. Besides the donkeys and blind men, the third place is where he mentions two demoniacs healed (Matt. 8.28). When it comes to the angels at the tomb, it's *Matthew* who mentions one while *Luke* mentions two. The so-called pattern of Matthew's doubling is an exaggeration.

them runs to offer him sour wine. John does not record the saying, "My God, my God, why have you forsaken me?" but only John mentions that Jesus said, "I am thirsty" (John 19.28). John then records that one of the bystanders offered him sour wine. There is no contradiction at all between John and the Synoptics at this point. There is no reason why Jesus could not have said both, "My God, my God, why have you forsaken me?" and "I am thirsty." As I will discuss further in Chapter 8, thirst would have been a very natural part of the sufferings of crucifixion. Both of these sentences from the cross express Jesus' suffering. In fact, Jesus' saying, "I am thirsty" would explain even better why one of the bystanders offered him something to drink. He could even have said these two things at about the same time. If John, the Beloved Disciple, was standing near the cross, as John 19.26 says, he would have been in a position to hear things that others who were farther away didn't hear.

Only Luke mentions that Jesus cried out, "Father, into your hands I commit my spirit" (Luke 23.46), but that doesn't mean that there is a contradiction with other Gospels. They just don't mention it, though both Matthew 27.50 and Mark 15.37 mention a loud cry. Perhaps Luke is recording the words of that cry. Matthew, Mark, and Luke all indicate that Jesus died shortly after this, while John 19.30 mentions that he said, "It is finished" before dying. But again, there is no contradiction here. These both express things that Jesus might well have said just before he died, and each sentence takes only a second or two.

These are easy examples of reconcilable variation, because it is only from the perspective of an over-thinking critic that there even *appears* to be a conflict. If Jesus could quite easily and plausibly have said all of the things recorded on the cross, there is no reason, from a commonsense perspective, *not* to put together the various sayings recorded in the Gospels to get a fuller picture. If one Gospel mentions one blind man and another mentions two, this is no reason to doubt that there were two present. These are just variations. The accounts wouldn't be better if they were all identical. In fact, if they were all identical, we would have less information about what happened.

3. More challenging differences: The Easter stories

Sometimes the differences between the Gospels present more of a challenge. It can be helpful to look at some of these cases in more detail to see whether an application of a reasonable amount of real-world imagination shows them to be compatible. When this is the case, it gives us resources for responding to objections, just as we could do in a modern case.

It is important to realize what a natural activity this is and how it comes up often, perhaps without our fully realizing it, in ordinary life. Cold-case detective J. Warner Wallace tells of a case like this. One witness to a robbery stated that the suspect left the scene of the crime on foot, walking across the parking lot. Another witness stated that the robber left by driving away in a four-door Nissan. Surely they couldn't both be right, could they? But as it turned out, they were both right in what they said they saw. The two witnesses were simply looking out of the window from different angles. The Nissan was just out of the first witness's line of sight, so all that person saw was the robber walking away across the parking lot.[2]

The Gospel accounts of Jesus' resurrection contain quite a few of these reconcilable variations. These stories come under a lot of pressure from both popular and scholarly critics who say that they are hopelessly contradictory, which (supposedly) means that they have been changed and embellished, either by the authors of the Gospels or by people who told the stories to the authors.

There are a number of differences in the Gospel accounts of the women who came to the tomb on Easter Sunday morning. Ultimately, these differences are quite interesting and fruitful, providing us with a real-life, many-faceted picture of what happened after Jesus rose again.† At the end of this section, there is a chronological list of the events as I'm sketching it here. You can look ahead to that list and follow along if desired.

The Synoptic Gospels all tell about a group of women, including Mary Magdalene among others, who came to the tomb and found it empty. Matthew says that Mary Magdalene and another woman, also named Mary,‡ came to the tomb (Matt. 28.1), and from that point on, Matthew says that various things happened to a plural group of women (vss. 5, 8–9, 11).

If we had only Matthew to go on, we would assume that this group included Mary Magdalene all the way through the passage. If one makes that assumption, then one will assume that she met Jesus on the road (Matt. 28.9). But that assumption would create a problem: John 20.1–18 gives us a detailed account of Mary Magdalene's movements that shows that she *didn't* meet Jesus on the road and that she was almost certainly alone when she first saw him. According to John, Mary Magdalene came to the tomb at first, saw the stone rolled away, and ran to Peter and "the other disciple" (John) to tell them that someone had taken away Jesus' body. John makes it quite clear that Mary Magdalene did not see Jesus until she returned to the tomb and stood weeping outside. We have discussed this moving scene in detail in Chapter 4. This is clearly quite a different meeting from the one that Matthew describes on the road.

---

† I highly recommend a little book by John Wenham, *Easter Enigma* (Eugene, OR: Wipf and Stock, 1992), on this topic, though I don't agree with every one of his suggestions.

‡ Don't forget what we learned in Chapter 2 about the popularity of the name "Mary."

Can we reasonably put together the movements of the women on that morning? Was John just making up a story about how Mary Magdalene met Jesus? Did Matthew change his story? Or did both stories come to Matthew and John through a "telephone game," passed from one person to another, in the course of which they became garbled?

To see how these accounts fit together requires a little historical imagination, but that is a reasonable tool to apply. The most important thing to recognize is that people who are part of a group at one time don't have to continue to stay with that group. Mary Magdalene came to the tomb with several other women, though Matthew mentions only Mary Magdalene and "the other Mary." We know that more women were there from Luke, who indicates that a woman named Joanna and several others (whom he doesn't name) were with the two Marys at the tomb (Luke 24.10). Mark confirms this as well, for he names Salome as one of the women (Mark 16.1). This variation of the women's names shows that the Gospel authors weren't just getting their stories from each other. Probably their accounts represent the different details that different women remembered. In John, there is even a hint that other people were involved, because Mary Magdalene says to Peter and John, "We do not know where they have laid him" (John 20.2). This doesn't mean that the other women are still with her then, but it shows that she was with others when they found the tomb empty.

The solution to the movements of the women on Easter morning depends on recognizing that real life resembles a movie, not a set of still shots. And it certainly doesn't resemble a series of stone statues. Just because several people are together at one time, it doesn't follow that they stay together. They can start out in a group and then separate. Mary Magdalene and the other women weren't chained together on Easter Sunday.

When Mary Magdalene saw that the stone was rolled away, she left the other women behind, perhaps after a hurried consultation, and ran to tell Peter and John that someone took the body. We can think of John's "camera" as following Mary Magdalene as she goes away. Meanwhile, the other women went to the tomb, looked inside, and had the experiences described in Matthew, Mark, and Luke. Those evangelists' "cameras" follow the other women. After hearing from the angels that Jesus had risen, they ran to tell the disciples, meeting Jesus on the road, as explained in Matthew.

It's not clear whether or not Matthew heard about the fact that Mary Magdalene left the group and met Jesus later alone, nor is it clear that he knew that there were four or more women present. But he doesn't deny such a meeting between Mary and Jesus. He says that "they" met Jesus on the road. Once we realize (by reading both Luke and Mark) that there were more than two women present to begin with, Matthew's "they" makes sense even after Mary Magdalene is no longer there. Several women received the message from the angel(s) and met Jesus on the road.

This is a good case of reconcilable variation. The accounts differ but can be put together like a puzzle to form a plausible picture. This outcome makes sense if the authors are drawing on different witness accounts of reality.†

Another difference between the accounts concerns the mention of Galilee. In Mark and Matthew, the angel tells the women that Jesus is going before the disciples into Galilee and that they will see him there (Matt. 28.7, Mark 16.7). They are to carry this

---

†There is another difference about the angel. Matthew mentions that he rolled away the stone and sat down on it; he then mentions the angel talking to the women in a way that might give the impression that they were still outside at this point. But as John Wenham explains, the Greek verb tense that Matthew uses here doesn't have to mean that all of these events occurred quickly, one right after the other. The angel could have rolled the stone away and gone into the tomb before the women arrived.

message to the male disciples. Luke doesn't mention this message but mentions instead that the angel reminded the women of something that Jesus told them while he was in Galilee—that he would suffer and die and rise again (Luke 24.6–8). Luke even emphasizes that the women remembered Jesus' prediction.

Some scholars have tried to say that this message of the angel is Luke's invention. Because Luke, they say, didn't want to mention a trip by the disciples to Galilee (see the next point), supposedly he changed the reference to Galilee to something quite different—a reminder of Jesus' prediction, made in Galilee, of his own death and resurrection. This is one of the many strained scholarly theories that are too clever to be plausible.[3]

Part of this implausible theory is that Luke wanted to eliminate the angel's reference to the trip to Galilee because he was going to move Jesus' first appearance away from Galilee to Jerusalem. But the theory doesn't even hang together well. If Luke wanted to do that, why wouldn't he just drop the angel's mention of Galilee altogether? Why make up some *other*, unrelated mention of Galilee to replace it? Why think that Luke had some attachment to the word "Galilee," so that he felt he had to keep that word while changing the facts? Scholars have an unfortunate tendency to be captivated by verbal resemblance. Since the word "Galilee" appears in both accounts of what the angel said, they suggest that Luke was "adapting Mark" while hanging on to the word "Galilee." But such a strained effort on Luke's part to keep that one word while inventing a different angelic message simply doesn't make sense.

Luke's record of the angel's words actually fits very well with repeated references in the Synoptic Gospels to a group of women who came with Jesus from Galilee. (Remember that this list of women also features in an undesigned coincidence about Joanna, the wife of Chuza.) Here is Luke's first bit of information about these women, back in Luke 8:

> Soon afterward he went on through cities and villages, proclaiming and bringing the good news of the kingdom of God. And the twelve were with him, and also some women who had been healed of evil spirits and infirmities: Mary, called Magdalene, from whom seven demons had gone out, and Joanna, the wife of Chuza, Herod's household manager, and Susanna, and many others, who provided for them out of their means. (Luke 8.1–3)

The women listed are Mary Magdalene, Joanna, and Susanna, though Luke notes that there were others as well. Luke says that they traveled with Jesus and gave money to him. Luke connects this group with Galilee both by the reference to Magdala (on the coast of the Sea of Galilee, south of Capernaum) and by the previous chapter's reference to Jesus as being in Capernaum and in Nain, about six miles south of Nazareth (Luke 7.11). So these women very likely were indeed with Jesus in Galilee.

Fast-forward to the crucifixion, and we find that Matthew, Mark, and Luke all mention that there were women at the cross who had followed Jesus to Jerusalem from Galilee. Luke mentions this briefly just after recounting Jesus' death (Luke 23.49) but names none of them at that point. He says that the women who followed Jesus from Galilee as well as some of Jesus' (male) acquaintances "stood at a distance watching these things." Later in the chapter (vss. 55–56) Luke again mentions "the women who had come with him from Galilee" and says that they saw the tomb and how Jesus was laid and then returned home to prepare spices and ointments. Again, Luke gives no names at this point.

But Matthew and Mark do. Here is Mark 15.40–41 on the women at the cross:

There were also women looking on from a distance, among whom were Mary Magdalene, and Mary the mother of James the younger and of Joses, and Salome. When he was in Galilee, they followed him and ministered to him, and there were also many other women who came up with him to Jerusalem.

Matthew's list is similar, though not identical to Mark's in wording:

There were also many women there, looking on from a distance, who had followed Jesus from Galilee, ministering to him, among whom were Mary Magdalene and Mary the mother of James and Joseph and the mother of the sons of Zebedee. (Matthew 27.55–56)

Possibly Salome was the mother of the sons of Zebedee. Isn't it interesting that the only overlapping name between Matthew's and Mark's lists of women from Galilee here and Luke's list in 8.1–3 is Mary Magdalene? Yet it really looks like the same group of women is in view in all three passages. Matthew and Mark expressly refer to the women from Galilee at the cross as those who traveled with Jesus and ministered to him, which sounds an awful lot like the group Luke mentions in Chapter 8.

Furthermore, Luke does record that Jesus predicted his death and resurrection while he was in Galilee, so it's very probable that these women did hear him say this while they were all there (Luke 9.21–23, 43–44).

That brings us back to Easter. At first, Luke does not expressly name the women who went to the tomb on Easter morning, though one infers from the continued use of "they" from the previous chapter that it was the same group of women from Galilee who had gone home to prepare spices. And sure enough, these very women from Galilee remember Jesus' words (Luke 24.8a–11).[4]

New Testament scholar Richard Bauckham suggests that the variations in the names of the women at the tomb indicate scrupulousness and a variation in the access that the authors had to the women. Perhaps Matthew and Luke had not spoken to Salome, but Peter or Mark did. Joanna is mentioned only in Luke's Gospel; no one else mentions her. John Wenham refers to Luke as our "Joanna source."[5] John may have had Mary Magdalene's personal account of meeting Jesus at the tomb, and thus he gives it in vivid detail, as we discussed in Chapter 4. Matthew may not have talked with Joanna but knew of the presence of Mary Magdalene and "the other Mary"—probably Mary the mother of James and Joses.

What does all of this mean? The Synoptic accounts of the angel's words and the names of the women present exhibit reconcilable variation: The angel referred to Galilee in both ways—both as the place where Jesus' followers were to meet him (confirmed by both Matthew and Mark) and as the place where he previously predicted his death and resurrection (recorded by Luke). Some of the women remembered one part of the message (about where Jesus would later meet them), and others told Luke about the other part (reminding them of Jesus' prediction).

This brings us to another area where the Gospel resurrection accounts are said to be hopelessly conflicting: Where did Jesus first appear to his group of male disciples—in Galilee or in Jerusalem? After telling the story of the guard at the tomb and how they were bribed to tell a lie about the disciples stealing the body of Jesus, Matthew says that the eleven proceeded to Galilee and met Jesus there (Matt. 28.11–16). It would take at least several days to travel to Jerusalem. So if this were the first time that the eleven met Jesus, they didn't first meet him on Easter Sunday. But was the meeting in Galilee the first meeting?

Unexpected Harmonies | 149

Luke 24.36ff describes an appearance of Jesus on the very evening of Easter Sunday to his gathered disciples in the upper room in Jerusalem, and John 20.19–29 describes two such meetings, a week apart, both in Jerusalem. Almost certainly, the first meeting that John describes is the same one that Luke 24 tells about. These meetings give the disciples ample opportunity to verify Jesus' identity; the second meeting a week after Easter even convinces Doubting Thomas.

Not only does Matthew not describe any meeting between Jesus and the male disciples in Jerusalem, but at the meeting in Galilee, Matthew 28.17 says that "some" were doubtful when they saw Jesus. If the eleven had already met Jesus in Jerusalem as described in Luke and John, why would any of them still be doubtful when they met him in Galilee? This looks like a problem for the Gospels.

It goes without saying that critics have seized on these differences to say that some of the appearances must be made up or garbled. On the critical view, John and Luke may have just invented the appearances in Jerusalem. Maybe Luke "moved" the first appearance to Jerusalem. Maybe Matthew is contradicting Luke and John by saying that the very first appearance happened in Galilee. Did Matthew make up the meeting in Galilee?

Not so fast! Something we saw with Jesus' first meeting with Mary Magdalene is relevant here as well: It's important not to insist that a document means *only* what we would have thought the first time we read it, without any input from any other account. How many of us have had the experience of thinking that someone meant one thing and then deciding later that he must have meant something else? Another thing that happens all the time is that we make a mental picture based on just one account and then correct it later. If one person mentions that Joe and Jamie were at the party and doesn't mention his close friend Chris, we might go away thinking that Chris wasn't there, even though the witness didn't say that. What he said was true as far as it went. Maybe he didn't happen to notice Chris there, for example. If we hear from someone else that Chris was at the party, we have to revise our opinion. The commonsense willingness to change our minds and our interpretations needs to be applied to the Gospels as well as to ordinary conversations. Just because Matthew doesn't mention any appearances of Jesus in Jerusalem, and just because we wouldn't have heard about them without John or Luke, we shouldn't conclude that Matthew is *denying* that the disciples saw Jesus in Jerusalem.

It's especially important not to use the mere silence of one account to make us dismiss another account that we have some reason to trust. Suppose that your spouse mentions an accident at a prominent intersection, while a teenager who drove home from work past that intersection doesn't mention it. Should you doubt your spouse's account because the teen driver didn't happen to mention the accident? Of course not. There could be lots of reasons why the teenager focused on talking about other things, even if he saw the accident scene. Or maybe it was cleaned up by the time he passed by.

We have to be willing and able to take in new information and correct our initial mental picture. No mention of meetings in Jerusalem in Matthew? Okay, but there *are* such descriptions in John and Luke, so we learned something new!†

---

†The ending of the Gospel of Mark printed in many Bibles is known as the "long ending," beginning at 16.9. It probably was not part of the original manuscript of Mark. I think that it was added later as a summary of Jesus' resurrection appearances to replace the original ending, which appears to have been lost. So we don't know what resurrection appearances Mark originally described. It is entirely possible that he described a meeting between the male disciples and Jesus in Jerusalem, as told in Luke and John, and it would not be accurate to argue that Mark leaves out any such

But there's more to be said. The women were charged by the angel (and according to Matthew, by Jesus) to tell his disciples to meet him in Galilee. The angel in Mark 16.7 mentions Peter specifically. At first, this seems like another problem for reconciling the accounts: If Jesus was going to see his eleven disciples, including Peter, in Jerusalem that very evening (as Luke and John say he did), why would he and the angels tell the women to carry this message to the eleven at all?

We find in Matt. 26.32 that Jesus had told the Twelve at the Last Supper that after he was risen he would meet them in Galilee. It's entirely possible that, for them, the women's reference to meeting them in Galilee was meant to function like a password. Why? Because it really looks like *only* the Twelve were there at the Last Supper. So if that was the only time that Jesus predicted meeting the disciples later in Galilee, the women wouldn't have heard that prediction. The male disciples should have known that the women had received a real message from Jesus, due to the mention of going before them into Galilee. The women would have had no other way of knowing about that. Although it seems that the men didn't draw the right inference (Luke 24.11 says they doubted the women's word), the mention of going ahead of them into Galilee should have provided a clue that the women's story of seeing Jesus and angels was true.

Also, the eleven were probably not the only ones to whom the women carried the message to meet Jesus in Galilee. According to Luke 10.1, Jesus sent out seventy disciples on a special mission earlier in his ministry. According to the Apostle Paul in I Corinthians 15.6, more than five hundred people saw Jesus at once—something that couldn't have happened in the upper room. So the message the women were to carry was likely

---

appearance, since we don't have his original ending. We are simply left in the dark about what was included in it.

intended for a much larger group than just the ones who would see Jesus that very evening.

The idea that a larger group met Jesus in Galilee clears up a point about the ones who doubted in Matthew 28.17. Matthew mentions only the eleven traveling to Galilee. They probably went on that journey together. But that doesn't mean that they were the only ones who came together at the meeting that Matthew refers to.† If a larger group met and saw Jesus in Galilee, including some who had not seen him since his resurrection, then those who doubted in Matthew 28.17 need not have been those who were present at the meetings in Jerusalem. Those who met Jesus in Jerusalem had already had a full chance to have any doubts cleared up. They were invited to touch Jesus (Luke 24.39, John 20.27), they saw his hands and feet, they saw him eat (Luke 20.41–43). But in the hills of Galilee, it is plausible that a larger group met him at this designated location. Some who were present worshiped him, but some among this larger group doubted, at least when they first saw him. We can surmise that as the meeting continued, they also had a chance to have closer conversations with Jesus and to see that he was indeed alive and physically present.

John is helpful here in a special way, for he tells us openly that Jesus did meet his disciples both in Jerusalem and in Galilee. He tells of two meetings in Jerusalem in John 20 and then of a meeting in Galilee in John 21. I don't want to be unclear: I'm *not* saying that the meeting in Galilee in John 21.1–22 is the same one that Matthew tells about. It clearly isn't. John makes it clear that only seven disciples were present—Peter and six others who went out fishing all night (vs. 2–3). They saw Jesus unexpectedly on the

---

† Notice, too, that Matt. 28.16 refers to a specific mountain meeting place that Jesus had designated. While it's possible that he mentioned this at the Last Supper, a post-resurrection meeting with the disciples would have made an even more appropriate opportunity for them to take in this information.

shore the next morning. John specifies that this was the third time that the (male) disciples had seen Jesus since he rose from the dead (vs. 14). The point is that John, without even trying to do so, confirms that Jesus' core male disciples saw him in Jerusalem after he rose from the dead, then traveled to Galilee and saw him there as well. They probably waited until the end of the Jewish Feast of Unleavened Bread to make the several-days' journey north.

Later on still, they could have returned to Jerusalem. The idea that the disciples saw Jesus in Jerusalem, traveled to Galilee, and then returned to Jerusalem later clears up a possible confusion caused by Luke 24.49, where Jesus tells the disciples to remain in Jerusalem until they receive the promised Holy Spirit. Did Jesus say that on Easter Sunday? If he did, then that would create a contradiction with Matthew; they would have no chance to go to Galilee if they were supposed to stay in Jerusalem the whole time. Skeptics are rather fond of pointing this out and claiming a contradiction. Luke himself tries to clear up any potential confusion in Acts 1.3 by emphasizing that Jesus was with his disciples for forty days after his resurrection and gave them lots of evidence that he was real and had risen from the dead. A trip up to Galilee and back to Jerusalem could easily fit into that forty days, and we can assume that Luke just didn't have space to tell about it (or hadn't yet heard about it) at the end of Luke 24.

Putting all of this together, we get the following order of events:

1. Easter morning: Mary Magdalene and the other women come to the tomb and see the stone rolled away.
2. Mary Magdalene runs to tell Peter and John. Meanwhile, the other women go into the tomb, hear the message of the angels, and leave. (The angels remind the women that Jesus predicted his death and resurrection in Galilee

and also send word to Peter and Jesus' other followers that he will go before them into Galilee and that a group of them will meet him there.)

3. The other women meet Jesus on the road while they are running to tell the disciples.

4. Peter and John come back with Mary Magdalene, find the tomb empty, and leave.

5. Mary Magdalene remains crying. She speaks briefly to the angels without realizing that they are angels. She then sees Jesus and eventually recognizes him. She runs to tell the disciples what has happened.

6. The male disciples are confused by all that has happened and talk about it all day, but most of them don't believe the women.

7. Some time during the day, Jesus has a private meeting with Peter (Luke 24.34).

8. That evening, two disciples (probably but not certainly both male), who have not yet heard about Peter's private appearance, talk with Jesus on the road to Emmaus. After they recognize Jesus, they hurry back to Jerusalem to tell the others.

9. Shortly after the Emmaus disciples arrive, Jesus appears to ten of the eleven core disciples and the others who are with them. He shows his hands, feet, and side, eats some fish and honeycomb, and talks with them for an unspecified period of time.[†]

[†]There is a big difference between just being non-specific about how much time something takes and deliberately trying to make it look like something took less time than it really did. The former is a type of what I have called "achronological narration"—narration without specifying time. This seems to be what is going on in Luke 24. It's very important not to confuse this with an author's deliberately changing the facts about time.

10. Thomas, who wasn't there when Jesus appeared to the disciples on Easter evening, doesn't believe. A week later, in Jerusalem, Jesus appears to the eleven, including Thomas, and convinces him. (Meanwhile, word is going out to the larger group of Jesus' followers that there is to be a meeting in Galilee.)
11. Peter and the rest of the eleven travel to Galilee, following Jesus' instructions.
12. Peter and six others go fishing on the Sea of Galilee and meet Jesus unexpectedly on the shore the next morning. They eat breakfast and talk together.
13. The eleven and a larger group meet with Jesus in Galilee, almost certainly outdoors in the hills, at a place he has designated for the meeting. Some who haven't seen Jesus since his resurrection are doubtful initially.
14. Over the next several weeks Jesus meets with his disciples on some unspecified number of other occasions. Eventually they return to the Jerusalem area. Jesus meets with them again in that area and tells them to stay in Jerusalem until they receive the Holy Spirit.
15. Jesus talks with his disciples one last time (Acts 1.4–9). He returns to heaven in their presence.
16. Ten days later, they experience the coming of the Holy Spirit at Pentecost.

The picture here is coherent and plausible. Skeptics, of course, deny that the resurrection happened at all, because it is a miracle. But they will also specifically claim that the resurrection accounts are hopelessly contradictory and that they can be put together only by the most strained, ludicrous attempts. It's this latter claim that I am arguing against here.

These examples from the resurrection accounts are just a few cases among many where a similar approach can be fruitfully applied. Is it possible for attempts to combine accounts to be strained and unconvincing? Yes, it certainly is possible, and sometimes it actually does happen. There are cases where I myself am not convinced by the available harmonizations that I have seen.[6] Yet far more often, the Gospels exhibit the fascinating quality of reconcilable variation, just as we would expect from truthful eyewitness accounts. Harmonization is just putting accounts together, and there is every reason to attempt to do so in the Gospels, just as we rationally do in ordinary life. The bad rap that harmonization gets in some scholarly circles tells us far more about the scholars than about the Gospels.

We've already noted that modern law enforcement agents recognize the importance of putting accounts together. The naturalness of witness variation was also noticed long ago by prominent English jurist Thomas Starkie concerning witnesses in court:

> It has been well remarked by a great observer, that "the usual character of human testimony is substantial truth under circumstantial variety." It so rarely happens that witnesses of the same transaction perfectly and entirely agree in all points connected with it, that an entire and complete coincidence in every particular, so far from strengthening their credit, not unfrequently engenders a suspicion of practice and concert.[7]

At the end of his book *Easter Enigma,* John Wenham explains the value of harmonization in a way that is hard to beat:

> Forced harmonizing is worthless. The tendency today, however, is the opposite—to force the New Testament writings into disharmony, in order to emphasize their individuality. The current analytical approach to the gospels often has the effect of making

scholars more and more uncertain at more and more points, till eventually their view of Jesus and his teaching is lost in haze. The harmonistic approach, on the other hand, enables one to ponder long and conscientiously over every detail of the narrative and to see how one account illuminates and modifies another. Gradually (without fudging) people and events take shape and grow in solidity and the scenes come to life in one's mind. Such study is beautifully constructive....[8]

Chapter Summary

- We have reconcilable variation between accounts when they show some differences, but these differences do not amount to irreconcilable contradiction.

- Sometimes these variations are very simple and don't even *appear* to be contradictory. In other cases there is some tension between the accounts, but reasonable use of historical imagination allows them to be reconciled.

- This use of historical imagination is not a desperate, theological activity but rather the kind of activity that we use rationally in non-religious contexts.

Study Questions

1. What is harmonization in studying the Gospels or historical documents or testimonies?

2. What is real-world imagination in harmonization?

3. How does the connection between Bill's alibi and the store clerk's testimony represent a reconcilable variation? Why is it legitimate to harmonize these two statements?

4. How can we apply real-world imagination to the fact that Mark 10.46–52 mentions only one blind man whom Jesus healed

in Jericho (Bartimaeus) whereas Matt. 20.30–34 mentions two blind men when telling the same story? Why is it not a contradiction when one author mentions one person or thing while another author mentions two?

5. Using the chapter discussion as a guide, apply real-world imagination to the following verses: In Mark 15.34–36 Jesus says, "My God, my God, why have you forsaken me?" One of the bystanders then brings sour wine and offers it to him on a reed. In John 19.28–29, Jesus says, "I am thirsty." A bystander offers him sour wine. Some scholars have suggested that John changed, "My God, my God, why have you forsaken me?" into "I am thirsty." They apparently see a tension or contradiction between these verses because the thing Jesus says just before the sour wine is offered to him is different in the two Gospels. Based on the discussion in the chapter, what simple, commonsense response can we give to the claim that the two Gospels are in tension because they report Jesus saying different things at about the same time in the crucifixion?

6. The chapter suggests as a possibility the idea that if the women told the male disciples on Easter day that Jesus was going ahead into Galilee, this might have been a kind of "password" to show that the women really had a message from the risen Jesus. Based on the chapter discussion, explain why the male disciples should have recognized this message as a sign that the women really were giving a message from Jesus. Hint: Were the women present at the Last Supper? When did Jesus tell the male disciples that he would go ahead of them into Galilee (Matt. 26.32)?

7. Digging deeper: Why is there an *initial* appearance of contradiction between the Gospels concerning the question, "When did Mary Magdalene meet Jesus on Easter?" Hint: Look at Matt. 28.1–10 and compare it with John 20.1–18. What might you think

about where and how Mary Magdalene met Jesus on Easter if you had *only* the passage in Matthew, and how would this differ from John's narrative? The chapter suggests that real-world imagination helps to solve this problem by leading us to remember that life is more like a moving picture than a series of still shots. What probably really happened to Mary Magdalene and to the other women?

8. Digging deeper: Skeptic Bart Ehrman points readers to Luke 24.49 and says that Jesus is telling the disciples, on Easter day, to stay in Jerusalem until the Holy Spirit comes. According to Acts 1–2, the Holy Spirit did not come until after Jesus ascended into heaven. But in Matt. 28.16 and following and in John 21, the disciples go to Galilee and see Jesus there while he is still on earth after his resurrection. Skeptics argue that this is a contradiction, since they couldn't go to Galilee and see Jesus there if they had to stay in Jerusalem from Easter Sunday until Pentecost. According to the chapter, how is this alleged contradiction answered? When did Jesus tell the disciples to stay in Jerusalem? Hint: You can apply the concept of achronological narration, which is just being non-specific about times, to the hurried narrative at the end of Luke 24.

For Discussion

1. If you know of one, describe a time when you mistakenly thought that someone was lying or mistaken because there seemed to be a contradiction between what he said and something else you knew or had heard. How did finding out that the person was right all along affect your evaluation of his trustworthiness?

2. Consider the following situation: Jan says that she saw Lori in the park alone with her children yesterday afternoon. Julie says that she saw Lori and Jessica together with their children in the park yesterday afternoon. How can Jan and Julie both be right?

3. Does the concept of using real-world imagination to harmonize Bible accounts seem surprising or new to you? Discuss whether or how this concept led you to see the Gospels in a different way.

4. Did any of the alleged discrepancies in the resurrection accounts (such as the question about the movements of the women) surprise you? Do you think such allegations of contradiction would be likely to cause doubt for yourself or others?

5. How would you answer a non-Christian who said, "You just harmonize these discrepancies in the Bible because the Bible is your holy book"?

6. Pick one or more of the alleged discrepancies or differences between the resurrection stories discussed in the chapter that you have heard, noticed, or wondered about before. Do you find the explanation in the chapter satisfying? Why or why not? If not, do you have a different explanation that you think is better?

7. Consider the fact that people often have an unspoken "about" idea in mind when they describe a number or a time. E.g. "It was 3:30," "There were ten people at the party." Someone might say these things while meaning "around 3:30" or "about ten people." This kind of approximation is one real-world tool that can help us to recognize reconcilable variation. One skeptical objection to the Gospels is the claim that Jesus is wrong in Matt. 13.32 when he says that the mustard seed is the smallest seed, since there are literally smaller seeds in the world. How would common sense and the idea of approximate numbers allow you to answer this type of objection? Hint: Imagine an American southerner saying, "It was the cutest thing you ever saw!"

Resources for Further Study

T. R. Birks, *Horae Evangelicae: or, the Internal Evidence of the Gospel History* (London: Seeleys, 1852), <https://tinyurl.com/TRBirks>.

J. H. A. Ebrard, *The Gospel History: A Compendium of Critical Investigations*, translated by James Martin (Edinburgh: T & T Clark, 1863), <https://tinyurl.com/EbrardGospelHistory>.

Lydia McGrew, "Arguments From Silence: The Good, the Bad, and the Ugly," *Lydia McGrew YouTube Channel*, April 3, 2022, <https://tinyurl.com/argumentfromsilence>.

Lydia McGrew, "Artificial Disharmonization," *Lydia McGrew YouTube Channel*, November 12, 2021, <https://tinyurl.com/Disharmony1>.

Lydia McGrew, "Artificial Disharmonization 2," *Lydia McGrew YouTube Channel*, November 28, 2021, <https://tinyurl.com/Disharmony2>.

Lydia McGrew, "Did John Move the Crucifixion Date?" Lydia McGrew YouTube Channel, April 10, 2022, <https://tinyurl.com/JohnCrucifixion>.

Lydia McGrew, *The Mirror or the Mask: Liberating the Gospels from Literary Devices* (Tampa, FL: DeWard Publishing, 2019), Chapter XII, "Still More Evidence for the Reportage, Model," section 3, pp. 316–321, Chapters XIII, "Utterly Unforced Errors," XIV, "Fictions Only Need Apply," XV, "Over-Reading," XVI "Fictionalizing Literary Devices and the Resurrection Accounts," pp. 339–479.

Lydia McGrew, "Time and Narrative: Clarity and Chronology in Reading the Gospels," *Journal of Greco-Roman Christian-*

ity and Judaism 17 (2021), pp. 62–87, <https://tinyurl.com/McGrewonChronology>.

Lydia McGrew and Timothy McGrew, "The Argument from Miracles: A Cumulative Case for the Resurrection of Jesus of Nazareth." In *The Blackwell Companion to Natural Theology*, edited by W. L. Craig and J. P. Moreland (Oxford: Wiley-Blackwell, 2009), pp. 593–662, <https://tinyurl.com/McGrewsResurrection>.

Thomas Starkie, *A Practical Treatise of the Law of Evidence* (Philadelphia: T. and W. Johnson, 1876), <https://tinyurl.com/StarkieTreatise>.

J. Warner Wallace, *Cold-Case Christianity: A Homicide Detective Investigates the Claims of the Gospels* (Colorado Springs, CO: David C. Cook, 2013), Chapter 4, "Principle #4: Test Your Witnesses," pp. 69–85.

John Wenham, *Easter Enigma: Are the Resurrection Accounts in Conflict?* (Eugene, OR: Wipf & Stock, 1992).

7

Unified Personalities

1. Real people are hard to fake
In the Gospels, we meet real people, not cardboard cutouts nor mere foils for Jesus' theological brilliance. Without any appearance of attempting to mimic one another, the four evangelists portray not only Jesus himself (whose consistent personality we'll discuss in the next chapter) but also several subsidiary characters in a variety of settings and stories, always recognizably themselves. As David Marshall points out in *Jesus is No Myth*,[1] this is not what we find in the non-canonical "gospels," where supporting characters are not fleshed out.

Accustomed as we are to movie prequels and sequels and long-running TV shows, we may too easily overlook the unity of characters in multiple stories as a mark of truth. But it is hard to pull off in fiction, especially when multiple authors are involved. I vividly remember binge-watching the show *Monk* and being frustrated by variations in the character of detective Adrian Monk over different seasons. In the first season, while he did struggle with his obsessive-compulsive disorder, he was not a mere caricature, and he solved crimes by a real genius for observation and inference. The pilot episode, "Mr. Monk and the

Candidate," introduces him as an inspired observer and reasoner, able to focus to an uncanny extent on a crime scene, noticing every tiny bit of physical evidence and drawing brilliant inferences from each of them. This is why the police call him in as an expert. But as the series went on, his OCD became such a focus of the episodes as a comic device that it came to dominate the show, leaving little space for detection. This change was frustrating to me, since I love the puzzle-like nature of detective fiction. For example, the third-season episode "Mr. Monk Takes Manhattan" is almost entirely taken up with Monk's painful distraction due to the unfamiliarity of New York City. He solves that case largely by the lucky chance of noticing the ear lobe of the murderer in an interview he sees on a screen. There is none of the laser-like focus and little of the Sherlock Holmes-like brilliance that characterized the Monk of the pilot. Even in a show with all the resources of modern film-making at the writers' disposal, the character of Monk was, it seemed to me, not consistent, because some of the writers got carried away with exaggerating his disability and trying to wring humor out of it.

The Gospel authors do better than that, because they are reporting real events happening to real people.

2. Peter

One of the most striking characters in the Gospels is Peter. Christians have heard so many sermons about Peter that by this time they may take for granted the Gospels' consistent portrayal of him. We shouldn't underestimate the historical and apologetic importance of Peter's personality. It would not be easy for authors who were making up stories to make this character consistent, recognizable, but not caricatured, through so many different scenes and situations. It's especially interesting to notice how Peter's personality shows across all four Gospels, and for that reason I'll often be noting here when a story is unique to one Gospel.

One of the consistent characteristics of Peter is his extravagance in feeling and expressing emotion. This quality sometimes takes the form of boasting but sometimes comes out in expressions of humility. Sometimes it takes the form of physical action. E.g., Peter flings himself at Jesus' feet after the first great catch of fish, begging him to leave him, for he is a sinful man (Luke 5.8). (This incident is unique to Luke.)

Peter's impulsive, extravagant nature reveals itself often in words as well. In his study of Peter's character, 19th-century scholar J. S. Howson comments,

> Most men find it difficult to be silent at critical moments of their lives. And all this is particularly true of vehement and impulsive natures. Such persons speak promptly, and speak unaffectedly, when they are under emotion. And such a character was St. Peter's.[2]

Naturally, it is Peter and not any other disciple who asks Jesus to invite him to come to him when he sees Jesus walking on the water—an aspect of that scene unique to Matthew (Matt. 14.28–31). Nor does this seem to be *just* showing off, though perhaps it is that as well. Such an impulse to go to Jesus on the water arises naturally from Peter's love. Says Howson,

> He is prompt and forward alike on the good side and on the bad side. On the one hand, a strong impulse of vigorous faith is displayed; on the other hand, he manifests a very wilful presumption.[3]

At the scene of the Transfiguration, Peter bursts out with the suggestion that they should construct three tabernacles, one apiece for Jesus, Elijah, and Moses. Mark 9.6–7 says that Peter didn't know what to say, because they were all terrified. It's just like Peter, when he doesn't know what to say, that he says something anyway! Howson remarks pointedly, "[W]e cannot imagine this utterance coming from any other of the Twelve Apostles."[4]

It is Peter who boasts on the night of the Last Supper that, even if all of the other disciples fall away from Jesus, he never will (Mark 14.29). Howson comments, "We remember, as we ought to remember, the sin which followed this presumption. But we ought not forget the true, honest, ardent faith which inspired his rash promise."[5] When Jesus says that he is going away and that Peter cannot follow him now but will follow later, Peter asks touchingly, "Lord, why can I not follow you right now? I will lay down my life for you" (John 13.37), a comment reported only in John. It is characteristic of Peter at this stage in his life that he does not really know himself, believing that he has more courage than he really has. It is, of course, Peter who strikes off the ear of the high priest's servant in defense of Jesus (John 18.10, Mark 14.47, Matt. 26.51, Luke 22.50). But after that, he doesn't have the courage to stand up to those who accuse him of being Jesus' disciple.

When Mary Magdalene reports that the tomb is empty on Easter morning, it is Peter who jumps up instantly with the Beloved Disciple and runs to the tomb (John 20.3). When Jesus appears on the shore of the Sea of Galilee and the Beloved Disciple recognizes him, it is Peter who leaps into the water, not waiting for the boat to come to land (John 21.7). These two incidents are told only in John. Throughout all of these varied scenes, the warmhearted, unwise, and undisciplined personality of Peter comes through loud and clear.

Closely connected to Peter's impulsive and emotional nature, though not mentioned as often, is his tendency to argue.[6] There is nothing remotely literary about this aspect of Peter's personality.

We feel that we know him. He is like the annoying student who so often thinks that he knows better than the teacher. But Peter is not merely annoying and argumentative. Rather, this touch of arrogant aggressiveness is intertwined inextricably with his overwhelming love for Jesus. The combination is unmistakable, unique to Peter, and (again) consistent all across the Gospels.

Several of the incidents already named illustrate this trait. Before the great catch of fish in Luke, Peter protests, "Master, we worked hard all night and caught nothing," though he immediately adds, "but I will do as you say and let down the nets" (Luke 5.8). One can sense that Peter thinks that Jesus doesn't know much about fishing. No doubt the memory of his own skepticism is part of the reason why Peter feels such awe and embarrassment after the miracle of the great catch. As it turned out, Jesus knew more about fishing than Peter thought he did!

But though he is overawed for the moment in Luke 5, in some later incidents he is even more pushy. When Jesus begins teaching the disciples plainly that he is going to be killed, Peter has the gall to take him aside and rebuke him (Mark 8.32). Matthew gives his words at this point as, "God forbid it, Lord! This shall never happen to You" (Matt. 16.22), illustrating yet again the combined forwardness and affection in Peter's nature. This incident comes after Peter's confession that Jesus is the Messiah, the Son of God; Matthew introduces the incident in verse 21 with the phrase "from that time Jesus began to show his disciples" that he must die. It seems that Jesus began right away to try to correct any false ideas of imminent messianic earthly reign, but Peter would not accept this. Jesus' breathtakingly stern rebuke, "Get behind Me, Satan; for you are not setting your mind on God's interests, but man's" (Mark 8.33) may dampen Peter's tendency to argue for a while, but not for long.

When Jesus wants to wash Peter's feet on the night of the Last Supper, he first protests that Jesus must never wash his feet (John 13.8). When Jesus says that he must wash his feet, or Peter will have no part with him, Peter immediately tells Jesus to wash his hands and head as well. He cannot simply let Jesus do what Jesus wants to do, which is what he is doing to everyone else. Peter has his own ideas about what Jesus should be doing and presses them repeatedly.

Even his boast that he will never forsake Jesus, though all the rest do, is an example of his contrariness. Jesus has just predicted that they *will* "all fall away" (Mark 14.27). Peter's loving heart is hurt at the implication that he will do anything of the kind, regardless of what the others do. It does not seem to occur to him that Jesus knows more about the matter than he does. By this time he seems willing to admit that Jesus might really die, but he insists (contrary to Jesus' own prediction) that in that case he will die with him (Mark 14.31).

Peter's forwardness, though tempered after his own great failure in denying Jesus, is visible to some extent even in the scene after the resurrection where Jesus calls forth Peter's humility at last. In John 21 Peter no longer boasts that he loves Jesus more than the others. He simply tells Jesus that, as Jesus knows, he loves him. He is learning.†But even then, when he turns and sees the Beloved Disciple following, he feels curious (perhaps we should say nosy) and can't resist asking, "Lord, and what about this man?" (John 21.21–23) Jesus has to take him down a peg yet again, reminding him that his plans for the other disciple are not really

---

†There is an undesigned coincidence here. John never mentions that Peter has boasted (Mark 14.29) that he loves Jesus more than the other disciples and will never forsake him even if they do. Jesus' line of questioning here in John is surprising, especially since he usually discourages comparison and competition between the disciples. The explanation is Peter's boast in Mark. Jesus wants to call forth Peter's humility instead.

Peter's business. Though Peter is not precisely arguing with Jesus here, the scene does seem to be a part of the pattern in which Peter puts himself forward with an inappropriate question, argument, rebuke, or suggestion and has to be reined in.

It would be incredible if the Gospel authors had contrived to portray Peter again and again in ways that show such a consistent personality across such a variety of incidents. It is one thing to copy a story from someone else. It is another thing for several different authors to make the reader feel that he recognizes the character portrayed in entirely different scenes. The character portraits of Peter have the mark of historical memoirs. Howson comments,

> This study, short and scanty as it has been...contains evidence of the truth of the Gospel narratives. A certain very remarkable aspect of character in the case of St. Peter has been brought to view from an examination of several passages. It is the self-same aspect which comes to view in all of them; and the passages relate to scenes very various in their circumstances and details. Such uniformity with diversity cannot be the result of accident. Still less can it be the result of fraudulent design. No one can suppose that in any degree these passages are copied from one another, so as to produce the impression of identity in the personality of St. Peter. And let it here be added that, without exhausting the instances that might be adduced, examples have been purposely taken from all the four Gospels. If the...reader of Holy Scriptures will look into all this closely, he will see that it contains an evidential argument of no inconsiderable weight.[7]

A few more points concerning Peter are worth discussing. The Gospels and Acts show a remarkable consistency in their connection of Peter with John. On three occasions in the Synoptic Gospels, Jesus singles out Peter with the two sons of Zebedee, James and John, to go with him while others are left behind. These are the raising of Jairus's daughter (Mark 5.37), the Transfiguration (Mark 9.2), and Jesus' agony in the Garden of Gethsemane (Mark 14.32). The author of Luke records in Acts a completely different set of scenarios where Peter and John are the most prominent leaders of the early church and are confronted by the Jewish leaders (Acts 3.1–4.21). (Luke makes no attempt to include James the son of Zebedee in these scenes, showing once more his care in specifying what happened. If he did not know that all three—Peter, James, and John—were together in a particular incident, he was not going to bring in James.)

John shows this same pattern, putting Peter and John together, by associating Peter with the Beloved Disciple.† Peter asks the Beloved Disciple by signals to try to find out who will betray Jesus (John 13.23–24). The Beloved Disciple (here called the "other disciple") gets permission for Peter to enter the high priest's courtyard (John 18.15–16). Peter and the Beloved Disciple are apparently lodging together when Mary Magdalene brings news of the empty tomb early on Easter morning, and they run together to investigate (John 20.1–10). The Beloved Disciple tells Peter when he recognizes Jesus on the shore (John 21.7). Peter and the Beloved Disciple are close to one another in the scene in John 21, prompting Peter's question to Jesus,

---

†I've argued elsewhere for the traditional position that the Beloved Disciple (mentioned repeatedly in John) is John the son of Zebedee himself. See Lydia McGrew, *The Eye of the Beholder: The Gospel of John as Historical Reportage* (Tampa, FL: DeWard Publishing, 2021), Appendix. Some scholars argue that the Beloved Disciple was the author of the book but was another disciple named John. See Richard Bauckham, *Jesus and the Eyewitnesses: The Gospels as Eyewitness Testimony*, 2nd ed. (Grand Rapids, MI: Eerdmans Publishing, 2017), chapters 15–17, 20. That position is in principle consistent with thinking that the Gospel of John is completely historical, but if you take Bauckham's position, you won't think that the connections between Peter and the Beloved Disciple fit with the explicit connections between Peter and John the son of Zebedee elsewhere, as in Acts. On the other hand, that in itself would be a rather surprising coincidence.

"What about this man?" (John 21.20–21) This close association between Peter and John is another aspect of the unity with which the Gospels (and Acts) portray Peter.

The church fathers tell us that Mark was the disciple of Peter, and parts of Mark's Gospel seem to come from Peter's perspective,[8] but it's important to notice that there is unique information about Peter in the other Gospels, too. Here are a few more examples: Only John reports the earliest meeting between Jesus and Peter. This is the first time that Jesus gives Peter his nickname (John 1.40–42)—Cephas, the rock. John also records a unique confession by Peter to Jesus' Messiahship (John 6.67–69). This incident, containing the famous words, "Lord, to whom shall we go? You have the words of eternal life" illustrates yet again Peter's warm-hearted, expressive personality. It is difficult to imagine any other disciple uttering those words.

Matthew has a few unique stories: Peter's walking on the water in Chapter 14 and his specific words of rebuke to Jesus in Chapter 16. Mark does *not* report that Peter went out and wept bitterly after he denied Christ and the cock crowed. That item is found only in Matthew and Luke (Matt. 26.75, Luke 22.62). And only Luke 22.61 includes the further, poignant detail that Jesus looked at him just about the time the cock was crowing.

Further evidence of Luke's contact with Peter comes from a fascinating study by classicist and New Testament scholar Colin Hemer of small differences between Luke's and Mark's records of the Transfiguration scene. Hemer suggests that this means Luke talked personally with Peter about this scene. Mark says that this scene occurred six days after Jesus' previous sayings (Mark 9.2). Luke says that it occurred "some eight days" after the same sayings. Hemer comments on this, "It may be the mark of a careful writer to be *imprecise* where definiteness is not warranted:

he [Luke] is unwilling to press the current hesitancy of an informant into the convenient mold of other tradition."[9] In other words, if Peter was less precise about exactly when the Transfiguration occurred when talking with Luke than he was when Mark heard him, Luke was not going to substitute Mark's statement about the number of days. Instead, he represented accurately his own independent evidence.

This is a good example of "reconcilable variation," which I discussed in the previous chapter. Mark mentions six days while Luke mentions eight, but "some eight days" is compatible with six days. The difference very likely comes from two different accounts, which may both have come from Peter himself. We all know what it's like to remember something slightly differently at different times and to use different expressions to tell when something happened. There isn't any contradiction here, and the variation probably means that Luke and Mark got their information in different ways. Luke isn't just using Mark for this scene.

Hemer also notes the following points of difference: Only Luke points out that Jesus went up to the mountain to pray and that the Transfiguration occurred while he was praying (Luke 9.28). In fact, Luke specifies that the appearance of his face began to change during his prayer. Luke's account mentions that there were two men with Jesus before Luke gives their identities as Moses and Elijah (vs. 30). The subject of the conversation (Jesus' death) is mentioned only in Luke (vs. 31). Only Luke notes that the disciples were extremely sleepy, but he carefully says that they were fully awake when they saw Jesus' glory and the two men with him (vs. 32). One can imagine that perhaps they became sleepy as Jesus prayed for a long time but awoke just before the Transfiguration began. Only Luke notes that Peter made his suggestion of three tabernacles at the moment when the other two

(Moses and Elijah) were parting from Jesus (vs. 33). Only Luke specifically notes that the disciples were afraid as they entered the cloud that overshadowed Jesus (vs. 34).

Several of these details in Luke could very well indicate eyewitness testimony. The progress from the sight of two men (some men or other) with Jesus to their identities sounds like it comes from someone who saw what happened and only gradually decided who these people talking with Jesus were. The statement that the disciples had been sleepy is rather embarrassing to the disciples. It is hard to see what motive Luke could have in including it except a belief that it was true. The information about their sleepiness could well have come from Peter, and perhaps the clarification that they were awake when they saw the Transfiguration itself came from him as well.

Hemer makes the fascinating conjecture that these details may be answers to questions that Luke posed directly to a participant: "How long after?" "What was the first thing you saw?" "Did you hear what they said?" "If you were so sleepy, are you really sure about what you thought you saw?" And so forth. He also points out that, even if Mark's Gospel was available to Luke before the final version of his Gospel was written, Luke could have been gathering materials for his own Gospel before he read Mark's.[10] And he conjectures that Luke could have come into personal contact with Peter during Paul's imprisonment at Caesarea in approximately AD 57–59.[11]

Often, biblical critics will assume, without any good reason, that any differences between Luke and Mark, when they are telling the same story, are the result of Luke's non-factually adding things to Mark—just using his imagination to make a better story. Colin Hemer is a welcome exception. He keeps his real-world imagination alive and doesn't forget that Luke is a reporter rather than an inventor. This allows Hemer to shed far more light on the Transfiguration scene than a critic who assumes that Luke is just "redacting" Mark.

Is Peter the only character whose vivid personality shines through in the Gospels? Not at all. In fact, Jesus is the most obvious example of such a character! But Jesus is so important that the remarkable consistency and vividness of his personality deserves a chapter all to itself, and that is the last chapter in this book. What about other supporting characters? There are other vivid character sketches in the Gospels. For example, the man born blind in John 9 is an intensely real, believable person. I've discussed him in *The Eye of the Beholder*. Here I want to talk about three other people whose personalities are consistent and vivid across multiple stories: Mary and Martha, and the disciple Thomas.

3. Mary and Martha

Both Luke and John tell about Jesus' special friendship with the household of Mary, Martha, and Lazarus, across three different stories. Two of the stories are in John, and one is in Luke. In all of these incidents, Jesus' interactions with Mary and Martha flow from his knowledge of them.

In the well-known story in Luke 10.38–42, Martha is frazzled by her dinner preparations and frustrated by the fact that Mary is sitting quietly listening to Jesus. Martha demands that Jesus tell her sister to help her. Jesus' reply shows his insight into the personalities of both sisters:

> But the Lord answered and said to her, "Martha, Martha, you are worried and bothered about so many things; but only a few things are necessary, really only one, for Mary has chosen the good part, which shall not be taken away from her." (Luke 10.41–42)

Unified Personalities | 175

This is a rebuke to Martha, but a gentle and affectionate one. The personalities of the sisters are sketched with both economy and vividness, as is Jesus' attitude toward them.

The stories about this family in John's Gospel manifest the same personalities of Mary and Martha and similar friendships between them and Jesus. When Jesus comes to Bethany after Lazarus has died, it is the active, forceful Martha who first goes out to meet him with the words, "Lord, if You had been here, my brother would not have died. Even now I know that whatever You ask of God, God will give You" (John 11.21–22). Is she hinting that Jesus might raise Lazarus from the dead? It seems as though she might be, but when Jesus does tell her that her brother will rise again (vs. 23), she takes him to be referring to the final resurrection, accepted by many of the Jews of the time (vs. 24). In this dialogue, Jesus deals with Martha according to her nature. She is somewhat argumentative but also curious. She is frustrated that he did not come sooner, but she loves him and is willing to trust him. Jesus challenges her, asking if she believes that he is the resurrection and the life (vss. 25–26). She replies that she believes that he is the Messiah and then goes to call her sister.

When Mary arrives, things are the same, yet different. Mary says the same half-reproachful words: "Lord, if You had been here, my brother would not have died" (John 11.32). But Jesus does not have a dialogue with Mary, and he does not challenge her as he did Martha. Instead, when he sees her weeping and those with her weeping, he is deeply moved. He asks where they have laid Lazarus, and then he weeps (11.33–35).

Naturally, it is the practical, outspoken Martha who questions Jesus' order to roll away the stone. She worries openly that Lazarus' body will smell (vs. 39). Jesus reassures her by reminding her that he promised her that she would see the glory of

God if she believed (vs. 40). Then he makes good on his promise and calls Lazarus forth from the tomb. One can't help thinking that Martha may be one of the first to run forward and unwrap the grave clothes when Jesus says, "Unbind him, and let him go" (vs. 44).

The other story about Mary and Martha in John is about a meal where Mary anoints Jesus' feet. This seems to be the same story told in Mark 14.3–9 and Matt. 26.6–13, but those Gospels don't mention Mary and Martha.† John gives the name of the woman who anoints Jesus (Mary) and adds further details, including a mention of Martha. It is *of course* Martha who serves (John 12.2) at the meal, just as she does in Luke. Matthew and Mark say that this happened at the home of someone named Simon the leper. This doesn't mean that he was still a leper; "the leper" would have been a further indication of which Simon one was talking about, since "Simon" was such a common name. (See Chapter 2 on disambiguation and name statistics.) The accounts in the Synoptics agree with John that the meal took place in Bethany, which would not have been a large city. Martha could have been involved in serving a meal at Simon's house.

It is Mary, consistent with her nature, who lavishly pours out the costly ointment on Jesus' head (Mark 14.3) and feet (John 12.3). In one of those sensory details that are characteristic of his Gospel, John mentions that the whole house was filled with the smell (12.3). And, just as Jesus has had to defend Mary to her busy sister in Luke, here he must defend her to Judas Iscariot (and perhaps others as well, according to Mark 14.4–5), who say that the perfume has been wasted and should have been sold and the money given to the poor. Just as Jesus interprets and defends Mary's having chosen the better part in Luke, here he relates her

---
†Luke 7.36–50 appears to be a separate incident in which a different woman anointed Jesus earlier in his ministry.

gift to his burial and points out that they do not have him always with them (John 12.7–8, Mark 14.6–9).

There is not as much material in the Gospels about Mary and Martha as there is about Peter, but what there is shows the same characteristic of truthful memoirs. These people come across as real; their consistent, vivid personalities are manifested in different stories told in different Gospels.†

4. Thomas

Thomas is mentioned in the Synoptic Gospels, but only in their lists of the twelve apostles (Matt. 10.3, Mark 3.18, Luke 6.15). He speaks in several places in John's Gospel, and even though all of these stories occur in John, the portrayal of his personality still deserves mention for its appearance of truthfulness, which comes out in subtle and apparently casual ways.

Thomas is like the character Puddleglum in C.S. Lewis's book *The Silver Chair*. Like Puddleglum, Thomas is blunt and outspoken. Like Puddleglum, he is loyal. And like Puddleglum, he is pessimistic. Sometimes the evidence for more than one of these characteristics comes from the same passage.

In John 11.7–8, Jesus decides to go to Judea because of the message that Lazarus is sick. The disciples attempt to talk him

---

†There is an interesting little mystery here in the stories about Mary and Martha: the silence of Lazarus. By contrast with his sisters, Lazarus never speaks, and we hear nothing about his personality or what he does. Jesus loves him, John tells us, but Martha acts more like the head of the family. In fact, Luke doesn't even mention him! We can only conjecture about the reason for this. One conjecture is that the parents of all three died relatively young and that Lazarus himself is much younger than his sisters, perhaps a teenager. Martha could easily be a bossy big sister who has had to run the house since the parents died, and the sisters' love for Lazarus may be a somewhat maternal older-sister love for a little brother. This, of course, is only a guess. But it is very interesting that John tells about Lazarus and puts him at the center of an important story, but he never records anything that he says or does besides dying and being raised by Jesus. This oddity is a mark of authenticity in itself. If the story were invented, we would expect a bit more fleshing out of the central character.

out of going, because the people tried to stone him when he was in Jerusalem not long before. (Bethany was quite close to Jerusalem.) But Jesus is determined. In verse 16, Thomas says, "Let us also go, that we may die with him." This shows all three characteristics. Thomas does not mince words. His comment could even be taken as a criticism of Jesus' judgement. He is certainly very pessimistic. But he is also loyal, willing at least in principle to go and die with Jesus. We know that he fled along with the other disciples when push came to shove in the Garden of Gethsemane, but at least his *intention* was to be brave and to stick by Jesus. In this respect he is like Peter, yet their personalities are quite distinct. Peter is the louder, brasher disciple, boasting that he is braver than all the others. Thomas is the "wet blanket," the disciple who says that it's probably hopeless but that they should all go together and not abandon Jesus.

On the night of the Last Supper, Jesus utters the comforting words, "In my Father's house are many dwelling places…I go to prepare a place for you" (John 14.2). Jesus tells the disciples further that they know where he is going and that they know the way. Thomas interrupts impatiently, "Lord, we do not know where you are going; how do we know the way?" (14.5) This is, as one might say, the "set-up" for an "I am" saying. Jesus replies, "I am the way, the truth, and the life. No one comes to the Father but through me" (14.6). Thomas was probably asking a more literal question. In fact, given Jesus' many ambiguous references to "going away" on that night (and the fact that some of them doubtless referred to his death, not to his returning to heaven), it was quite reasonable for Thomas to ask for clarification. Jesus' theological reply may have been rather frustrating, though John does not record that Thomas asked any further questions. The exchange reveals Thomas's blunt personality. Jesus, cryptic as he so often is, tells them that they already know where he is going and know the way, and Thomas speaks up and says frankly and perhaps in some exasperation, "No, we don't!" Implicitly, he is asking Jesus to be less theological and more clear in literal terms.

With these scenes in place, it should come as no surprise that Thomas, happening not to be with the other disciples during Jesus' first meeting with them after his resurrection, is skeptical of the resurrection claim, despite the assurances of the others—a pessimistic skepticism that has earned him his famous title of Doubting Thomas:

> But Thomas, one of the twelve, who was called Didymus, was not with them when Jesus came. So the other disciples were saying to him, "We have seen the Lord!" But he said to them, "Unless I see in His hands the imprint of the nails, and put my finger into the place of the nails, and put my hand into His side, I will not believe." (John 20.24–25)

It would be too easy to see this as mere stubbornness on Thomas's part, and certainly he states his requirements for belief in extreme terms. If we demanded to see the risen Jesus personally as he insisted, none of us, two thousand years later, would ever believe. But before we judge Thomas too harshly, we should remember how astonishing his fellow disciples' claims must have seemed. None of them really expected Jesus to rise again, despite some thoughts (as reflected in Luke 24.21) about his prediction that he would rise. Confronted abruptly with the other disciples' proclamation no more than seventy-two hours after Jesus was brutally slain on the cross, the grieving Thomas reacts by angrily dismissing their claims. Perhaps he shouldn't have done so, but the reaction reflects, among other things, his glass-half-empty outlook. That Jesus has literally returned from death seems to the gloomy Thomas too good to be true.

We find one other important characteristic in Thomas—the willingness to admit that he's been wrong. When Jesus appears the second time to the disciples in Jerusalem and challenges Thomas directly, his response is unequivocal. He declares Jesus to be his Lord and God:

> Eight days later His disciples were again inside, and Thomas was with them. Jesus came, the doors having been shut, and stood in their midst and said, "Peace be to you." Then He said to Thomas, "Place your finger here, and see My hands; and take your hand and put it into My side; and do not continue in disbelief, but be a believer." Thomas answered and said to Him, "My Lord and my God!" (John 20.26–28)

This, too, fits with Thomas as we begin to know him in the Gospel of John. He is the kind of person who values truth above comfort. This leads to his pessimism. He assumes that it's better to expect the worst and be pleasantly surprised than to expect the best and be disappointed. The surprise he gets when Jesus shows up and invites him to touch his scars is the best kind of surprise, and Thomas, consistent with his commitment to the truth, accepts Jesus, the Truth, and worships him immediately.

The Gospel authors did not have the literary precedents we are so used to. They didn't have the concept of spinoffs, prequels, or TV series. Nor did Luke (for example) have access to John's stories of Mary and Martha. He doesn't even seem to have known what village they lived in (Luke 10.38). Yet the characters in the Gospels are obviously the same people. A casual similarity, seen in many subtle little touches, pervades the characters of Peter, Mary, Martha, and Thomas across different stories. This is a sign that the Gospels are testimonies to the truth.

Chapter Summary

- The Gospels make clear the reality of a number of supporting characters by casual similarities in their personalities, seen across a variety of stories.

- It would be hard to fake this similarity, since it comes out in incidental ways in the stories. It is even hard to do in modern fiction like serial TV, and would be all the harder for the Gospel authors if they were not telling the truth.

- The characters of Peter, Mary, Martha, and Thomas are consistent but not exaggerated.

Study Questions

1. List two or three characteristics of Peter that are consistent across multiple Gospel stories.

2. For one of the characteristics named in answer to question 1, find at least two incidents in different Gospels that illustrate that characteristic.

3. With what other disciple do the Gospels and Acts specially associate Peter? Give examples from multiple Gospels.

4. Give several illustrations of Martha's active, practical personality from different stories in the Gospels.

5. Give several illustrations of Mary's character from different stories.

6. How does Thomas's statement that the disciples should go and die with Jesus illustrate his personality?

7. How do both Thomas's doubt of Jesus' resurrection and his later change of mind illustrate the same personality?

8. How does consistency of characters across multiple stories confirm the truth of the stories?

For Discussion

1. The chapter makes a distinction between consistent but superficial caricatures and realistic, consistent character portrayals. In fiction, we sometimes have stereotypes, such as a person who is always boasting, a person who eats too much, a person who is annoyingly clever, and so forth, but these tend to be one-note. "Stereotype consistency" or "caricature consistency" is different from the consistency of the characters that we find in the Gospels. How might the stories in the Gospels be different if Peter or one of the other characters discussed in the chapter were merely a caricature?

2. Describe a person whom you have known well in your own life who has a consistent character. Reflect on the ways in which his personality was manifested in different ways in different situations. You might add as a bonus, if you can think of one, a situation where it might have seemed that he was acting out of character, but on deeper reflection it actually revealed character consistency.

3. The chapter briefly mentions the story of the man born blind in John 9. Even though the man born blind is found in only one story, it is still instructive to see how vivid his personality is. Read the story and discuss how his characteristics are revealed in the details of the story.

4. If you had been Thomas and had heard from the other disciples that they had seen Jesus risen from the dead, would you have believed them? Discuss.

5. Describe a character in a TV show that you believe is not consistently portrayed across various episodes. What do you think the writers' motives might have been in portraying him in these different ways?

Resources for Further Study

Colin Hemer, *The Book of Acts in the Setting of Hellenistic History*, WUNT 49 (Tübingen: J. C. B. Mohr, 1989), pp. 355–358.

J. S. Howson, *Horae Petrinae, or Studies in the Life of St. Peter* (London: The Religious Tract Society, 1883), <https://tinyurl.com/JSHowson>.

David Marshall, *Jesus is No Myth: The Fingerprints of God on the Gospels* (Kuai Moo Press, 2016).

Lydia McGrew, *The Mirror or the Mask: Liberating the Gospels from Literary Devices* (Tampa, FL: DeWard Publishing, 2019), Chapter XII, "Still More Evidence for the Reportage Model," section 4, pp. 321–329.

8

Unmistakable Jesus

1. Knowing Jesus, the ultimate goal
All of the other chapters in this book have been leading up to this chapter. Why are we interested in the Gospels at all? Because they tell us about Jesus. Most of us wouldn't be all that interested in Thomas, Peter, Mary, or Martha if it weren't for the fact that they are friends and followers of Jesus. Ultimately, we want to know Jesus. But the only way that we can know Jesus from the Gospels is if they are reliable records of what he did and taught.

The reliability of the Gospels in telling us about Jesus is important, then, because of the need to know him (Phil. 3.10). So, for example, if believers want to base theological doctrine on Jesus' teachings, they need to know that they have a good record of his teachings. It won't do to say that the evangelists put into Jesus' mouth what they believed was the correct *interpretation* of his *other* teachings. As the ancient church father Papias said, he didn't want to know "someone else's commandments" but rather the memories of the commandments "given by the Lord...and proceeding from the Truth itself."[1] It would seriously undermine our justified confidence in the Gospels' picture of Jesus if, as some have suggested, Jesus didn't recognizably say, "I and the Father are one" (John 10.30) but only taught more implicitly that he was God, after which John created this more explicit teaching to draw out the meaning of some quite different saying. If you thought that, how could you confidently use John 10.30 to teach that Jesus claimed to be God? How could you use it, for example, in talking with Jehovah's Witnesses about who Jesus really was?

Jesus' teachings are important for our personal devotion. In that same chapter, Jesus told the crowds that his sheep hear his voice and know him and that no man will take them out of his hands (John 10.27–29). These are rich teachings and comforting ones. We need to be confident that, if we had been standing there and had known the language, we could have recognized this saying on Jesus' lips. To be sure, this does not mean that every word is recorded verbatim. No doubt Jesus said much more at the time, and he may have been speaking Aramaic. Even very reliable memory often produces a degree of harmless, recognizable paraphrase in a record. If Jesus said that his lambs hear his voice, you could still easily have recognized the saying in John 10 if you had been there and knew the relevant language. The point is that, for confidence in using these words of Jesus, we need to know that they are authentic historical records of what Jesus told people at that time and place, as the Gospel tells us, not a result of John's literary invention. For that purpose, there is no substitute for Gospel reliability.

We need to have Gospel reliability in portraying Jesus because of the command to commit to him and follow him. Jesus repeatedly tells his disciples and others to follow him, and there is no question that we should understand this call to apply to those who, having not seen him, love him (John 20.29, I Peter 1.8). To follow the command to follow Jesus, we need information. What was Jesus like? What would it have been like to know him, day in and day out? If we are his followers, at two thousand years' distance of time, we need reliable records of his personality and character.

And finally, we need Gospel reliability because of the call to tell others. In Romans Paul says that the way to salvation is to confess with one's mouth the Lord Jesus and believe in one's heart that God the Father raised him from the dead (Rom. 10.9). Paul praised the beautiful feet of those who bring this Good News to the world (Rom. 10.15). To have good evidence for the gospel (the Good News), we need the Gospels. These are the books in which we find out *why* the disciples were so committed to Jesus that they risked their lives for him (as recorded in Acts). These are the books in which we find out what sort of experiences they told about after his resurrection—unmistakably physical experiences in which they recognized him, spoke with him at length, ate with him, and were invited to touch him. From these records we know that the disciples were not jumping to conclusions when they taught that he was risen indeed. They were not deluded or hallucinating. Such interactions with the risen Jesus made it entirely *reasonable* for them to believe that he had conquered death and that he came to them in a physical body. If we want to tell others, inviting them to be ready to die for Jesus, we as Christians need to be prepared to present this case convincingly to the world. And that requires Gospel reliability.[2]

It's certainly true that the Gospels don't tell all the same stories about Jesus, though the Synoptics—Matthew, Mark, and Luke—tell a lot of the same ones. John fills in, telling many important things not found in the others. The different selection of material produces different emphases in the Gospels. Yet despite that fact, we can be confident that it is the same Jesus portrayed.

It is unfortunate that the uniqueness of John has caused critical scholars to argue that John has altered or at least tweaked the portrayal of Jesus, putting discourses in his mouth that he didn't recognizably utter, making him teach more clearly about his own deity than he really did, and more. Fortunately, all such insinuations turn out to be quite false.[3] In this chapter, we'll observe the unity of Jesus' personality as portrayed consistently in a variety of scenes and stories throughout *all* the Gospels. This unity-in-variety has tremendous evidential force, just as we saw in the case of Peter. And there is even more material with which to make the argument when it comes to Jesus. Here we will see just some of it.

2. Witty Jesus

In Luke 13.10–17, Jesus heals a woman with an affliction that makes it impossible for her to stand up. He heals her on the Sabbath, and this causes a dust-up. The ruler of the synagogue, perhaps afraid to tackle Jesus directly, launches into a lecture to the people standing around, scolding them for coming to be healed on the Sabbath. "There are six days in which work should be done. Therefore come during them and get healed, and not on the Sabbath day" (vs. 14).

This, as you can imagine, does not go over well with Jesus, and he shoots back:

> "You hypocrites, does not each of you on the Sabbath untie his ox or his donkey from the stall, and lead him away to water him? And this woman, a daughter of Abraham as she is, whom Satan has bound for eighteen long years, should she not have been released from this bond on the Sabbath day?" And as He said this, all His opponents were being humiliated; and the entire multitude was rejoicing over all the glorious things being done by Him. (Luke 13.15–17)

What the bystanders probably found especially enjoyable in Jesus' sharp reply to the pretentious synagogue official was the very Jewish play on words. Jesus' opponents will *untie* an animal on the Sabbath to lead it to water, but they attempt to forbid his *untying* this daughter of Abraham on the Sabbath, though she has been bound by disease for eighteen years.

Now compare the account of a completely different episode, found in John. In John 5.1–18, Jesus heals a crippled man at the Pool of Bethesda in Jerusalem. He tells him to take up his pallet and walk. The Jewish leaders complain both because the man has performed "work" by carrying his pallet on the Sabbath (which Jesus told him to do) and because Jesus healed him on the Sabbath. Jesus, so far from trying to calm them down, implies his equality with the Father and the Father's approval of his miracle (John 5.17). This only makes them angrier and more determined to kill him.

Since John 5.1 just mentions a festival but doesn't tell us which one it was, it's difficult to be sure how much time passed between this incident and the Feast of Tabernacles in John 7. It was apparently not that long, because at that feast, Jesus mentions the healing of the crippled man to the people and expects at least some of them to remember it:

> Jesus answered and said to them, "I did one deed, and you all marvel. "On this account Moses has given you circumcision…, and on the Sabbath you circumcise a man. If a man receives circumcision on the Sabbath that the Law of Moses may not be broken, are you angry with Me because I made an entire man well on the Sabbath? Do not judge according to appearance, but judge with righteous judgment." (John 7.21–24)

We've already discussed this passage in Chapter 2, where we noted that Jesus' comments are in keeping with rabbinic literature; they did indeed circumcise a boy child on the Sabbath day if the child's eighth day happened to fall on the Sabbath. This was not considered forbidden work. Now I want to point out how this manifests Jesus' personality: Here, on the same topic but in an entirely different incident, is the same turn of thought, the same rhetorical flair, and the same sharp wit found in Luke 13.15–17. It is permitted to circumcise (cutting something off) on the Sabbath, but when Jesus made a man's entire body whole on the Sabbath, the leaders were furious.

In Chapter 2 we saw the very same pattern of mind in this passage in Matthew:

> "Woe to you, scribes and Pharisees, hypocrites! For you tithe mint and dill and cummin and have neglected the weightier provisions of the law: justice and mercy and faithfulness; but these are the things you should have done without neglecting the others. You blind guides, who strain out a gnat and swallow a camel!" (Matt. 23.23–24)

Once again, Jesus points out the lack of a sense of perspective. The leaders are more concerned about nit-picky matters of their interpretation of the law of Moses, which leads them to weigh out lightweight herbs, than about far heavier matters such as justice, mercy, and faithfulness.

This is clearly the same man and the same mind. Again and again, Jesus exposes hypocrisy and misplaced priorities concerning the observation of the law, and he loves to do it using witty word parallels—untying an animal vs. untying a person, circumcising vs. making whole, light vs. heavy. But who would have invented such a thing? The best explanation is that this is really what Jesus was like. It was really how his mind worked.

3. Teaching Jesus

William Paley was an 18th-century Anglican bishop. He originated the argument from undesigned coincidences discussed in Chapter 3, applying it mainly to the book of Acts and Paul's letters. He had an excellent sense for a point I have mentioned frequently in these pages—the evidential importance of casualness. The Gospel authors don't appear to be trying to do any of this. The connections between their stories arise from the fact that they are telling the truth.

Paley has a useful passage where he talks about Jesus' manner of teaching and how it shows the same Jesus in all the Gospels:

> It is known to every reader of scripture, that the passages of Christ's history preserved by St. John, are, except his passion and resurrection, for the most part different from those which are delivered by the other evangelists....But what I observe in the comparison of these several accounts is, that, although actions and discourses are ascribed to Christ by St. John, in general different from what are given to him by the other evangelists, yet, under this diversity, there is a similitude of *manner*, which indicates that the actions and discourses proceed from the same person....Such uniformity, if it exist, is on their part casual; and if there be, as I contend there is, a perceptible resemblance of *manner*, in passages, and between discourses, which are in themselves extremely distinct, and are delivered by historians writing without any imitation of...one another, it affords a just presumption, that these are, what they profess to be, the actions and the discourses of the same real person; that the evangelists wrote from fact, and not from imagination....The article in which I find this agreement most strong, is in our Saviour's mode of teaching, and in that particular property of it, which consists in his drawing of his doctrine from the occasion; or, which is nearly the same thing, raising reflections from the objects and incidents before him....[4]

What Paley is talking about here is the fact that Jesus used both object lessons and the events and scenes around him as opportunities to teach. Sometimes he created these object lessons himself. Sometimes they simply arose from the circumstances. He was always quick to seize the opportunity if it presented itself or to make an illustration if needed. This concreteness in his teaching is a consistent characteristic across all four Gospels, in different scenes.

In Mark 3.31–35 (a story also found in Matthew), Jesus' family members (his mother and brothers) come to confront him, because some of them are saying that he is out of his mind.† When he is told that they are outside the ring of the crowd, wanting to speak with him, he takes the opportunity to say that those who obey his commandments are his true family members—mother, brothers, and sisters.

In Matt. 16.5–12 (a story also found in Mark), Jesus takes the occasion when the disciples have forgotten to bring bread to tell them to beware of the leaven of the Pharisees and Sadducees. Of course, they misunderstand, worrying that he is rebuking them in a roundabout way for their forgetfulness. Jesus has to explain and also remind them that he is able to produce physical bread. His teaching has a "hook"—the fact that they forgot to bring bread. This no doubt made it more memorable. Matt. 16.12 says that eventually they took the point; Jesus was warning them about false teachings of the Pharisees and Sadducees.

In Mark 10.13–16 when young children are brought to Jesus to be blessed and his disciples turn them away, he rebukes the disciples and stresses the need to receive the kingdom of God as a little child. (This story is found only in Mark.) The opportunity

---

† I myself am inclined to think that Mary, his mother, did not believe that he was crazy. She had the evidence of having conceived Jesus when she was a virgin. She must have known (at a minimum) that he was above such judgements on her part. In any group of people, there will be multiple opinions and reasons for being involved. Mary may have gone with the family group in the hopes of moderating the dispute; the Gospels certainly don't say anything to rule this out.

arises from the actions of the parents and the wrong response of the disciples; Jesus is quick to use it as a teaching moment.

Jesus makes a similar point in Matt. 18.1–4 (parallel in Mark 9.35–37), but there he has to create the object lesson. The disciples have been arguing among themselves on the road about who will be the greatest. Jesus enters a house in Capernaum (possibly Peter's house, though this is conjecture) and places a child among them. (Peter, who was married, may have had children. The child appears to have been in the house.) Jesus tells them that whoever wishes to be the greatest among them must humble himself as a little child. This lesson of self-sacrificing love is in keeping with what he has just been teaching them (Mark 9.31) about the fact that he must die. It appears to have occurred shortly before his finally leaving Galilee (Mark 10.1) for the Jerusalem region, where he will die.

This tendency to seize (or create) a concrete illustration as an occasion for spiritual teaching is also evident in John's Gospel. Jesus' conversation with the woman at the well is a famous instance. First, he asks her for a drink. No doubt he really was thirsty, but this is also an opportunity to offer her living water so that she will (spiritually) never thirst again (John 4.7–14). When the disciples return to the well and offer him food, he says that his food is to do the will of the Father who sent him (4.32–34).

When the people follow Jesus after the feeding of the five thousand, he urges them not to labor for the food that perishes but for that which will endure to everlasting life (6.27). He gives the Bread of Life discourse in the rest of the chapter, while the recent feeding is fresh in the minds of many of his hearers. He teaches them that he is the true spiritual bread.

In John 7.37–38, as discussed in Chapter 2, Jesus uses the water-pouring ceremony during the Feast of Tabernacles as an opportunity to cry out, "If anyone is thirsty, let him come to me and drink," promising rivers of living water.

In John 9.2–4, when Jesus and his disciples meet the man born blind, Jesus immediately tells them that he must work while it is day and that while he is in the world, he is the light of the world. He makes references to light and blindness in connection with this miracle in 9.39–41; within the Pharisees' hearing, he refers to their spiritual blindness. They are far more blind than the blind man was before he was healed, because they do not even recognize that they are blind.

Most notably, in John 13.1–17, in a scene told in meticulous detail, Jesus rises from supper and washes the disciples' feet. As we saw in Chapter 3, there is an undesigned coincidence here with Jesus' words in Luke 22.27, "I am among you as the one who serves." As told in Luke 22.24, but not in John, the disciples were once more bickering about who would be the greatest in the kingdom. In the Synoptics, Jesus responded to an earlier quarrel on the same topic by placing a child among them. Now, he rises from supper, lays aside his outer garment, girds himself with a towel, and washes their feet.

If we imagine Jesus rising from supper amidst the childish quarreling, we can hear that a hush falls as he engages in actions that no one expects—taking upon himself the work of a slave. When he sits back down, as recorded in Luke 22.25–27 and John 13.12–17, he makes the lesson plain. He who would be the greatest must be the servant of all, following the example of their master. Just as he has washed their feet, they must wash one another's feet.

This is what Paley means by a "resemblance of manner" in the teaching of Jesus throughout the Gospels. He points out shrewdly, "[N]othing of this *manner* is perceptible in the speeches recorded in the Acts, or in any other but those that are attributed to Christ....[I]n truth, it was a very unlikely manner for a forger or fabulist to attempt; and a manner very difficult for any writer to execute, if he had to supply all the materials, both the incidents, and the observations upon them, out of his own head."[5]

4. Disconcerting Jesus

Jesus must have been an extremely disconcerting person to spend time with. Sometimes he read thoughts outright. At other times, he showed an uncanny knowledge of human nature. And yet he did not do these things out of a childish desire to show off. While his thought-reading, and his mentioning the fact that he knew thoughts, illustrated his power, his goal was always to speak to the heart for the good of his hearers and followers.

We find this quality of knowing the hearts and thoughts of others repeatedly in the Synoptics. In Mark, the religious leaders are angry with Jesus because he told the paralytic that his sins were forgiven, but they don't say so out loud. Jesus confronts their tacit accusation of blasphemy:

> And immediately Jesus, aware in His spirit that they were reasoning that way within themselves, said to them, "Why are you reasoning about these things in your hearts? Which is easier, to say to the paralytic, 'Your sins are forgiven'; or to say, 'Arise, and take up your pallet and walk'?"(Mark 2.8–9)

They, of course, can neither forgive sins nor tell a lame man to stand up and walk. Jesus shows his authority to forgive sins by performing a miracle; he puts the religious leaders on the spot by reading their thoughts and directly addressing their criticism.

The disciples would have preferred that Jesus not know about their dispute over who would be the greatest while walking on the road. But Jesus confronts them by asking the uncomfortable question, "What were you discussing on the way?" (Mark 9.34). He then proceeds to address their spirit of competition.

We find this same uncomfortable quality of Jesus' personality in completely different scenes in John. Imagine Nathanael's embarrassment when, having just dismissed Jesus with thoughtless regional bigotry as a mere Nazarene (John 1.46), he finds Jesus at first complimenting him (having never met him before) and then saying that he saw him under the fig tree:

> Jesus saw Nathanael coming to Him, and said of him, "Behold, an Israelite indeed, in whom is no guile!" Nathanael said to Him, "How do You know me?" Jesus answered and said to him, "Before Philip called you, when you were under the fig tree, I saw you." (John 1.47–48)

Jesus does not mention Nathanael's comment, "Can any good thing come out of Nazareth?" but it must have been in Nathanael's mind. "If he saw me under the fig tree, does he know what I said to Philip about his home town?" Jesus is indeed trying to impress Nathanael, but his goal is to win Nathanael's heart. Knowing that Nathanael is an honest lover of the God of Israel, Jesus wants him as a follower.

Jesus leads the woman at the well to admit that she has no husband, then tells her pointedly (but not unkindly) that she has had five husbands and that the man she is currently living with is not her husband at all (John 4.16–18). By revealing that he knows of her lifestyle without being told, Jesus moves the conversation onto a plane where she will have to consider that he might indeed be the Messiah and that she needs to change.

In John 16.16–19, he perceives that his disciples are afraid to ask him what he means by "a little while," and he points it out. We might even say that this sort of thought-reading was a common way in which Jesus communicated with his disciples.

In the restoration scene with Peter after the resurrection (John 21.15–17), we can well imagine that Peter would rather Jesus not allude so pointedly to his own boast about loving Jesus more than the others do. Apparently, he and Jesus had already spoken in private (Luke 24.34). Peter must have wondered why they couldn't just leave it at that. But Jesus had a purpose in this embarrassing conversation, so he asked Peter, "Do you love me more than these do?" He wanted to make it clear to the others by the dialogue that Peter was restored. He wanted Peter to express his humility before the others. He wanted to emphasize Peter's leadership role in feeding the sheep. And no doubt he wanted to impress these commands on the memory of Peter himself. Still, it was undoubtedly uncomfortable for all the disciples. The others had nothing to boast of, either. While they did not deny Jesus, they didn't even try to follow him on that dreadful night. They just ran away! If they, with Peter, are to feed his sheep, they must do better than that.

After his resurrection, Jesus is very much the same person he always was, and no easier to live with than he was before he died. Commanding and compelling but unpredictable, a superb teacher but not inclined to answer questions he considers impertinent or unnecessary. (See, for example, his "that's none of your business" response to Peter's question about the Beloved Disciple in John 21.21–22 and his refusal to answer the disciples' question in Acts 1.6–7 about restoring the kingdom to Israel.) In John 20.27, he makes a nearly word-for-word allusion to Thomas's own demand to see his wounds, showing that he knows quite well what Thomas said to the other disciples when Jesus was not present. This must have been embarrassing for Thomas: "Place your finger here, and see My hands; and take your hand and put it into My side; and do not continue in disbelief, but be a believer." (John 20.27). There may be a touch of amusement in Jesus' tone, together with a serious invitation to Thomas.

The post-resurrection Jesus is not particularly soothing. Matthew records that he says he is with the disciples always (Matt. 28.20), but he tells Peter almost in so many words that he will suffer agonizing martyrdom (John 21.15–19). He is strengthening the disciples for the task before them and for the trials they will have to face.

All of these incidents taken together give us a vivid understanding of what it must have been like to be with Jesus. If there was something you didn't want him to bring up, he was almost sure to bring it up. You never knew when he would reveal things you preferred not to have revealed. You might feel nervous to ask him about something but also nervous about *not* asking him.

In all of this, Jesus' goal was not to humiliate but to teach, to confront falsehood and confusion, to cut through pride and evasion, and to bring his followers forward in their walk with himself. It is the same Jesus everywhere, which gives us confidence that we are meeting the real Jesus in all four Gospels.

5. Sarcastic Jesus

Who would ever think that Jesus would be sarcastic? Generally, we don't associate sarcasm with Jesus at all, and this is probably because we ourselves find it difficult to be sarcastic without having sinful attitudes of cruelty or pettiness. Yet Jesus, though sinless, did sometimes use sarcasm to get his point across.

One finds a sarcastic Jesus in Luke 13.32–33 when some of the Pharisees warn him that Herod Antipas wants to kill him:

> And He said to them, "Go and tell that fox, 'Behold, I cast out demons and perform cures today and tomorrow, and the third day I reach My goal.' Nevertheless I must journey on

today and tomorrow and the next day; for it cannot be that a prophet would perish outside of Jerusalem."

In Chapter 1, I've discussed the way that this incident relates to the chronology and geography of Jesus' ministry. Here I want to relate it to Jesus' personality. The statement, "It cannot be that a prophet would perish outside of Jerusalem" is quite harsh. It is not merely that Jesus calls Herod a fox. He also speaks almost with bitterness of Jerusalem and its relationship to the death of prophets, a topic he expands upon with painful love in the next few verses (Luke 13.34–35). Jerusalem is the city that kills the prophets. Jesus says wryly, with a bit of exaggeration, that a prophet can't perish anywhere else. Yet he longs to gather Jerusalem's children as a hen gathers her chicks and grieves over the impending destruction of the city, which occurred in AD 70.

Jesus' words in the "woes to the Pharisees" in Matthew show a similarly savage wit:

> "Woe to you, scribes and Pharisees, hypocrites! For you build the tombs of the prophets and adorn the monuments of the righteous, and say, 'If we had been living in the days of our fathers, we would not have been partners with them in shedding the blood of the prophets.' So you testify against yourselves, that you are sons of those who murdered the prophets." (Matt. 23.29–31)

One can almost hear his voice: "If *we* had been living in the days of our fathers, *we* would not have been partners with them in shedding the blood of the prophets." Jesus knows quite well that, even as he speaks, the Pharisees are plotting with the priestly Sadducees to kill him and even to kill Lazarus, whom he raised from the dead (John 11.53, 12.10–11, Mark 14.1–2).

In John, we hear the same tone from Jesus when the people are about to stone him. He asks them facetiously, "I showed you many good works from the Father; for which of them are you stoning me?" (John 10.32) He knows that it is his claim to be one with the Father (John 10.31) that has enraged them, as they are quick to tell him. But he cannot resist a poke at their attempting to kill a man who has done them nothing but good, a man who has healed the sick and raised the dead. He has previously pointed out that the crowds are seeking to kill him merely for telling them the truth (John 8.40).

Perhaps the closest resemblance between Jesus' sarcasm in John and that in Luke is found in John 5.39–43:

> "You search the Scriptures, because you think that in them you have eternal life; and it is these that bear witness of Me; and you are unwilling to come to Me, that you may have life. I do not receive glory from men; but I know you, that you do not have the love of God in yourselves. I have come in My Father's name, and you do not receive Me; if another shall come in his own name, you will receive him."

Jesus shrewdly points out that his audience would actually prefer a Savior who was more self-promoting. It is quite plausible that these verses are a real prophecy of the military messianic claims of Simon bar Kokhba, who led a revolt against the Romans in about AD 132. But whether Jesus intended his words to be such a specific prophecy or not, his biting wit is the same: They search the Scriptures and they watch and pray for the Messiah to come, but when the Messiah stands right before them, they will not recognize him. They see one who has come in the name of the Father, but what they want is one who comes in his own name. This is the same Jesus who says, in much the same tone, "It cannot be that a prophet would perish outside of Jerusalem."

6. Lonely Jesus

It is a basic Christian doctrine that Jesus is both God and man and that as a man, he suffers. The book of Hebrews emphasizes this, saying that our high priest (Jesus) can be touched with our griefs and infirmities (Heb. 4.15). One of the areas that is most striking in this regard in the Gospels is Jesus' loneliness, and this aspect of his character is evident throughout all four Gospels. Jesus is not a kill-joy. In fact, he suggests that the Pharisees criticized him for not fasting often enough, for eating and drinking (Luke 7.34). But as Isaiah had predicted hundreds of years before, he is a man of sorrows and acquainted with grief (Is. 53.3).

What is perhaps not noticed as often is the fact that some of Jesus' greatest mental suffering arises from his friends' abandonment. He knows the hearts of men so well that he is constantly predicting that others will fail him; we will see this predictive aspect of his character in a later section. What I want to emphasize here is how much this hurts him and how much he relates things to himself. In a manner of speaking, you could say that Jesus takes things personally.

We can see this in the middle of his ministry, when many of those who at first followed him fall away, after he teaches about "eating his flesh" and "drinking his blood":

> As a result of this many of His disciples withdrew, and were not walking with Him anymore. Jesus said therefore to the twelve, "You do not want to go away also, do you?" (John 6.66–67)

There is something painful about this. Jesus turns to his trusted Twelve and asks if they, too, will go away. Even Peter's loving proclamation that Jesus has the words of eternal life and that they are sure that he is the Messiah, the son of God (John 6.68–69) does not seem to cheer him up much, for he reflects on Judas: "Did I myself not choose you, the twelve, and yet one of you is a devil?" (John 6.70).

Jesus knows exactly what is going to happen, but he suffers over it nonetheless. It is the same way with Jerusalem: He *personally* has wanted to gather the inhabitants of Jerusalem to himself. He *personally* has been rejected. And he personally grieves as he foresees the city's desolation (Luke 13.34–35, 19.41–44, Matt. 23.37–38).

On the night of the Last Supper, this sense of personal loneliness becomes intense. Jesus reaches out to the human companionship of his disciples, despite knowing that they will fail him. When they are all reclining at the table, he says, "I have earnestly desired to eat this Passover with you before I suffer" (Luke 22.15). But just a little while later, after he has washed their feet, we learn from John, "He became troubled in spirit, and testified, and said, 'Truly, truly, I say to you, that one of you will betray Me'" (John 13.21).

Those of us who love the Narnia books of C.S. Lewis will remember that Lewis captures this atmosphere very well. In *The Lion, The Witch, and the Wardrobe*, Lucy and Susan cannot sleep one night—it is to be the night of the death of Aslan, the noble lion, for the sin of Edmund, who has been a traitor. The girls get up in the night and find that Aslan is walking away, all alone, his glorious head hanging low in grief. They run after him. When he finds them there, he says at first (thinking of their danger) that they should not have come, but he then reflects that he would be glad to have company on that night, so he gives them permission to come along, if they promise to stop when he tells them to do so and to leave him to continue alone: "I am sad and lonely. Lay your hands on my mane so that I can feel you are there and let us walk like that."[6]

Like the women in the Gospels, the girls follow Aslan and are witnesses of his death and resurrection. But in the Gospels, Jesus asks in vain for the comfort of his male disciples, even after he warns them to watch and pray in the Garden of Gethsemane:

> And they came to a place named Gethsemane; and He said to His disciples, "Sit here until I have prayed." And He took with Him Peter and James and John, and began to be very distressed and troubled. And He said to them, "My soul is deeply grieved to the point of death; remain here and keep watch." And He went a little beyond them, and fell to the ground, and began to pray that if it were possible, the hour might pass Him by. And He was saying, "Abba! Father! All things are possible for Thee; remove this cup from Me; yet not what I will, but what Thou wilt." And He came and found them sleeping, and said to Peter, "Simon, are you asleep? Could you not keep watch for one hour? Keep watching and praying, that you may not come into temptation; the spirit is willing, but the flesh is weak." And again He went away and prayed, saying the same words. And again He came and found them sleeping, for their eyes were very heavy; and they did not know what to answer Him. And He came the third time, and said to them, "Are you still sleeping and taking your rest? It is enough; the hour has come; behold, the Son of Man is being betrayed into the hands of sinners. Arise, let us be going; behold, the one who betrays Me is at hand!" (Mark 14.32–42)

It is not possible to discuss Jesus' loneliness, and the way that this is a consistent aspect of his personality in the Gospels, without mentioning his great cry on the cross, "My God, my God, why have you forsaken me?" (Mark 15.34) I will not attempt here to delve too deeply into the theology of this cry. I certainly would never say that there was, or could be, any real, metaphysical separation between the persons of the Godhead—Father and Son.

And I recognize that Psalm 22, from which this is clearly a quotation, does end with the speaker's deliverance and victory. At the same time, it seems to me unconvincing to say that *in no way* does this cry from the cross reflect an actual feeling that Jesus had. Can we really say that Jesus on the cross is merely *citing a text* to call attention to his own expected vindication by God? The speaker of the Psalm itself seems to *feel* (at first) that he has been abandoned by God. The Psalm as a whole reflects a *movement* from grief and horror to calm confidence.

I think it is easy to be too rigid and not to take Jesus' human nature with full seriousness. We are not forced to choose between "a Jesus" who is confident that the Father is with him and therefore that he is never alone (John 16.32) and "a Jesus" who feels abandoned on the cross. It is all the same Jesus. Even on the cross, we should not think that Jesus' words "into your hands I commit my spirit" (Luke 23.46) and "it is finished" (John 19.30) cannot come from the same man who has, perhaps only a short time before, cried out in real grief and loneliness. Don't we ourselves find our feelings changing from one minute to the next when in grief or physical pain? Don't we ourselves feel, at one time, "Well, at least *God* will never abandon me, so I am never alone" and then, just a short time later, feel emotionally that God *has* abandoned us and that we *are* alone? And then perhaps only a short time later shift back to feelings of confidence? Surely we do! I have experienced this turmoil myself, often.

Perhaps we shouldn't be too quick to assume that such emotional upheaval is in and of itself sinful or the fruit of a sin nature. These are mysterious matters, and I make no claim to have understood them completely. We know that Jesus prayed in the Garden that if it were possible, the cup might pass from him. Feelings of fear, painful hope, loneliness, and grief, and even their rapid alternation with confidence, are not intrinsically sinful, just as experiencing physical pain is not intrinsically sinful. Such alternations in us, sinful humans that we are, are sometimes accompanied by bitterness toward God and distrust, but they need not be. Most Christians have probably wondered at one time or other what it really means for Jesus to be at all points tempted as we are, yet without sin. Perhaps here we come close to the heart of that doctrine. And so it may very well be that the loneliness of Jesus comes to its climax in his cry of desolation on the cross itself, only to be countered shortly thereafter by the confiding prayer, "Into thy hands, I commit my spirit" (Luke 23.46, taken from Psalm 31.5),[7] and the triumphant, exhausted final gasp, "It is finished."

7. Suffering Jesus

It may seem that the previous section has exhausted the topic of Jesus' suffering and his unity of character through all four Gospels as a man of sorrows. There we saw his loneliness and his desire for personal loyalty and companionship. There is more to the sufferings of Jesus.

The topic is worth stressing, because skeptics and even (unfortunately) some Christian scholars have suggested a *disunity* in Jesus' character at precisely this point. That is, they have suggested that Jesus, especially in John, does *not* really suffer as he does in the other Gospels and that even the cross itself is "for John" Jesus' glorification rather than his place of greatest torment. The skeptical scholar Bart Ehrman has taken this claim to great lengths, even saying that Jesus' crucifixion in John is not agonizing for him. He says that, since John says that Jesus expressed thirst with the intention that Scripture might be fulfilled (John 19.28), this means that it was not even a genuine expression of suffering![8] (This, it should go without saying, doesn't follow.)

So it's important to emphasize that Jesus' suffering, physical humanity is a point of similarity throughout the Gospels and, as such, an argument for their truthfulness. The real evidential situation is exactly the opposite of what Ehrman claims.

Take, for example, the matter of weeping. While it is common in scholarly circles to imply that "John's Jesus" is superhuman, in fact, only Luke and John mention that Jesus wept (Luke 19.41, John 11.35). Luke says that Jesus wept over Jerusalem; John mentions his weeping at the grave of Lazarus.

His mental sufferings during his last week come not only from anticipating that his friends will forsake him but also from anticipating the physical agony and humiliation of the cross itself. In John 12.27–28a, Jesus muses aloud about his "hour" (that is, his death), which is coming toward him: "Now My soul has become troubled; and what am I to say? 'Father, save Me from this hour'? But for this purpose I came to this hour. Father, glorify Your name." Should he ask the Father to save him from the cross? Yet for this very reason he was born. The occasion is clearly different from the prayer in the Garden of Gethsemane, quoted in the last section, but the content is similar. If you knew that you were going to be crucified, wouldn't you think of it, and pray about it, on more than one occasion? Of course. John does not record the prayer in Gethsemane. Probably he knew that Matthew, Mark, and Luke had already done so. But he remembered and recorded this earlier occasion when Jesus was in mental anguish about his forthcoming death.

C.S. Lewis comments helpfully on Jesus' mental makeup and the fact that he dreaded the cross:

> God c[ould], had He pleased, have been incarnate in a man of iron nerves, the Stoic sort who lets no sigh escape him. Of His great humility He chose to be incarnate in a man of delicate sensibilities who wept at the grave of Lazarus and sweated blood in

Gethsemane. ...[Otherwise] [w]e should...have missed the all important help of knowing that He has faced all that the weakest of us face, has shared not only the strength of our nature but every weakness of it except sin. If He had been incarnate in a man of immense natural courage, that w[ould] have been for many of us almost the same as His not being incarnate at all.[9]

It is worth noting that no Gospel states *directly* that Jesus experienced pain on the cross. Here once again we see the restraint of the Gospels, noted already in Chapter 4 on unnecessary details. The evangelists, unlike ancient (or, for that matter, modern) orators whose goal is to produce a strong emotional response in hearers or readers, write of Jesus' sufferings in a style that is almost matter-of-fact. This is what happened. This is what the soldiers did. This is what Pilate ordered. And so forth. But there are plenty of indications even in these terse statements: The servants of the high priest struck him in the face and mocked him while he was blindfolded (Mark 14.65). He was scourged by order of Pilate, at least once and possibly twice (John 19.1, Mark 15.15). The soldiers placed a crown of thorns on his head (Mark 15.17). Herod's soldiers mocked him and in all probability knocked him around (Luke 23.11). The fact that Simon of Cyrene was compelled to carry the cross-beam to Jesus' cross (Mark 15.21) must have meant that Jesus was by that time unable to carry it all the way to Golgotha and that the soldiers, who had their orders to crucify him, did not want him to die before he was nailed up.

New Testament scholar Richard Bauckham points out the well-known shame and horror of crucifixion for a first-century audience. They did not need pain and suffering stressed. They had witnessed crucifixions themselves:

That the Johannine passion narrative could be read as a triumph *rather than* as a narrative of abject humiliation is intrinsically very unlikely. Everyone in the ancient world knew that crucifixion was an excruciatingly painful way to die, and that—even more important for the social values of the time—[it was] the most shameful way to die, the fate of slaves, enemies of the state and others who were treated as subhuman, deserving of this dehumanizing fate. This is why none of the Gospel narratives need to say explicitly that Jesus suffered physical pain or to point out the humiliation of such a death. The mere telling of the familiar tale of events entailed in death by crucifixion—familiar to people from observation, though rarely recounted in ancient literature—was more than enough to convey the agony and the shame.[10]

Bauckham's point is a welcome correction to over-clever scholars who think that Jesus' cross in the Gospel of John cannot be a place of suffering because John treats it as his glorification. The *whole point* in John's Gospel is that paradoxical combination—that the place of greatest suffering and shame is the place where the Son of Man is glorified. Hence the grim pun when Jesus says, "And I, if I be lifted up from the earth, will draw all men to myself." (John 12.21) He is going to be "lifted up" in two different senses. In Isaiah 52.13, the Suffering Servant is said to be "exalted." Jesus uses this concept both in the straightforward sense that he is to receive praise (especially from the Father) and in the gruesome sense that he is to be lifted up on the cross. It takes an ear of tin (which, unfortunately, some biblical critics seem to possess) not to see that the two come together in John's own themes.

And indeed, it is only in John that we hear that on the cross Jesus expressed physical thirst (John 19.28). This was of course quite probable. Loss of blood and dehydration would have been a part of the torments of crucifixion. But only the Beloved Disciple, who witnessed the scene, mentions it.†

---

† One of the stranger events in recent evangelical biblical criticism is the advocacy by two well-known evangelical scholars, Daniel Wallace followed by Michael Licona,

There is no need to make a pronouncement on whether physical pain or mental pain is hardest to bear. In the providence and foreknowledge of God, Jesus, God the Son made man, was spared neither. All of the Gospels agree on this fact and complement one another in showing us one Jesus, suffering in different concrete ways.

8. "I told you so" Jesus

Most of us don't like it when someone says, "I told you so." This often happens after the person has warned us about what will happen if we don't heed his advice, we haven't listened to the warning, and sure enough! That very thing happened. "I told you so!" says the gloomy prognosticator, and we grind our teeth.

Jesus said, "I told you so" quite a bit, but he usually said it *before* the events, and then emphasized it over and over. Of course, the restoration scene with Peter, which we've talked about repeatedly in these pages, is more like the kind of "I told you so" that we see with mere humans: Jesus predicted Peter's denial, Peter said he would never deny him, then Peter denied him. So after Jesus' resurrection, he points this out, only slightly indirectly, as a part of restoring Peter to his place of leadership. More often, Jesus' method is to hammer home his own predictions and the reason for them.

It sounds obvious to say that Jesus often predicts the future. But we can get more specific than that. It's not just that he predicts the future. He is repetitive and emphatic about his predic-

---

of the theory that Jesus never literally said, "I am thirsty," nor anything recognizable as that to a bystander, while on the cross. Rather, John's report is, according to these scholars, supposed to be a transformation of the entirely different saying, "My God, my God, why have you forsaken me?" from the Synoptic Gospels. Allegedly, John invented this saying to express a metaphorical, spiritual thirst, even though John records it as a literal saying, heard as such by those standing by. Apparently, only modern biblical critics can discern this hidden meaning in John's Gospel. See Michael Licona, *Why Are There Differences in the Gospels? What We Can Learn from Ancient Biography* (Oxford: Oxford University Press, 2017), pp. 165–166; Daniel B. Wallace, "*Ipsissima Vox* and the Seven Words From the Cross," unpublished paper presented to the Society for Biblical Literature Southwest Regional meeting, March 5, 2000, pp. 6–10.

tions. There are certain things that he wants to warn his disciples about, and he doesn't even try to avoid repeating himself. We find this emphatic nature in Jesus' predictions in all four Gospels. Sometimes he takes matters a step further and tells them that he *has told* them, emphasizing the *fact that* he is making a prediction ahead of time so that they will be ready.

Jesus is especially emphatic and repetitive about predicting his own death. Mark explicitly records such a prediction more than once (Mark 8.31–32, 9.31–32), and in both of these cases Mark emphasizes that he taught his disciples from that point onward about his own coming death. Matthew records yet another occasion when Jesus predicted his death, after his Triumphal Entry (Matt. 26.1–2). In John, Jesus refers a bit more cryptically to being "lifted up" (John 3.14, 12.32), but it is interesting to note that the crowd who hears him in John 12.32 seems to know quite well that he is referring to his death, since they consider his prediction as being in tension with the statement that the Messiah abides forever (12.34). Jesus' urgent message to his disciples in the Farewell Discourse is his repeated, cryptic reference to "going away" soon. Sometimes this refers to his ascension, but other times it refers to his imminent death (John 13.33, 16.5, 6, 16). And in John 16.20, he predicts that they will weep and mourn, but their mourning will turn to joy.

Jesus is just as emphatic in all the Gospels about predicting what the disciples will do. Throughout the Gospels, he predicts that one of them will betray him (Mark 14.18–21, Matt. 26.21–25, Luke 22.21–23, John 13.18, 21–26), that Peter will deny him (Mark 14.26–31, Luke 22.33–34, John 13.37–38), and that they will all be scattered (Mark 14.26–31, John 16.32). Some of these passages, especially those set at the Last Supper where Jesus predicts that one of them will betray him, probably describe the same occasion when he made the prediction, though they give differing details. Others probably represent different occasions. It looks like Jesus predicted twice on the night of his betrayal that Peter would deny him that very night—once during supper and once after they had left the table.[11] The same is probably true of the prediction that they will all be scattered and leave him alone; one such prediction appears to occur while they are on the way to the Garden of Gethsemane and the other after they have arrived. If these matters were on his mind, he could easily have repeated them. Again, this tendency to emphasize predictions is a feature of Jesus' personality throughout the Gospels.

The predictions that he is going to die and that Peter will deny him are deeply intertwined with Jesus' relationship with Peter. The prediction that he is "going away" and the disciples' realization that something dark is coming lead to this touching exchange:

> Simon Peter said to Him, "Lord, where are You going?" Jesus answered, "Where I go, you cannot follow Me now; but you shall follow later." Peter said to Him, "Lord, why can I not follow You right now? I will lay down my life for You." Jesus answered, "Will you lay down your life for Me? Truly, truly, I say to you, a cock shall not crow, until you deny Me three times." (John 13.36–38)

The ironic question, "Will you lay down your life for me?" has something in common with the "sarcastic Jesus" of an earlier section, but here Jesus' tone seems more gentle, tinged with pain and love.

In several places, Jesus is quite explicit that he is making predictions so that the disciples will be ready to apply his words later, whether for comfort, warning, or in order to take some action. For example, this passage in Mark:

"And then if anyone says to you, 'Behold, here is the Christ'; or, 'Behold, He is there'; do not believe him; for false Christs and false prophets will arise, and will show signs and wonders, in order, if possible, to lead the elect astray. But take heed; behold, I have told you everything in advance." (Mark 13.21–23)

The context here is false messiahs; Jesus' prediction leads to a warning not to be taken in by them.

When Jesus predicts that they will all be scattered that night, he adds an instruction about the time after his resurrection:

"You will all fall away because of Me this night, for it is written, 'I will strike down the shepherd, and the sheep of the flock shall be scattered.' But after I have been raised, I will go before you to Galilee." (Matt. 26.31–32)

So when his prediction is fulfilled and he, the shepherd, is struck down and the sheep (his disciples) are scattered, they are to know that he is not finished with them. After his resurrection, they are to gather again and return to obeying his instructions.

In John, Jesus emphasizes that he has predicted what will happen so that his disciples will believe:

"You heard that I said to you, 'I go away, and I will come to you.' If you loved Me, you would have rejoiced, because I go to the Father; for the Father is greater than I. And now I have told you before it comes to pass, that when it comes to pass, you may believe." (John 14.28–29)

Even though his death is imminent, and even though later he will return to heaven and not be with them physically anymore, he wants them to take comfort from his foreknowledge. These terrible things that are about to happen do not lie outside of the Father's plan and providence, just as they do not lie outside of Jesus' knowledge. He is telling them what will happen so that they will have more confidence and trust in him.

Jesus does the same when he predicts the persecution that will follow:

> "These things I have spoken to you, that you may be kept from stumbling. They will make you outcasts from the synagogue, but an hour is coming for everyone who kills you to think that he is offering service to God. And these things they will do, because they have not known the Father, or Me. But these things I have spoken to you, that when their hour comes, you may remember that I told you of them. And these things I did not say to you at the beginning, because I was with you." (John 16.1–4)

> "These things I have spoken to you, that in Me you may have peace. In the world you have tribulation, but take courage; I have overcome the world." (John 16.33)

Here he predicts persecution, sometimes from their fellow Jews. He emphasizes, as in Mark, that he has told them these things ahead of time on purpose. His purpose here is to strengthen their faith so that they will not be shaken by persecution; they will know that it lies within the plan of God.

There is, finally, a happy "I told you so" in the words of the angel at Jesus' tomb. The angels are acting as Jesus' messengers, so this can be regarded as a case where Jesus is indirectly saying, "I told you so," but it is joyful rather than annoying:

> ...And as the women were terrified and bowed their faces to the ground, the men said to them, "Why do you seek the living One among the dead? He is not here, but He has risen. Remember how He spoke to you while He was still in Galilee, saying that the Son of Man must be delivered into the hands of sinful men, and be crucified, and the third day rise again." And they remem-

bered His words, and returned from the tomb and reported all these things to the eleven and to all the rest. (Luke 24.5–9)

"He is risen," says the angel, "*just as he said*" (Matt. 28.6). Through his messenger, here is Jesus telling them, with a gleam in his eye, "See!? I told you so! Don't you remember?" And the women, filled with joy and fear that cannot be disentangled, remember his words. Yes, indeed, he *did* tell them so, and now it has come to pass.

9. The Real Jesus of the Gospels

I don't for a moment claim that in this chapter I have touched on all of the elements of Jesus' unified character and personality that one could use in a similar argument for the Gospels' reliability. I could, for example, have written another section on Jesus' capacity to deal with people as individuals and his sensitivity to their real needs. I could have written on his fascinating relationship to the Jewish law—at times ruthlessly criticizing the Pharisees' additions to the Law of Moses but at other times complying with rules that he knew to be unnecessary. I could have talked about his combination of authority with gentleness. Jesus is a figure we will never get to the bottom of, which is exactly as it should be.

One possible result of this chapter is that it will unsettle certain ideas we have about Jesus. He was a much more abrasive person, or must have seemed so to both his friends and his enemies, than we are sometimes led to think. It is in a way easier to love and surrender to "gentle Jesus meek and mild" or to a baby in a manger than to the man who emerges from this study. Indeed, at times I have been a little worried that he would not have liked me very much if he had met me. Or, perhaps worse, that maybe *I* would not have always liked *him*! But following Jesus is life itself to the Christian believer. We are not permitted to pick and choose.

C.S. Lewis encountered some uneasiness when he first read the Gospels, as he recounts in a letter:

> My own experience in reading the Gospels was at one stage even more depressing than yours. Everyone told me that there I should find a figure whom I couldn't help loving. Well, I could....Indeed some of His behaviour seemed to me open to criticism....
>
> Now the truth is, I think, that the sweetly-attractive-human-Jesus is a product of 19th-century scepticism, produced by people who were ceasing to believe in His divinity but wanted to keep as much Christianity as they could. It is not what an unbeliever coming to the records with an open mind will (at first) find there. The first thing you find is that we are simply not invited to speak, to pass any moral judgement on Him, however favourable: it is only too clear He is going to do whatever judging there is: it is we who are being judged, sometimes tenderly, sometimes with stunning severity, but always *de haut en bas* [from high to low]. (Have you ever noticed that your imagination can hardly be forced to picture Him as shorter than yourself?)
>
> The first real work of the Gospels on a fresh reader is, and ought to be, to raise very acutely the question, "Who or What is this?" For there is a good deal in the character which, unless He really is what He says He is, is not lovable or even tolerable. If He is, then of course it is another matter: nor will it then be surprising if much remains puzzling to the end. For if there is anything in Christianity, we are now approaching something which will never be fully comprehensible.[12]

Exactly. And in this, too, there is comfort. For if Jesus is who he says he is, then he already knows all my thoughts and feelings anyway, and there is no point in my worrying about "liking" at all. He, as Lewis says, is going to do whatever judging there is to be done, but he has given his life for the sheep. He is the Judge with nail prints in his hands and feet, and we can trust him to judge justly and to show mercy upon all who fall down before him. He is the one who has said to come to him and he will give us rest. He is the Shepherd whose voice his sheep hear and trust. He has assured us that the one who comes to him in humility will never be cast out. And he told his disciples that he calls them his friends.

When I was much younger, there was a song, a very inspiring-sounding song, that advised the audience to rely only on themselves, not on any other human being. Some of the words went like this:

> Everybody's searching for a hero,
> People need someone to look up to.
> I never found anyone who fulfilled my needs;
> A lonely place to be. So I learned to depend on me.
> I decided long ago never to walk in anyone's shadow.
> If I fail, if I succeed, at least I lived as I believed.
> No matter what they take from me, they can't take away my dignity.
> Because the greatest love of all is happening to me....
> Learning to love yourself, it is the greatest love of all.[13]

Such a creed of self-reliance is all very well until the world comes crashing down around you, one way or another. There comes a time in each of our lives when we realize that we have failed or that we have insufficient strength in ourselves to go on. You will fail to live up to your own ideals. You will fail others. You will fail yourself. You will find yourself weak and afraid. You will let you down. If secular inspiration is all that you have at those moments, that is indeed a lonely place to be.

Of course we also need finite human heroes. I'm not saying that Jesus should be the only person we admire, though he is the only human being we should worship. But if ordinary human heroes let you down, deciding to rely only on yourself isn't the answer. "Depending on me" will go just as badly wrong as depending on any other sinful human being for your life's entire meaning and dignity. Depending on God Incarnate is better than either.

If Jesus is to be the center of our lives, we must encounter him as a fully historical figure, a real man who walked and talked, cried, laughed, and loved, and who also was God, which is why he can never ultimately let us down. The study in this chapter is just a short stage on that journey of learning to know, love, and trust Jesus of Nazareth. We can be eternally grateful that God has given us historically reliable Gospels to help us in that quest.

Chapter Summary

- Gospel reliability is important chiefly because the Gospels are our original records of the life, death, and resurrection of Jesus.
- The Gospels show a remarkable unity in the characteristics and personality of Jesus, across many different stories.
- This unity concerns the way that Jesus' mind works, the way he taught, what he was like to be around, and how he suffered.
- Jesus is clearly the same person both in John and in the Synoptic Gospels.
- Jesus' personality has surprisingly tough aspects.
- Jesus' sufferings, both mental and physical, help us to trust him.

Study Questions

1. List at least three reasons given in the chapter for the importance of Gospel reliability.

2. Give at least two places where Jesus uses witty word-play to make his point.

3. What is a notable characteristic of the way that Jesus teaches in all of the Gospels?

4. In what way was Jesus a disconcerting person to spend time with?

5. How does Jesus speak somewhat sarcastically in John 10?

6. Give at least one example from John and one from the Synoptic Gospels of Jesus' loneliness and/or his mental suffering due to the knowledge that his friends will forsake or betray him.

7. Give one passage from John that shows that Jesus was dreading his crucifixion.

8. How would you answer someone who said that Jesus suffers physically in his passion in Mark but not in John?

9. What does it mean to talk about "I told you so Jesus"?

10. Many of Jesus' "I told you so" moments concern sad events. Which one concerns something joyful?

For Discussion

1. It might seem that a characteristic of Jesus like sarcasm is useful for showing that the Gospels are all portraying the same person but *not* useful for our own imitation, since sarcasm in fallen human beings is often unkind. Discuss how traits of Jesus like sarcasm and thought-reading (being disconcerting) might be applicable in our own lives. How can Jesus' combination of love with tougher characteristics be especially helpful for Christians in leadership positions?

2. Do you agree or disagree with the implication in the chapter that on the cross Jesus really *felt* as if the Father had abandoned him? Why or why not? How does this issue relate to our own relationship with Jesus and with God the Father?

3. Choose at least two character traits of Jesus from this chapter that are manifested in multiple Gospels (in John as well as the Synoptics) and think about how you would use these character traits to answer the claim that Jesus is "so different" from one Gospel to another. Be prepared to argue that the unity of Jesus' character in all four Gospels is actually evidence for the truth of the Gospels.

4. Name another characteristic or characteristics of Jesus' personality that are not discussed in the chapter in detail and that are illustrated in multiple stories in the Gospels.

5. Discuss C.S. Lewis's comment that Jesus' character would have been much less helpful for us if he had been a man of steel nerves. Do you agree with this comment? Why or why not? Relate your answer to Hebrews 4.15–16.

6. Discuss the idea that a "sweet" Jesus became more popular when theologians were letting go of the deity of Jesus. Do you think that a "sweet" Jesus is easier to reconcile with a concept of Jesus as merely human? Do you think that we have a similar problem in contemporary Christian circles with not accepting characteristics of Jesus that might seem harsh?

7. Has your perception of Jesus changed as a result of reading this book, especially Chapter 8? Discuss.

Resources for Further Study

Tom Gilson, *Too Good to be False: How Jesus' Incomparable Character Reveals His Reality* (Tampa, FL: DeWard Publishing, 2020).

Stanley Leathes, *The Witness of St. John to Christ* (London: Rivingtons, 1870), pp. 300–320, <https://tinyurl.com/Leathes>.

Lydia McGrew, *The Eye of the Beholder: The Gospel of John as Historical Reportage* (Tampa, FL: DeWard Publishing, 2021), Chapter XII, "A High-Resolution Jesus," pp. 376–415,

Lydia McGrew, "Is Jesus John's Mouthpiece? Reconsidering Johannine Idiom," *Conspectus* 32 (2021), pp. 43–57, <https://tinyurl.com/McGrewMouthpiece>.

William Paley, *A View of the Evidences of Christianity in Three Parts*, T.R. Birks, ed. (London: The Religious Tract Society, 1848), pp. 243–253, <https://tinyurl.com/PaleyEvidence>.

Study Guide Answers

Chapter 1 Study Question Answers

1. Due to the lack of resources for research, such knowledge would have to be based on firsthand experience. They would have to have actually been there.

2. Confirmations from small details that are hard to get right. (As opposed to names of very famous people or famous locations of the time.)

3. Familial relationship. It turns out, based on an inscription, that there was a Lysanias ruling in Abilene at the time of Jesus who may have been the son of the Lysanias who is mentioned by Josephus.

4. The author's intention was just to convey that events happened, not specifically when they happened. So the author may group events or sayings together and narrate them out of order, but without intending to "make" them happen in a different order from reality. If there is confusion caused by this, it is accidental, not intentional.

5. A dialogue with some of the religious leaders implies that Jesus was in a region ruled by Herod the tetrarch (Herod Antipas) even after Jesus had left Galilee. Herod Antipas also ruled Perea.

6. It means "oil press." It is significant because the Gospel authors do not explain the name, but they say that the garden was on the Mount of Olives.

7. Because Capernaum is on the shore of Galilee and Cana is in the hills. So you really would have to go *down*.

8. The scene includes Jesus' saying, "I and the Father are one," which is more explicit than the claims to Jesus' deity in the Synoptic Gospels.

9. Bethany's approximate distance from Jerusalem.

10. (Two of the following.) Pool of Siloam, Pool of Bethesda, Solomon's Porch, Cana, Sea of Tiberias.

Chapter 1 Discussion Answers

1. Answers will vary but should include the idea that when you mention something like this casually, you're just trying to relate the incident, not show off. This kind of casual mention in the course of telling about something else indicates real familiarity and a truthful intention.

2. Answers will vary.

3. The answer should include the fact that the Gospel locations are much more specific than just New York City and therefore are much harder to get right. (E.g. Specific pools and structures within Jerusalem.) Perhaps also mention the connections between obscure rulers and specific locations. If those in the discussion don't bring up the destruction of Jerusalem in AD 70, the discussion leader should bring it up. That would make references to highly specific locations there even harder to get right.

4. Skeptics would use that to argue that the Gospels are unreliable and to undermine the truth of their stories. So the fact that they get them right should count in favor of their stories.

5. The correct answer is that it is easier to get a detail of this kind wrong (by misspeaking or misremembering, etc.) while getting the rest of one's story correct than it is to get such a detail right while getting the rest of one's story wrong. Those discussing may not agree with that, and the main point is to get interesting discussion going. As the previous question indicates, the more important point is that skeptics have an obvious double standard: Alleged errors in external facts are allowed to count against the Gospels, whereas proven accuracy isn't allowed to count for the Gospels.

Chapter 2 Study Question Answers

1. Roman and Jewish. There was a constant mingling of legal authority, rulers at different levels, and cultural practices.

2. The Romans had deposed Annas and made Caiaphas high priest, but Annas was still alive. Josephus uses the title "high priest" for two different people in a similar situation later in the century.

3. The Jewish people in Judea tended to look down on the Jewish people in Galilee as "hicks." They even made fun of their accent. Answers will vary on other references. Could include the references to Peter's accent when he is in the high priest's courtyard, the religious leaders' statement that no prophet comes from Galilee, and in Acts the surprise of the religious leaders at the confidence of the "uneducated" Peter and John.

4. The rabbis really did have to rule on whether or not it counted as "work" to circumcise a baby boy on the Sabbath, which is what Jesus refers to. In Matthew 23 Jesus refers to tithing dill and cumin, and there were real rabbinical discussions about how to tithe herbs.

5. The narrator doesn't pretend that Jesus actually mentioned the Holy Spirit. He separates his own interpretation from Jesus' historical words.

6. A guard of four Roman soldiers. This was the normal number for a guard. John mentions that they divided Jesus' clothes into four parts, one for each soldier.

7. They use "extra" names when they give a name that was especially common in that time and place. That is how "extra" names were really used, so that people knew which Mary, Judas, etc. was intended. The common or uncommon names varied in different places even at the same time.

8. The narrator just refers to him as "Jesus," because he would only be thinking of one person named Jesus. But the people in the stories use an "extra" term to refer to him (like "Jesus of Nazareth"), because his name at that time and place was quite common. This is how the people would really have spoken of him.

Chapter 2 Discussion Answers

1. Answers will vary.

2. Answers will vary but should include the idea that even before the Internet you could go to a library and use encyclopedias and reference works to read up on other cultures and their odd customs, but this was not available in the time when the Gospels were written.

3. Answers will vary.

4. Answers will vary.

5. The general idea should be that we found that common names in the list needed "extra" designations to avoid any ambiguity, whereas uncommon names did not.

6. Answers will vary. The general idea is complexity when different levels or types of government all have some authority within the same geographical region. One historical example with which people in the discussion may or may not be familiar is the relationship of the British Empire's colonial government to various local governments in India, Africa, etc., in the 19th and early 20th century. Often the British officials would let the traditional governments have a measure of independence while stepping in only occasionally. A more familiar type of contemporary example in the U.S. would be the way that federal regulations and state regulations overlap, sometimes duplicating and occasionally even conflicting, making things difficult for businessmen. (I once had a contractor tell me that state and federal regulations told him conflicting things concerning how to remove lead paint from a house.) Another example would be that local governments and school districts have sometimes had additional Covid regulations for schoolchildren beyond the state regulations. These are all examples of the complexity of different types of rules and types of authority in a region, which are the kinds of things that the Gospels get right.

Chapter 3 Study Question Answers

1. In an undesigned coincidence, statements made in different accounts fit together even though it doesn't look like the authors were trying to make them fit together. Often this involves a question and answer between two accounts.

2. Matthew, Mark, and Luke. Critical scholars assume that if a story in Matthew or Luke has similar wording to the wording in

Mark, then the other Gospel authors had no other access to what really happened. Therefore, if there is anything additional in such a passage in Matthew or Luke, they assume that they just made it up.

3. Joanna was the wife of Chuza, who was Herod's steward. Joanna was a follower of Jesus and could have passed on this information. (Bonus: We learn about Joanna only in Luke.)

4. Jesus healed the man born blind in Jerusalem. Jerusalem is much closer to Jericho where Bartimaeus was than Galilee, where Jesus healed other blind people. (Bonus: Bartimaeus is mentioned only in the Synoptic Gospels. The healing of the man born blind is mentioned only in John.)

5. His washing the disciples' feet, found only in John.

6. It isn't the same event. The rebuke in Mark occurred earlier, when James and John asked to sit on his right and left hand in the kingdom. The rebuke in Luke happened on the night of the Last Supper. The disciples often bickered about this topic, and it looked like Jesus said things that were similar but not identical. (Bonus: Since the words, "I am among you as the one who serves" are only in Luke and are confirmed by an undesigned coincidence, it looks like Luke knew what Jesus really said on that night. He didn't "move" the rebuke from a different place to make it fictionally look like it happened that night.)

7. Jesus told him that his kingdom was not of this world.

Chapter 3 Discussion Answers
1. Answers will vary.

2. Answers will vary but should include something to the effect that it's good for laymen to have some preparation to respond to

such criticisms. It can help laymen to recognize what someone is referring to and not to be thrown by it because it is completely new.

3. When an account mentions only the question or only the answer, this means that the author was not trying to make the connection, so he appears to be mentioning it just because he knows that it is true. If he mentioned both the question and the answer, that definitely wouldn't mean that what he was saying was not true, but it would lose that characteristic of casualness which has special evidential value.

4. The fact that John doesn't mention the other part of the coincidence in the same story means that he doesn't seem to have been trying to build on the other story. For example, when he wrote about the feeding of the five thousand, he may not even have remembered that Luke said that it happened near Bethsaida. He might not even have thought about how this was connected with Jesus' speaking to Philip. If one author were trying to build on another author's story and make up a connected fact, why would he leave out the fact (such as the location of the feeding) that he was trying to connect it with?

5. A sample answer might be that two children telling about an event they were both present at might imitate each other's language (if they heard each other telling the story) while having noticed different specific facts and having variation at those points.

6. Answers will vary.

Chapter 4 Study Question Answers

1. Real people often include details in their stories for no special reason, just because that's how they remember it and because it occurred to them.

Study Guide Answers | 227

2. Two or three of the following:

Liars do it because it really does make their stories look true. So unnecessary details are on the face of it a sign of truth unless there's evidence to the contrary.

- Many of the unnecessary details in the Gospels can be checked and turn out to be true.
- The Gospels present themselves as true history, so they are not like a novel or a partly fictionalized movie, since those present themselves as at least partly non-historical.
- The hyper-realistic modern novel didn't exist at the time of the Gospels, so such a comparison is anachronistic.
- The Gospels don't use details in the same way that modern novels do.

3. Jesus was asleep on a pillow.

4. He gives the specific name of the tree (sycamore) which Zacchaeus climbed. Extra information that may be included: This botanical name is similar to but not the same as the tree in Jesus' saying about faith and telling a tree (sycamine) to be cast into the sea. (Bonus: Sycamore trees did grow in Jericho, where Jesus met Zacchaeus.)

5. Multiples of three. John sometimes gives times that are even more specific, like the tenth hour or the seventh hour.

6. Answers will vary but could include the 46 years that the Temple was in the process of being built, the 38 years that the man at the Pool of Bethesda had been crippled, the approximate number of gallons that the water jugs could hold at the wedding at Cana, or the approximate distance the disciples had been rowing in the storm before they saw Jesus.

7. Answers will vary and can be checked from the text. The scenes discussed in the text in detail are the raising of Lazarus, the Last Supper (including the foot washing and Jesus' giving the sop to Judas, followed by Judas' exit), the race to the tomb followed by the view of the grave clothes, Mary Magdalene's meeting with Jesus outside the tomb, and the great catch of fish in John 21.

8. They use enough details to look like eyewitness testimony but they don't use those details consistently throughout a scene in the style of a modern novelist. Also they are not over-the-top like ancient fiction or rhetoric. They are just right.

9. Quintilian told them to be "over-the-top" in order to involve the emotions of their audience. The Gospels are matter-of-fact and don't seem to be trying to excite emotion.

Chapter 4 Discussion Answers

1. Answers will vary.

2. Answers will vary. An example to get discussion going: If someone tells truthfully around Christmas time about an accident in which a red car hit a green car, it would be rather silly to suggest that he's trying to symbolize Christmas by telling about the colors of the cars.

3. God seems to have inspired the authors of the Gospels to write them in the way that real-world witnesses speak. The unnecessary details are not necessary to the story, nor do they have to have hidden symbolic meanings, but they do show that the stories have the quality of true witness testimony. Also, sometimes these details can be verified, and this increases our confidence in the Gospels. So they can be unnecessary to the story while serving other purposes in an historical book.

4. Participants will select different passages. As a discussion starter, you may find the video suggested in the chapter resources to be helpful: "Gospel Details in the Goldilocks Zone." There I read a passage from modern realistic fiction and point out the differences.

Chapter 5 Study Question Answers

1. An unexplained allusion would probably not be understood by at least some members of the original audience, and the author would have known that. This shows that the author included it in an unselfconscious way.

2. It would distract from the story without adding anything to the reader's experience.

3. It is unexplained within that book or account.

4. A story that explains why Jesus called them that.

5. It occurs in the Gospel of Luke, and Luke's original audience probably wouldn't have known what this was about. Luke apparently just included it because it was what Jesus said.

6. John the author doesn't tell us what the dispute was about or how John the Baptist resolved the dispute.

7. If John thought it was okay to make up Jesus' teaching, he would have made Jesus refer more clearly to a specific Old Testament quotation.

8. He said, "Destroy this Temple, and in three days I will raise it up." (Referring to his resurrection.) What he really said is reported in John. The accusation that he said he would destroy the Temple is reported in the Synoptic Gospels as something the witnesses said at his trial before the Sanhedrin. It's unexplained

in the Synoptic Gospels and forms an undesigned coincidence with the saying in John.

Chapter 5 Discussion Answers

1. Answers will vary. The explanation of why it is a mark of truth should have something to do with the idea that the speaker would have his eye on the audience if he were making something up rather than throwing in something the audience doesn't know anything about.

2. The answer to this is related to the idea that a "world-building" fantasy or science fiction author does have a meaning in mind for the allusion (e.g., to the name of a king or a backstory) and intends to make it known eventually to readers or viewers of a series of movies. Or he has made it known in some other part of the series or in a background book (like Tolkien's book *The Silmarillion*). Another answer might be that a good author of this kind will sometimes deliberately provide additional information as the reader goes along in that book or in a television series to allow him to answer a question like, "Who is this person?" So the allusion is not ultimately unexplained. Another answer could be that world-building is expected in fantasy and that unexplained allusions can be a part of that. The author imitates this aspect of reality in, say, a conversation between characters who know the rest of the story. The Gospels present themselves as historical. Therefore the simplest explanation is that they are reporting real things that happened or were said, without worrying about whether their audiences know the backstory.

3. If John thought it was okay for him to put his own words into Jesus' mouth, he didn't need to pause and tell the readers separately what his own interpretation was in the voice of the narrator.

John 14.26 is evidence against that view of inspiration because it says that the Holy Spirit will help them to remember what Jesus actually said. The teaching of the Holy Spirit may also help them to understand it better, but that isn't the same thing as pretending that Jesus said something that he didn't historically say.

4. Answers will vary but will probably include the idea that spontaneity and narrating events as they come to the mind will make an unexplained allusion more probable. Its inclusion also means that the account is not highly edited, which fits with the "no word processing" point.

5. Answers will vary. Some possibilities are that you don't have a lot of time to tell about the sermon, that it isn't necessary for the audience to know about the event that the preacher is referring to in order to get his point, that the backstory would be a long one, that you don't think about it one way or another, and that you yourself don't know the backstory.

Chapter 6 Study Question Answers

1. Harmonization is putting accounts together when they vary and suggesting ways that they are compatible even if they look contradictory at first.

2. Real-world imagination is the ability to think about how things might have happened that puts together multiple pieces of evidence instead of assuming they are contradictory.

3. It might seem like they are contradictory, but the clerk said "about" when referring to the time. His being at the store at "about" 3:30 is compatible with what Bill said about when he left the gym. The store clerk's independent testimony actually strengthens Bill's alibi.

4. Saying that there was one blind man isn't the same thing as saying that there weren't two. One author (such as Mark) might have only heard about one or only mentioned one while the other author (such as Matthew) has heard about and mentions both.

5. Jesus could have easily said both "My God, my God, why have you forsaken me?" and "I am thirsty" at about the same time, even one right after the other.

6. It seems like the women weren't present at the Last Supper, when Jesus told his male disciples that he would go ahead into Galilee after his resurrection. If this was the only time he mentioned it, the male disciples wouldn't expect the women to know about it. Therefore, if the women said that they had a message on Easter that the risen Jesus would meet his disciples in Galilee, this should have been a hint to the male disciples that the women's story of seeing an angel and Jesus who gave them this message was true.

7. Matthew names Mary Magdalene and another Mary and as the passage goes on says that "they" saw Jesus on the road after seeing the angel. So if you had only Matthew's account, you would be inclined to think that Mary Magdalene met Jesus after his resurrection when she was with the other women, leaving the tomb. John describes Mary Magdalene as leaving the tomb to get Peter and the Beloved Disciple, coming back and weeping there by herself, and meeting Jesus when she is alone. The explanation given in the chapter is that there were more women than just the two mentioned by Matthew. (Luke and Mark make this clear.) John's "camera" followed Mary Magdalene when she left the group, ran to tell Peter and John, returned to the tomb, and saw Jesus alone. The "camera" in the other three Gospels follows what happened to the other women when they went into the

tomb after Mary ran, saw the angel and heard his message, left the tomb, and saw Jesus while they were together on the road.

8. Jesus told the disciples, "Stay in Jerusalem" after they had already gone to Galilee and returned to Jerusalem. There was plenty of time for this during the forty days that he was on earth with them. The end of Luke 24, especially from verse 44 onward, gets somewhat rushed and just doesn't specify on what day the things in those last few verses took place (achronological narration). Luke clears this up in Acts 1 when he clarifies that Jesus was on earth for forty days. So the command, "Stay in Jerusalem" in Luke 24.49 actually took place somewhat later, not on Easter Day itself.

Chapter 6 Discussion Answers

1. Answers will vary. The general idea is that their confidence in the other person is increased after realizing that the person was right after all.

2. Different answers are possible. Perhaps Jessica had taken her children to the park's bathroom at the time that Jan was there. Perhaps Jessica hadn't arrived yet or had already left. The idea from the chapter is that people are not chained together. They can move around and be with someone at one time and not with that person at another time.

3. Answers will vary. It is possible that some in the discussion will be uncomfortable with the idea of applying real-world imagination to the Bible. Perhaps this might seem irreverent in some way. It is important in that case to emphasize that if these events really happened, we can see that there might be a need to "fill in" or "connect the dots" between accounts. As long as we recognize that our own guesses about how these things fit together are not

inspired by God, we can treat the Gospels as real history without being over-confident about extra-biblical speculation.

4. Answers will vary. Some may say that these alleged discrepancies wouldn't cause doubt for them but might do so for someone else, such as a seeker or a new believer. Some who are adult converts may say that these sorts of issues kept them from Christianity at first. One thing that would be worth stressing is the importance of not avoiding or squelching questions when they arise.

5. You point out that this is a reasonable thing to do outside of the Bible, for other documents, for witnesses to an event, for people you know, etc. So the skeptic should be open to these explanations in the Bible and should not be so quick to assert that they are contradictory.

6. Answers will vary. This will probably be a lively discussion.

7. Jesus was probably saying only that the mustard seed is very small, not that it is literally the smallest seed in the whole world. People in the discussion may give other examples in their experience where people mean only to be giving approximate numbers. The "southern dialect" hint is meant to prompt the idea that a person who says that is merely emphasizing that the thing in question was extremely cute. It would be missing the point to say, "Oh, wasn't this other thing you once saw even cuter?"

Chapter 7 Study Question Answers

1. Two or three of the following: Speaks without thinking, extravagant and emotional in his words and gestures, impulsive in his actions, argues with Jesus, argues because he loves Jesus, loving/warmhearted, promises (boasts) beyond what he can deliver.

2. Answers will vary and can be checked from the text or from the Gospels cited.

3. He is associated with John. Jesus takes Peter, James, and John with him on several occasions: Transfiguration, into the house when he raises Jairus' daughter, further into the Garden when he prays. Peter asks John (the Beloved Disciple) to find out who will betray Jesus. Peter and the Beloved Disciple are staying together and go to the tomb together on Easter. Peter and John act as spokesmen for the Christians before the religious leaders in Acts.

4. She is the one serving the meal in Luke and a different meal in John; she is the first one to go out to meet Jesus after Lazarus dies; she worries that Lazarus's body will stink after four days.

5. She sits at the feet of Jesus (in Luke); she falls at Jesus' feet in John; she weeps in John; she pours out the ointment on Jesus' feet.

6. He is pessimistic but loyal.

7. He always wants to know the truth even if it is uncomfortable.

8. When different people are writing different fiction stories about the same character, it is hard to make the different stories agree in illustrating the same complex character traits.

Chapter 7 Discussion Answers

1. Answers might focus on the fact that a caricature follows a shallow formula, whereas that isn't the case with Peter in the Gospels. The similarities are more subtle. If Peter were merely a caricature, he might boast all the time but not show his love for Jesus at the same time. Or he might be unable to be authentically

humble later on (as in the scene in John 21). He would be likely to show just one or two characteristics in formulaic stories.

2. Answers will vary.

3. Some possible answers would include his sense of humor, shown when he asks if the rulers also want to be Jesus' disciples, his wit, when he says that they don't know where Jesus is from but that he was able to open his eyes, and his courage, shown in his willingness to confess Jesus before the rulers.

4. Answers will vary.

5. Answers will vary.

Chapter 8 Study Question Answers

1. The need to support doctrine based on Jesus' teachings; the need to know what Jesus was like on earth so that we can follow him; the need for good evidence for his resurrection (which we need to invite others to commit themselves to him).

2. (Two of the following.) They will untie an animal on the Sabbath but are angry when he unties a woman who was not able to stand upright. They will circumcise a boy baby on the Sabbath if it falls on the eighth day but are angry that he made a man's body whole on the Sabbath. The Pharisees tithe lightweight herbs but neglect the weightier matters of justice and mercy.

3. His use of object lessons.

4. He could read thoughts and would bring up things that you preferred he would not bring up.

5. When the people are about to stone him, he asks what good work they are trying to stone him for.

6. Check from text of chapter from the section "Lonely Jesus."

7. In John 12 Jesus says that his soul is troubled and rhetorically asks if he should ask the Father to save him from the approaching hour of his death.

8. One could point out that John states just as the Synoptics do that Jesus was scourged. Also, the statement that Jesus was crucified would have been more than enough for an audience of the time to know of his physical sufferings. Also, only John describes his cry of thirst on the cross.

9. In all the Gospels, in different teachings, Jesus emphasizes that he is predicting things ahead of time so that the disciples will recognize them when they happen and do something he wants them to do.

10. The angel reminds the women that Jesus predicted ahead of time that he would rise again.

Chapter 8 Discussion Answers

1. Answers might include the idea that God can use our insight into the inconsistencies of human nature and a sense of humor. Discussion participants may also talk about parents or leaders whom they have appreciated who have combined the characteristics of confidence and firm authority with love and kindness.

2. Answers will vary. If they agree, an obvious application would be that it is not a sin to *feel* abandoned by God, but that our feeling that way doesn't make it true. We are not really abandoned by God in those times and can continue in the path of obedience as Jesus did.

3. Answers will vary and can be checked from the text.

4. Answers will vary, but make sure that the chosen characteristic can be found in more than one incident.

5. Answers might include the idea that even a man of steel nerves will be afraid of being crucified. Some might want to be careful to emphasize that Jesus' value to us is chiefly as a redeemer, not as someone to imitate. Hebrews 4.16 says that we can come boldly to the throne of grace because Jesus is a high priest who can be touched with our feelings. We want to know that in our emotional suffering we are also participating in Jesus' sufferings.

6. It does seem that a "sweet" Jesus fits better with a concept of Jesus as merely human, since a mere man would not have as much authority to speak strongly and harshly. People in the discussion will have different opinions about whether or not contemporary Christians have a problem with portraying Jesus as merely sweet. Perhaps one way to direct discussion would be to the widespread quoting of the words "do not judge" from Jesus' teaching, selectively avoiding both the context and the places where Jesus himself is clear in condemning sin. A similar area for discussion would be the claim that Jesus "hung out with" prostitutes, implying that Jesus was non-judgemental concerning on-going, unrepentant sin, whereas in fact it is clear in the contexts of the passages in question that those who came to Jesus were called upon to forsake their sin.

7. Answers will vary.

Endnotes

Chapter 1 – Location, Location, Location

[1] All Bible quotations are from the NASB unless otherwise stated.

[2] Josephus, *Jewish War* II, 9.2–4.

[3] Ibid. II, 6.3.

[4] Josephus, *Antiquities* XVIII, 2.2, 4.3.

[5] Ibid., XVII, 8.1.

[6] Ibid., XV, 4.1.

[7] https://wholestones.org/the-complete-text-of-the-abila-inscription-concerning-lysanias/.

[8] Josephus, *Antiquities* XVIII, 7.1.

[9] Peter J. Williams, *Can We Trust The Gospels?* (Wheaton, IL: Crossway, 2018), p. 61.

[10] https://www.biblicalarchaeology.org/daily/people-cultures-in-the-bible/jesus-historical-jesus/mark-and-john-a-wedding-at-cana-whose-and-where/.

[11] Williams, *Can We Trust the Gospels?*, p. 59.

[12] Tzippe Barrow and Julie Stahl, "Archaeologists Unearth Roman Era Stone Water Pots Near Biblical Cana," Christian Broadcasting Network News, August 15, 2017, https://www1.cbn.com/cbnnews/israel/2017/august/archaeologists-unearth-roman-era-stone-water-pots-near-biblical-cana.

[13] E. M. Blaiklock, *Jesus Christ: Man or Myth?* (Homebush West, NSW: Anzea Books, 1983), p. 65.

[14] Josephus, *Antiquities* XVIII, 2.3.

[15] Josephus, *Jewish War* III.3.5 and IV.8.2.

[16] https://www.abarim-publications.com/Meaning/Siloam.html.

[17] "The Siloam Pool: Where Jesus Healed the Blind Man," *Bible History Daily*, Biblical Archaeological Society, May 12, 2018, https://www.biblica-

larchaeology.org/daily/biblical-sites-places/biblical-archaeology-sites/the-siloam-pool-where-jesus-healed-the-blind-man/.

[18] Unfortunately, such critical scholars include some known as evangelical, such as Craig A. Evans and Michael Licona. For documentation and further discussion, see Lydia McGrew, *The Eye of the Beholder: The Gospel of John as Historical Reportage* (Tampa, FL: DeWard Publishing, 2021), pp. 6–12, 156, 280–282.

[19] Josephus, *Antiquities* XIII, 11.3, XX.9.7.

[20] "Al-Eizariya," Welcome to Palestine, https://www.welcometopalestine.com/destinations/jerusalem/al-eizariya/.

[21] https://www.biblicalarchaeology.org/daily/news/has-dalmanutha-from-the-bible-been-found/.

[22] https://www.biblicalarchaeology.org/daily/news/baptismal-site-bethany-beyond-the-jordan-added-to-unesco-world-heritage-list/.

Chapter 2 – Customs and Culture

[1] George Rawlinson, *The Historical Evidences of the Truth of the Scripture Records: Stated Anew* (Boston: Gould and Lincoln, 1860), pp. 185–188. For a longer quotation and more discussion of this passage of Rawlinson in relation to the Gospels, see Lydia McGrew, "The Annotated Rawlinson," *Extra Thoughts,* April 29, 2015, https://tinyurl.com/McGrewRawlinson.

[2] Robert Taylor, *The Diegesis* (London: Richard Carlile, 1829), p. 135. I am indebted to Timothy McGrew for this reference.

[3] Josephus, *Antiquities,* XVIII.2.2, 4.3; "The Jewish Temples: High Priests of the Second Temple Period," Jewish Virtual Library, https://www.jewishvirtuallibrary.org/high-priests-of-the-second-temple-period; Emil Schürer, *A History of the Jewish People in the Time of Jesus Christ,* Second Division, Vol. 1, Trans. Sophia Taylor and Rev. Peter Christie (Edinburgh: T. & T. Clark, 1890), pp. 198–200.

[4] J. B. Lightfoot, *Biblical Essays* (London: Macmillan & Co., 1893), pp. 163–164.

[5] Josephus, *Antiquities* XX, 9.2.

[6] Lightfoot, *Biblical Essays,* pp. 158–159.

[7] Eruvin 53b.

[8] Solomon Schechter, Wilhelm Bacher, Johanan B. Zakkai, *Jewish Encyclopedia*, 1906. https://www.jewishencyclopedia.com/articles/8724-johanan-b-zakkai#anchor2.

[9] Hampton Keathley IV, "Raising the Widow's Son from Nain," Bible.org, https://bible.org/seriespage/13-raising-widow-s-son-nain.

[10] Craig L. Blomberg, *The Historical Reliability of the Gospels*, 2nd ed. (Downers Grove, IL: IVP Academic, 2007), p. 134.

[11] Shabbat 153a.

[12] "Stater," *International Standard Bible Encyclopedia Online*, https://www.internationalstandardbible.com/S/stater.html.

[13] Tacitus, *Annals*, 1.17.

[14] James Hastings, ed., *A Dictionary of the Bible*, vol. 3 (New York: Charles Scribner's Sons, 1911), p. 427.

[15] Josephus, *Jewish War*, II.12.3–7.

[16] Hilchos Milah, chapter 1, section 9. See also "Circumcision" in *The Jewish Encyclopedia*, 1906, http://www.jewishencyclopedia.com/articles/4391-circumcision.

[17] For more references on these ceremonies, see Craig Keener, *The Gospel of John: A Commentary* (Grand Rapids, MI: Baker Academic, 2012), pp. 722–723.

[18] m. Sukkot 5.1.

[19] Peter J. Williams, *Can We Trust The Gospels?* (Wheaton, IL: Crossway, 2018), p. 81.

[20] m. Maaseroth 4.5.

[21] Eduyoth 5.3.

[22] Justinian, *Digest*, 48.20.2, 6.

[23] John J. Rousseau, *Jesus and His World: An Archaeological and Cultural Dictionary* (Minneapolis, MN: Fortress Press, 1995), pp. 325–326.

[24] Polybius, *Histories* 6.33.4. See also Vegetius, *De Re Militari* 3.8; Philo, *In Flaccum* 13.2.

[25] Williams, *Can We Trust the Gospels?* p. 65; Richard Bauckham, *Jesus and the Eyewitnesses*, 2nd ed. (Grand Rapids, MI: Eerdmans, 2017), p. 85.

[26] Bauckham, *Jesus and the Eyewitnesses*, p. 89.

[27] Williams, *Can We Trust The Gospels?*, p. 65.

[28] Ibid., p. 68.

[29] Bauckham, *Jesus and the Eyewitnesses*, pp. 99–101.

[30] Williams, *Can We Trust The Gospels?*, p. 74.

[31] Ibid., p. 69.

Chapter 3 – Undesigned Coincidences

[1] John Wenham, *Redating Matthew, Mark, and Luke: A Fresh Assault on the Synoptic Problem* (Downers Grove, IL: Intervarsity Press, 1992).

[2] Lydia McGrew, "What I Think of the Synoptic Problem," https://tinyurl.com/McGrewSynoptic, discusses this possibility further.

[3] Lydia McGrew, "Confirmation, Coincidence, and Contradiction," *Synthese*, 2021, Online First 3/14/21, DOI https://doi.org/10.1007/s11229-021-03102-x.

[4] Lydia McGrew, *Hidden in Plain View: Undesigned Coincidences in the Gospels and Acts* (Chillicothe, OH: DeWard Publishing, 2017).

[5] See discussion in Lydia McGrew, *The Mirror or the Mask: Liberating the Gospels from Literary Devices* (Tampa, FL: DeWard Publishing, 2019), pp. 268–272.

Chapter 4 – Unnecessary Details

[1] See Lydia McGrew, *The Mirror or the Mask: Liberating the Gospels from Literary Devices* (Tampa, FL: DeWard Publishing, 2019), pp. 109–110, 147–151, 127–129; Lydia McGrew, "Is Jesus John's Mouthpiece? Reconsidering Johannine Idiom," *Conspectus*, 32 (2021), pp. 43–57.

[2] Josephus *Jewish War* 3.9.5; Ketubot 48a.

[3] For more on rainfall and this coincidence, see Peter J. Williams, *Can We Trust the Gospels?* (Wheaton, IL: Crossway Books, 2018), pp. 91–94.

[4] Ibid., p. 82.

[5] Craig L. Blomberg, *The Historical Reliability of the Gospels*, 2nd ed. (Downers Grove, IL: IVP Academic, 2007), p. 228.

[6] See *The Mirror or the Mask*, pp. 282–287.

[7] Lydia McGrew, *Hidden in Plain View: Undesigned Coincidences in the Gospels and Acts* (Chillicothe, OH: DeWard Publishing, 2017), pp. 113–118.

[8] Leon Morris, *Studies in the Fourth Gospel* (Grand Rapids, MI: Eerdmans Publishing Company, 1969), p. 172.

⁹ Richard Bauckham, *The Testimony of the Beloved Disciple: Narrative, History, and Theology in the Gospel of John* (Grand Rapids, MI: Baker Academic), pp. 192–193.

¹⁰ E. M. Blaiklock, *Jesus Christ: Man or Myth* (Homebush West, NSW, Australia: Anzea Books, 1983), p. 69.

¹¹ Morris, *Studies in the Fourth Gospel*, p. 141, quoting and here agreeing with N.E. Johnson.

¹² For further reading, in addition to Wenham, *Easter Enigma*, pp. 92–93, noted in a footnote, see Henry Latham, *The Risen Master* (Cambridge: Deighton Bell and Co., 1901), pp. 29–56.

¹³ Frédéric Louis Godet, *Commentary on Selected Books,* John 20:11–13, in loc. https://www.studylight.org/commentaries/gsc/john-20.html.

¹⁴ Quintilian, *Inst. Oratoria* 6.2.26ff.

¹⁵ Ibid., 8.3.62.

Chapter 5 – Unexplained Allusions

¹ For a fascinating discussion of the character of Pontius Pilate in non-biblical literature and its intersection with the stories in the Gospels, see E.M. Blaiklock, *The Compact Handbook of New Testament Life* (Minneapolis, MN: Bethany House Publishers, 1979), pp. 66–69.

² George Wesley Buchanan, "The Tower of Siloam," *The Expository Times,* Vol. 115 No. 2 (November 2003): 37–45, https://www.askelm.com/temple/t031205.htm.

³ Colin J. Hemer, *The Book of Acts in the Setting of Hellenistic History,* WUNT 49 (Tübingen: J.C. B. Mohr, 1989), Chapters 4 and 5, pp. 101–243.

⁴ Leon Morris, *Studies in the Fourth Gospel* (Grand Rapids, MI: Eerdmans Publishing Company, 1969), pp. 159–160.

Chapter 6 – Unexpected Harmonies

¹ T. R. Birks, *Horae Evangelicae, or The Internal Evidence of the Gospel History* (London: Seeleys, 1852), pp. v, 269–271.

² J. Warner Wallace, *Cold-Case Christianity: A Homicide Detective Investigates the Claims of the Gospels* (Colorado Springs, CO: David C. Cook, 2013), pp. 76–77.

³ Michael Licona, *Why Are There Differences in the Gospels? What We Can Learn from Ancient Biography* (Oxford: Oxford University Press, 2017), p.

180, referring to this change as "one element of a larger picture involving redaction in the Synoptics."

⁴ Richard Bauckham, *Jesus and the Eyewitnesses: The Gospels as Eyewitness Testimony*, 2nd ed. (Grand Rapids, MI: Eerdmans, 2017), p. 130.

⁵ Ibid., pp. 48–51. John Wenham, *Easter Enigma: Are the Resurrection Accounts in Conflict?* (Eugene, OR: Wipf & Stock, 1992), p. 68.

⁶ See, for example, my discussion of the centurion who came to Jesus. *The Mirror or the Mask: Liberating the Gospels from Literary Devices* (Tampa, FL: DeWard Publishing, 2019), pp. 375–381.

⁷ Thomas Starkie, *A Practical Treatise of the Law of Evidence* (Philadelphia: T. and W. Johnson, 1876), p. 831.

⁸ Wenham, *Easter Enigma*, p. 128.

Chapter 7 – Unified Personalities

¹ David Marshall, *Jesus is No Myth: The Fingerprints of God on the Gospels* (Kuai Moo Press, 2016).

² J. S. Howson, *Horae Petrinae, or Studies in the Life of St. Peter* (London: The Religious Tract Society, 1883), p. 141.

³ Ibid., p. 145.

⁴ Ibid., p. 7.

⁵ Ibid., pp. 147–148.

⁶ Howson refers to this characteristic as Peter's impatience. Ibid., pp. 7, 144–147.

⁷ Ibid., p. 148.

⁸ See, e.g., Richard Bauckham, *Jesus and the Eyewitnesses: The Gospels as Eyewitness Testimony*, 2nd ed. (Grand Rapids, MI: Eerdmans, 2017), Chapter 7.

⁹ Colin Hemer, *The Book of Acts in the Setting of Hellenistic History*, WUNT 49 (Tübingen: J. C. B. Mohr, 1989), p. 358.

¹⁰ Ibid., p. 358 n. 85.

¹¹ Ibid., pp. 354–55, 362.

Chapter 8 – Unmistakable Jesus

¹ Papias in Eusebius, *Hist. eccl.* 3.39.3–4. As translated by Richard Bauckham, *The World Around the New Testament: Collected Essays II* WUNT 386 (Tübingen: Mohr Siebeck, 2017), p. 154.

[2] See Chapter 6 on reconcilable variation. See the discussion of alleged discrepancies in the resurrection stories in Lydia McGrew, *The Mirror or the Mask: Liberating the Gospels From Literary Devices* (Tampa, FL: DeWard Publishing, 2019), Chapter XVI. See also "Minimal Facts vs. Maximal Data: Approaches to the Resurrection," April 12, 2018, Apologetics Academy, https://www.YouTube.com/watch?v=RUt3r3dXBr4.

[3] For a fuller treatment of objections to the historicity of John, see Lydia McGrew, *The Eye of the Beholder: The Gospel of John as Historical Reportage* (Tampa, FL: DeWard Publishing, 2021).

[4] William Paley, *A View of the Evidences of Christianity in Three Parts*, T.R. Birks, ed. (London: The Religious Tract Society, 1848), pp. 243–244.

[5] Ibid., p. 247.

[6] C.S. Lewis, *The Lion, the Witch, and the Wardrobe* (New York: Macmillan & Co., 1970), p. 147.

[7] Peter J. Williams, *Can We Trust The Gospels?* (Wheaton, IL: Crossway, 2018), pp. 79–80; G. K. Beale and D. A. Carson, eds., *Commentary on the New Testament Use of the Old Testament* (Grand Rapids, MI: Baker Academic, 2007), p. 398; b. Berakhot 5a.

[8] "Jesus and the Hidden Contradictions of the Gospels," National Public Radio, March 12, 2010, https://www.npr.org/transcripts/124572693.

[9] C. S. Lewis, *Letters of C. S. Lewis,* revised and enlarged edition, edited by Walter Hooper (San Diego, CA: Harcourt, Brace, Jovanovich, 1993), p. 383, Letter to Mrs. Frank L. Jones, Feb. 23, 1947.

[10] Richard Bauckham, *Gospel of Glory: Major Themes in Johannine Theology* (Grand Rapids, MI: Baker Academic, 2015), p. 199.

[11] McGrew, *The Mirror or the Mask*, pp. 414–420.

[12] C.S. Lewis, *Letters of C.S. Lewis*, pp. 344–345.

[13] Whitney Houston, "Greatest Love of All," Michael Masser (music), Linda Creed (lyrics), Arista Records, track 9 on *Whitney Houston*, 1985.

Index

Abilene 5–6

Achronological narration 7–8, 33 n. †, 154 n. †

Aenon near Salim 15

Annas 4, 22–25

Argument from silence 78, 150

Artlessness 117, 123, 130, see also casualness

Asides 36–37, 126 n. †

Bartimaeus 45, 65–67, 89–90, 138

Beloved Disciple 78, 86, 94 n. †, 98–105, 140, 166, 168, 170, 196, 207

Bethany beyond Jordan 15

Bethany, location 13–15, 67, 93, 95, 178

Bethsaida 62–64, 88

Boanerges 116–117

Caiaphas 4–5, 22–25

Cana 9–10, 92, 121–122

Capernaum 10, 29, 120–122, 146, 192

Casualness 3, 9–12, 16, 30, 39, 44, 51, 53, 61, 63, 65, 73, 89, 106, 117, 121, 177, 180–181, 189–190

Chronology, see achronological narration

Chuza 59–61, 146

Circumcision 33–34, 188–189

Contradictions 52–53, 58, 65, 77–78, 134–157, 172

between Easter stories, alleged 141–155

Cushion, Jesus asleep on 88, 115

Customs and culture 20–46 (Chapter 2)

Dalmanutha 14–15

Denarius 30–31

Destruction of Jerusalem 11, 21–22, 35, 198

Details, Goldilocks zone 87, 107–110

obscure 2–3

unnecessary 83–111 (Chapter 4)

Disambiguation 40–45

Discrepancies, see contradictions

Doublet 89

Doubling in Matthew, alleged 139 n. †

Emmaus, distance from Jerusalem 91

Ephraim 15

External evidence, definition ix–x

Faith and reason ix

Feast of Tabernacles (Feast of Booths) 7, 31, 35–37, 67, 123–126, 188, 192–193

Feeding of the five thousand 61–66, 88–89, 110 n. †, 192

Feeding of the four thousand 89

Fiction, ancient 2, 86–87 n. †, 109–110

modern 87, 107–109, 111, 130

modern, characters in 163–164, 181

Flute players, see mourning practices

Foot washing 70–75, 97–98, 168, 193

Forty-six years, building of the Temple 92–93

Galilee 4, 7–9, 25–29, 31–32, 37, 60, 63, 66–67, 103–104, 118, 121, 144–155, 192, 211–212 resurrection appearances 144–155, 211–212

Genre, partially non–factual 86

Gethsemane 9, 170, 177–178, 202–203, 205–206, 210

Gist 90

Golgotha 9 n. †, 206

Grave clothes of Jesus 91, 101

Green grass 85, 89, 110 n. †

Harmonization 64, 78, 134–157 (Chapter 6)

Herod Antipas 4–8, 11, 59–61, 88, 197–198

High priest 4–5, 21–26, 45, 94, 166, 170, 206

Independence 4, 23, 40, 50, 52–59, 65, 70, 73–75, 78–79, 90, 137, 156, 172, 180

Information, difficulty of gathering in ancient times 2–3, 16, 20–21, 29, 118

Internal evidence ix–x

Jesus,
  ability to read thoughts 194–197
  abrasiveness 213–214
  crucifixion 39–40, 86, 99–100, 139–140, 146–147, 179, 202–208
  deity claims 12, 37, 187, 214–216
  fear of crucifixion 205
  loneliness 200–204
  predictions 208–213
  sarcasm 197–199
  suffering 200–208, 218
  teaching with object lessons 189–194
  teachings and Gospel reliability 184–185
  thirst 207–208
  unified personality 184–216 (Chapter 8)
  wit 38, 187–189, 198

Joanna 57–61, 88, 143, 146, 148

John, Gospel of
  Jesus' humanity in 205–208
  physical detail in 96–107
  publication in Asia Minor 10, 26, 122
  scenes 95–107
  specific numbers in 91–93
  theology and accuracy 100

John the Baptist 3–6, 15, 24, 43, 59–61, 88, 92, 122–123

Judas Iscariot 43, 62, 94, 97–99, 176

Judas, not Iscariot 43, 93–94

Last Supper 97–100, 151–152, 166, 168, 178, 201, 209

Lazarus 13, 15, 41, 67, 95–97, 173–177, 198, 205

Liars 53, 84–85, 127

Locations in the Gospels 2–16 (Chapter 1)

Long ending of Mark 150–151 n. †

Lysanias 4–6

Man born blind 12, 44–45, 67, 174, 193

Markan priority 53–55, 173–174

Martha 13, 15, 67, 95–97, 173–177, 180–181, 184

Mary Magdalene 43–44, 100–103, 142–144, 146–149, 153–155, 166, 170

Mary of Bethany 13, 15, 67, 95–97, 173–177, 180–181, 184

Memoir 84, 87, 107, 169, 177

Mourning practices 13, 28–29, 88, 95

Nain 28–29, 146

Name statistics in the Gospels 40–46, 176

Nathanael 25–26, 28, 103, 195

Non-canonical "gospels" 45, 163

Paraphrase 128, 185

Perea 5–8, 59

Personal importance of Christian evidence xii, 185–186, 213–216,

Peter, unified personality in the Gospels 164–174, 181
Philip (disciple) 25, 61–65, 88, 195
Philip the tetrarch 4–5
Pontius Pilate 3–5, 61, 118, 123, 206
  Jesus' dialogue with 75–79
Pool of Bethesda 10–11, 33, 93, 188
Pool of Siloam 12, 35, 119
Precision 15, 90, 92–93, 95, 102, 135–136, 171–172
Puddleglum 177–178
Purification, dispute about 122–123
Q document 54, 57
Quaternion 39–40
Quintilian, advice on ancient rhetoric 109–111, 206
Raising of Lazarus *see* Lazarus
Realism in fiction, *see* fiction, modern and fiction, ancient
Real-world imagination xi, 56, 75, 78–79, 110, 141, 143, 159, 173–174
Recognition of Jesus after resurrection 103–105
Reconcilable variation x, 58, 64–65, 69 n. †, 134–157 (Chapter 6), 172
Reliability, Gospel, and knowledge of Jesus 184–187, 216
Resurrection appearances of Jesus, harmonization 141–155, 179–180
Resurrection of Jesus, argument for x, 186, 216
Sabbath observance 33–34, 87, 187–189
Samaritans 31–33
Sea of Galilee 10–11, 62, 103–107, 103–104, 121, 146, 155, 166
Self-reliance 215–216
Self-presentation of the Gospels 1, 53, 85–86
Stater 29–30
Statler Brothers 83

Solomon's Porch 12–13
Sons of thunder, *see* Boanerges
Synoptic problem 53–59, 79, 173–174
Temple tax 29–30
Texture of witness testimony 84–85, 87, 110
Theophilus 86, 118
Thomas 103, 149, 155, 174, 177–181, 184, 196–197
Tiberius Caesar 3–6, 11
Tithing herbs 37–38, 189
Tower of Siloam 119
Transfiguration 165–166, 170–174
Triumphal Entry 90–91, 209
  donkeys at 90–91, 138–139
Two-source hypothesis 54–56
Undesigned coincidences x, 8 n. †, 50–79 (Chapter 3), 85–89, 92, 115–116, 126–130, 135, 145–146, 168 n. †, 189, 193
Unexpected harmonies, *see* reconcilable variation
Unexplained allusions x, 26, 87, 114–130 (Chapter 5)
Unidentified locations 11–16
Unified personalities 163–181 (Chapter 7)
Unnecessary details, *see* details, unnecessary
Variations without apparent discrepancy, *see also* reconcilable variation 137–141
Wicked tenants, parable of 68–70
Witness separation 51–52, *see also* independence
Zacchaeus 90

Also by Lydia McGrew

The Eye of the Beholder
The Gospel fo John as Historical Reportage

Why is the Gospel of John different from Matthew, Mark, and Luke? Many scholars have suggested that John felt more free than the other evangelists to massage the facts in the service of his theological goals and to put embellishments into the mouth of Jesus. Such freedom supposedly accounts for the discourses in John, for Jesus' way of speaking in John, and for (at least) the time, place, and manner of various incidents. Analytic philosopher Lydia McGrew refutes these claims, arguing in detail that John never invents material and that he is robustly reliable and honestly historical. 495 pages. $24.99 (PB).

Also by Lydia McGrew

The Mirror or the Mask
Liberating the Gospel from Literary Devices

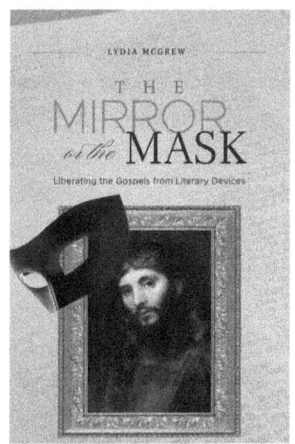

In recent years a number of evangelical scholars have claimed that the Gospel authors felt free to present events in one way even though they knew that the reality was different. Analytic philosopher Lydia McGrew brings her training in the evaluation of evidence to bear, investigates these theories about the evangelists' literary standards in detail, and finds them wanting. At the same time she provides a nuanced, positive view of the Gospels that she dubs the reportage model. Clearing away misconceptions of this model, McGrew amasses objective evidence that the evangelists are honest, careful reporters who tell it like it is. Meticulous, well-informed, and accessible, *The Mirror or the Mask* is an important addition to the libraries of laymen, pastors, apologists, and scholars who want to know whether the Gospels are reliable. 560 pages. $24.99 (PB).

Also by Lydia McGrew

Hidden in Plain View
Undesigned Coincidences in the Gospels and Acts

Hidden in Plain View revives an argument for the historical reliability of the New Testament that has been largely neglected for more than a hundred years. An undesigned coincidence is an apparently casual, yet puzzle-like "fit" between two or more texts, and its best explanation is that the authors knew the truth about the events they describe or allude to.

Connections of this kind among passages in the Gospels, as well as between Acts and the Pauline epistles, give us reason to believe that these documents came from honest eyewitness sources, people "in the know" about the events they relate. Supported by careful research yet accessibly written, Hidden in Plain View provides solid evidence that all Christians can use to defend the Scriptures and the truth of Christianity. 276 pages. $15.99 (PB).

For a full listing of DeWard Publishing Company books, visit our website:

www.deward.com

www.ingramcontent.com/pod-product-compliance
Lightning Source LLC
Chambersburg PA
CBHW022100090426
42743CB00008B/668